Mourant Brock

Rome

Pagan and Papal

Mourant Brock

Rome
Pagan and Papal

ISBN/EAN: 9783744792295

Printed in Europe, USA, Canada, Australia, Japan

Cover: Foto ©ninafisch / pixelio.de

More available books at **www.hansebooks.com**

ROME: PAGAN AND PAPAL.

BY

MOURANT BROCK, M.A.,

Formerly Incumbent of Christ Church, Clifton.
Author of
" *The Cross: Heathen and Christian,*" " *Short Chapters on the Sacraments,*" *etc.*

" *He being dead, yet speaketh.*"

London:

HODDER AND STOUGHTON

27, PATERNOSTER ROW.

MDCCCLXXXIII.

[*All rights reserved.*]

PREFACE.

FOR many years, both at home and while sojourning in other lands, I have been much interested in observing the various religions of the world, and in collecting such information respecting their traditions, ritual, and usages, as would enable me to comp arethem. And my intention was that, if it pleased God to grant me health, I would, after retirement from clerical duties, digest my miscellaneous papers, and shape them into a book.

But this was not to be: health failed, and my purpose was postponed from year to year. Last autumn, however, finding that a few of the papers which appeared in the *Rock* had met with much acceptance, I thought it might, perhaps, be well to revise and republish these together with some others. But feebleness of body again interposed, and rendered me quite unable to decide the question. So I called upon my friend Mr. Pember—author of "*Earth's Earliest Ages,*" and "*The Great Prophecies*"—with a bundle of MS. in my hand, and asked his opinion. He replied that the MS. contained much interesting information of a kind likely to be valuable at the present time.

This answer determined me; and when I further told him how unfit I felt to undertake the completion of my own work, he kindly consented to help me by digesting and revising the papers, verifying those extracts which were within the range of his library, and seeing the book through the press.

For the cuts of the Council of Florence, taken from the Bronze Gates of St. Peter's, I am indebted to the courtesy of the family of the late Rev. W. B. Marriott.

I have also to thank Dr. Lewis of Berkeley Square, Bristol, for the loan of many curious books from which I have culled much interesting matter.

Nor must I forget many other friends and acquaintances, who have most kindly helped me, either by gathering or copying notes, and to whom I beg to tender my grateful thanks.

MOURANT BROCK.

CLIFTON, *June*, 1883.

A few days after he had written his preface, the venerable author was called into the presence of Him who turneth the shadow of death into the morning.

He had requested that he might be spared to bring out a second edition of his useful "*Short Chapters on the Sacraments,*" and his petition was granted, so that he was enabled to send copies of that work to some of his friends on his eighty-first birthday.

He had conceived a dread of lingering illness, and was wont to pray that, if such were the will of God, it might not fall to his lot. This desire also was remembered by his gracious Lord.

On Friday, June 29th, he retired to rest in his usual condition, but became ill in the night, and, after an hour's laborious breathing, the command went forth—"Loose him, and let him go!"

A gentle calm stole over his face, he gasped out the words, "Old things are passed away; behold, all things are become new," and quitted the sick chamber for the Paradise of God so quietly that his sorrowing family scarce knew the moment of his departure.

"Yea, saith the Spirit, that they may rest from their labours; and their works do follow them."

G. H. P.

CONTENTS.

CHAP.		PAGE
I.	THE TWO CITIES	1
II.	THE RELATION OF PAGANISM TO THE ROMAN CHURCH	8
III.	THE EARLY CHURCH (PART I.)	14
IV.	THE EARLY CHURCH (PART II.)	19
V.	THE COMPROMISING SPIRIT OF THE EARLY CHURCH	25
VI.	FURTHER EVIDENCE TO THE COMPROMISING SPIRIT OF THE EARLY CHURCH	28
VII.	THE DARK AGES	35
VIII.	A DEVICE OF MAN FOR HIS OWN SALVATION	41
IX.	CELIBATES AND SOLITARIES	49
X.	MONKS AND MONASTERIES	55
XI.	THE SUPERSTITION AND IMMORALITY OF MEDIÆVALISM	64
XII.	CHARMS AS USED IN THE PAGAN WORLD (PART I.)	72
XIII.	CHARMS AS USED IN THE PAGAN WORLD (PART II.)	78
XIV.	CHARMS IN THE CHURCH OF ROME (PART I.)	86
XV.	CHARMS IN THE CHURCH OF ROME (PART II.)	90

CONTENTS.

CHAP.		PAGE
XVI.	CHARMS IN THE CHURCH OF ROME (PART III.).	97
XVII.	THE CONSECRATION OF HOLY FIRE AND HOLY WATER	104
XVIII.	THE FEAST OF THE PURIFICATION, OR CANDLEMAS	110
XIX.	THE IMAGES OF THE GODS	114
XX.	THE IMAGE OF ST. PETER AT ROME	121
XXI.	THE ADORATION OF IMAGES BY KISSING	125
XXII.	THE CLOTHING OF IMAGES	130
XXIII.	THE MOTHER AND CHILD	133
XXIV.	VOTIVE OFFERINGS	138
XXV.	THE NIMBUS	141
XXVI.	MARKS OF THE GODS	149
XXVII.	HOLY PLACES	156
XXVIII.	MODERN PILGRIMS	159
XXIX.	BLEEDING KNEES	164
XXX.	ST. GEORGE AND THE DRAGON	167
XXXI.	POPE JOAN	173
XXXII.	THE ELECTION OF A POPE	187
XXXIII.	ECCLESIASTICAL PAINTING: ITS SENSUOUSNESS AND PAGAN CHARACTER	194
XXXIV.	ECCLESIASTICAL SCULPTURE: ITS SENSUOUSNESS AND PAGAN CHARACTER	198
XXXV.	THE BRONZE GATES OF ST. PETER'S	204
XXXVI.	THE SHRINE OF ST. ANTHONY OF PADUA	212
XXXVII.	THE BURLESQUE SIDE OF SUPERSTITION	217

CHAP.		PAGE
XXXVIII.	ORVIETO AND TRANSUBSTANTIATION.	223
XXXIX.	THE CATHEDRAL OF ORVIETO (PART I.)	228
XL.	THE CATHEDRAL OF ORVIETO (PART II.)	234
XLI.	THE CATHEDRAL OF ORVIETO (PART III.)	244
XLII.	BOLSENA	248
XLIII.	BRIGANDAGE	253
XLIV.	THE PERSECUTING SPIRIT OF ROME	262
XLV.	MODERN JESUITISM	266
XLVI.	CONCLUSION	269

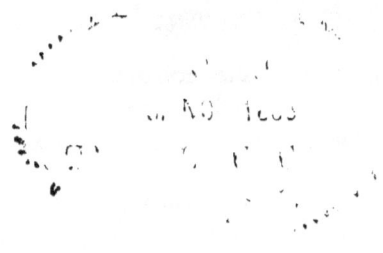

I.

THE TWO CITIES.

IN Southern Italy there are two cities hard by each other: the one teeming with life, the other a city of the dead.

These cities are Naples and Pompeii. The latter, accidentally discovered after an entombment of nearly seventeen centuries, began to be disinterred from the *débris* with which Vesuvius had overwhelmed it. This consisted, not of streams of lava, such as those beneath which Herculaneum was buried, but of ashes and pumice stone, intermingled with mud and water. By its removal an astonishing spectacle was presented to the modern world, a complete specimen of ancient civilization, with its arts, habits, and domestic arrangements, all laid bare to view; nay, even the very forms and features of some of the inhabitants of the overwhelmed city.

How, you will perhaps say, is the latter possible? Italian skill has cleverly solved the difficulty.

The volcanic ashes in which a human body was buried, were so delicately pressed upon every part of it by the water, which was also ejected from the mountain, that the form, whether male or female, was perfectly moulded. In process of time the body decomposed, but the impression upon the ashes which clasped the vanished form was still left.

Now mark the artist's skill. Professor Fiorelli—honoured be his name—has found a mould, and, see! he makes openings into the cavity, and pours in plaster of Paris, so as to fill it completely. He digs out the figure, now become solid;

he brushes off the ashes adhering to it ; and lo ! there comes forth from the ground a Pompeian man, matron or maid, horse or dog, an exact facsimile, whichever it may be, of its original.

The remains of the buried city disclose the fact that the habits of the ancient Roman differed but little from those of the modern Italian.

To this effect Professor J. J. Blunt, a most competent authority, in the third chapter of his *Vestiges of Ancient Manners* (Murray, 1828), writes as follows :—" From the discovery of Pompeii many connecting links between ancient and modern times may now be accurately traced. The same features present themselves in the general view of Pompeii as those of a modern Italian town. It exhibits indications, too, of the same gregarious habits as are still conspicuous. The ancient, like the modern, inhabitants of Italy ever preferred town to country life. The splendour of their sacrifices, the amusements of the Theatre, the Circus, the Baths, etc., have been succeeded by a magnificent Mass, the Opera, the Cafés, the Piazza, and the Corso. . . . Lapse of time, and the glories of history, have almost persuaded us that such men as the ancient Romans could not have thought, acted, and spoken like beings of this nether world. By a nearer acquaintance, however, the spell is broken, and the more that acquaintance is increased the more, I am convinced, shall we find that they resembled their present descendants."

We shall be able to test the truth of these remarks as we proceed, and shall see that in many points, and especially in matters of religion, the Italy of the present does indeed surprisingly resemble the Italy of the past. Let us illustrate this from what has been, and is daily being, disclosed in Pompeii, instancing some of the ordinary habits and usages of society.

An Englishman going for the first time to Naples, or indeed to any town of Italy, is surprised to find that, contrary to the custom of his own country, the grandest houses are built in the form of a square, with a garden and fountain in the centre; and that the ground floor and entrance to these mansions are occupied by shops, the best rooms being always upstairs. If he seeks the prototype of these modern dwellings, he will find it in the old Roman residences, and among them are those of Pompeii, where shops fronting the street are found in the basement story, and where the inner square with the little garden and fountain belonging to the dwelling, are the almost invariable rule.

These fountains are usually, as in Naples and other modern Italian towns, either jets or little cascades, to serve which there are leaden supply pipes, with cocks and the usual modern appliances. On these ancient pipes, too, may be seen, as now-a-days, the stamp marked with the plumber's name.

This correspondence of ancient with modern usage may be found also, in the Museum at Nismes, on a leaden pipe fished out of the Rhone, which in times of yore conveyed water through the river from a much esteemed fountain for the use of the dwellers on the opposite bank. In the Museum at Bath, too, there is a piece of a Roman leaden pipe similarly stamped.

No glowing fireplace cheered the occupants of a Pompeian saloon—poor enough truly is the modern Italian wood-fire—but in place of this northern comfort stood a brazier for charcoal. This is still the case in Naples, and in those towns of Italy where the English, and other northern visitors, have not yet taught the natives the use of fireplaces. Formerly nothing would have been found anywhere but these braziers and the miserable *scaldinos*, or open earthern pots of heated charcoal. I have even seen, at Pistoja in Tuscany, a bed heated with a *scaldino*. It was in the next room to mine, so I went to witness the operation.

The Pope's Swiss Guard, in their noble guard-room at the

Vatican, keep themselves warm by standing round a great open brazen vessel filled with live charcoal. As I contemplated them, I thought of Simon Peter, at the palace of the High Priest in Jerusalem, standing with the guard, and "warming himself," probably, at just the same kind of fire, the "fire of coals"—*i.e.*, charcoal—of the New Testament.

One may also see in Pompeii the shop-signs so common in modern towns. For example, the figure of a goat, or of a cow, to indicate the sale of milk; and so also the signs of various trades. Among them is a pictorial advertisement of a schoolmaster, found also at Herculaneum. Here you have it, reader.

And characteristic of the calling it certainly is, showing that pedagogues two thousand years ago were just as fond of torturing boys with the birch as they used to be in our own country in my boyish days. It made me twist as I looked at it, and thought of the petty tyrant who ground me with oppression in tender childhood. Not that I would be understood to imply that boys never require the rod. No doubt they do sometimes, and it would be a good thing if our magistrates could see that occasionally men do also.

At Siena, again, in the noble Piccolomini library adjoining the cathedral, there is, in one of the many illuminated choir books, an illustration of the same disagreeable subject.

As one walks along the deserted streets of Pompeii, the eye

is arrested by notices of municipal elections, with the names of the different candidates, which may still be seen upon the walls, where also the titles of the several guilds are yet to be read. Italy, always famous for its fraternities, received them from ancient Rome. For Sir W. Gell, in one of his charming volumes on Pompeii, says :—" In this street was an inscription of the Fruitsellers ; and it seems that there must have been a fraternity of almost every trade or profession."

Among these he mentions the corporations of Goldsmiths, Fishmongers, Woodmen, Carmen, Porters, Muleteers, etc.

Inscriptions, too, of a different kind may be seen upon the walls—scribbles, lampoons, personalities, scurrilities, and others of a still more objectionable character. Blackguards then, as blackguards now !

We have already noticed the similarity of mediæval shops in Italy to those of the ancient Romans at Pompeii. In the towns of the Rivièra of Nice such shops are still to be seen —stone counters and shutters, with an entire absence of glass For example, there are several of them in the old town of Mentone, in the " Rue Longue."

It is just the same with the kitchens. The Continental

Stove in kitchen of Pansa's house.

kitchen of the South is the kitchen of Pompeii, and it helps us to discover the kind of cooking which furnished Roman dinners —those of Lucullus for instance. For the old Roman, like the modern Italian, had the range of low arches supporting little hollow squares, for charcoal fires, upon which were fitted iron gratings for the stewpans. There you see the various utensils of the culinary art, much the same as those in present use. There, too, stand the jars, large and small, as conspicuously as in the kitchens of modern Italy or of the East, their great size frequently putting one in mind of Hadji Baba and the Forty Thieves.

An interesting instance of old Roman economy struck me in connection with these earthen amphoræ. I found that one or two of them, having been cracked, were stitched in several places with wire. And good the mending has proved to be, to have lasted, as it has done, through the best part of two thousand years. I have seen the same thing at Nismes, and with as enduring a result, in some similar Roman pottery.

But the Italians do not merely follow the Romans in the method of cooking their food,—the food itself is of the same character as that of their predecessors: and to this fact the discoveries at Pompeii give ample testimony. One of the disinterred streets has been named "The Street of Fruits," from the stores of fruits which were found in it. Figs, raisins, chestnuts, plums, fruit in glass bottles—think of that, English housewives!—oil, lentils, hempseed, etc.: all these have come to light in abundance. Bread, too, has been found, and various other things, such as money, scales, and moulds for pastry. And quite recently the tablets of a Pompeian gentleman, containing his private accounts, have been added to this curious list. In the Pompeian pictures, again, the old Roman taste is represented by sausages, hams, onions, garlic, and other savoury viands. In the Museum, one of the most curious relics of edible antiquity is some honey in the comb. With great interest I looked upon it—honey eighteen hundred years old!

The ancient Romans began their dinner with oysters: modern Europe has copied their example. As to sausages, they delighted in them; and let the shops of Naples or modern Rome testify how truly the Italian people prove their descent in this point. Only see them, reader, on the eve of Good Friday—that is the best time, and the place the Piazza Navona at Rome, or near the Pantheon; for in those localities the shops of the *Pizzicaruoli*, or porksellers, are to be found. A season of fasting it is, to be sure; but those sausage-shops do not look like it, splendidly illuminated as they are, and with their savoury and abounding goods arranged in varied and fantastic devices. Did one ever see such festoons of sausages as in modern Rome? But where are the pigs fed?

Oxford, the savour of thy sausages—how did it excite my undergraduate breakfast sensibilities! But the sausages of Imperial Rome: must not they have been, and still be, sublime? Perhaps; but I like the Oxford ones better.

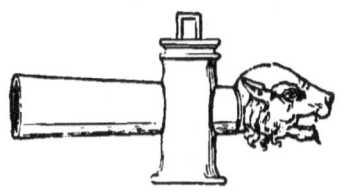

Water tap from Pompeii.

II.

THE RELATION OF PAGANISM TO THE ROMAN CHURCH.

IN the former chapter we illustrated the striking similarity of the secular arrangements and usages of modern Italy to those of the ancient Romans. That similarity may also be detected in matters connected with religious worship.

Paganism, or the rejection of the One God and the worship of other persons or things, is that to which the great masses of the human family have ever shown themselves inclined, and may, therefore, be considered to be the religion of human nature. And the element of Paganism, that in which it lives and breathes, is the material and the visible, and not, as is the case with Christianity, the immaterial and the unseen. Pagan worship is sensuous; that is, it belongs to the senses. Christian worship is not sensuous, but spiritual. For the object of Christian worship is God—a Being unseen, but revealed to faith by His Word, and not by sight.

There is, therefore, this distinguishing difference between Christianity and Paganism: that whereas the one is conversant with faith, the other is conversant with sense. "There be many that say, Who will show us any good?" "Show us good!" There is the voice of sense, of the sensuous or natural man, whether Pagan or baptized. And opposed to this voice is another, "Lord, lift Thou up the light of Thy countenance upon us." Such is the cry of faith, and of the spiritual man.

In these two voices we recognise the two religions of the

earth: the religion of nature, which naturally belongs to all men; and the religion of faith, which belongs to but few: the religion of Cain and of Abel, of the unregenerate and of the saints, of the world and of the Church.

In the following pages we shall see that the Church of Rome, though she holds some essential truth, allies herself most closely, by her materialism, to the sensuousness of natural religion, and so symbolizes with Pagan worship, from which also most of her ceremonies are derived.

Another means by which she corrupted Christianity, namely, by the adoption of Mosaic ceremonial, I do not notice. Suffice it to say that we Christians have nothing to do with Jewish ceremonies, or with temple-worship. Judaism was an infantine dispensation, the shadow of a Substance since manifested—that is, of Christ. It was but a voice, "the voice of one crying in the wilderness" of Heathendom. To the law belonged only beggarly elements long since done away in Christ. Woe to us if we seek to reinstate this effete dispensation! Christ is our "all in all," and Christ is to be worshipped, not with ceremonies, incense, bowings, and prostrations, but with the heart.

Christ loved not ceremonies. He invented none; only, out of the many which He was accustomed to see going on around Him, He partially adopted, or rather adapted, two—Baptism and the Lord's Supper. Both the rules and rites which He instituted for His new society were of the utmost simplicity, independent alike of place and of ritual.

I may, however, remark with respect to Jewish ceremonies in connection with Romish ritual, that I have been much struck by the little allusion made to them by Roman Catholic antiquarian writers. They freely refer to the Heathen origin of much in their Church, but to the Jewish element—so far as I have seen—there is seldom an allusion. And the reason I take to be partly as follows. While these ecclesiastical writers are well acquainted with the classical authors, they know their Bibles but little, or not at all. The writers in Picart, and Du Choul in his learned work full of classic lore, often refer Romish ceremonies to Heathen sources, but rarely ever mention Jewish rites. The inference, I apprehend, is that they were not acquainted with them.

It remains, therefore, a curious fact, that while Roman Catholics in England are apt to deem themselves insulted if one should refer any of their ceremonies to Paganism, their brethren on the Continent take quite a different view, and regard the adaptation of Pagan rites with satisfaction. To them it was a clever device on the part of their ancestors that they Christianized Heathen customs by appropriating them; so that, on this head, they have nothing in common with the feelings of our Roman Catholic neighbours. Ecclesiastics in Rome itself fully recognize what has been stated above, and rejoice in it.

It is more than thirty years ago since Hobart Seymour wrote the following words:—"In England, Romanists are usually indignant when it is said that their ceremonies were originally Heathen. In Italy, on the other hand, that origin is claimed for them as a proof of the wisdom of a Church which has converted a Heathen people and their Heathen customs into a Christian people and Christian ceremonies."—*Pilgrimage to Rome*, p. 228.

To have "a right judgment in all things" is good; and no doubt our Roman Catholic countrymen arrive at their more correct view of such a method of conversion through their intercourse with a people who are enlightened by the Word of God.

But the learned antiquarian Du Choul, "a good Catholic," thus expresses himself:—"If we closely investigate the subject, we shall perceive that many institutions of our religion have been taken and translated from Egyptian and Heathen

PAGANISM AND THE ROMAN CHURCH.

ceremonies. Of this kind are tunics and surplices, the crowns made by our priests, their bowings around the altar, sacrificial pomp, the music of the temples, adorations, prayers and supplications, processions, and litanies. These and many other things—*plusieurs autres choses*—which the folly and superstitious ignorance of the Heathen refer to their gods and deified men, our priests adopt in our mysteries, and refer to the One Sole God, Jesus Christ."—*Discours de la Religion des Anciens Romains, escript par Noble S. G. Du Choul, Conseiller du Roy, et Bailly des Montaignes Du Dauphiné: à Lyons,* 1580; 4to, p. 339.

The date of this book is about eight years later than that of the Massacre of St. Bartholomew (1572); so that our author may probably have witnessed the event.

He gives, observe, ten or eleven illustrations of our subject, and affirms that there are many others. And he is no mean authority, for Moreori writes of him that "he was of his day the greatest investigator into antiquity." He lived, too, at Lyons at a time when Roman antiquities were being continually disinterred.

This cut represents a baptismal font in the cathedral at Naples, of which I had a careful drawing made many years ago. A glance will show that it was originally a large Bacchic vase, for upon it may be seen the masks and thyrsi which were formerly used in the worship of the obscene god.

Font in Naples Cathedral, originally a Vase dedicated to Bacchus.

A similar vase—but not so fine—was, some years ago,

pointed out to me by the sacristan in the Church of the Bocca Veritatis at Rome; and it, also, though once consecrated to Bacchus, is now used for the Christian rite of baptism.

These fonts present a good illustration of the way in which Rome unites Christianity with Paganism. Indeed, in the one at Naples a third element is introduced: Christian baptism is carried on by means of a Heathen vase surmounted with a Jewish apex, representing the son of Zacharias baptizing Jesus!

In the cathedral at Syracuse—where also may be seen many noble pillars which once supported a Heathen temple—there is a third antique font, cut from marble, of vast size, and exhibiting a Greek inscription.

And at Naples there is yet a fourth vase, the prince of all these Heathen vessels in beauty, though not in size. It is of Greek workmanship, and its material is white marble, the base being exquisitely sculptured in relief. No doubt it once adorned some Bacchic temple: but in later times it seems, like a well known Venus, to have been used by boatmen as a column for mooring their craft, and the hawsers have left their indelible mark upon its beauty. Subsequently, it became the baptismal font of the church at Gaeta, but at last found a more fitting home in the splendid Museum of Naples.

The subject of the sculpture is Mercury giving the infant Bacchus to the Nymph Leucothea, who gladly stretches out her arms to receive him. But her neck, as well as the body of Mercury, is sadly cut by the sailors' hawsers. Dancing fawns with Bacchantes playing on musical instruments attend their god, and make up the total number of the figures to nine. There is a Greek inscription commemorating the fact that— "The Athenian sculptor made this."

Now, the adoption of these four vases—and no doubt other examples might be found—while it shows that the Christianity of Rome has no special horror of Paganism, at least so far as the worship of Bacchus is concerned, illustrates also the statement made above, that Roman Catholics on the Continent by no means shrink from that general adaptation of Heathenism which their English brethren so indignantly repudiate.

For see how freely the Italian priests use for the baptismal water of the Church those vessels from which once copious libations were wont to be poured out in honour of the Ogygian deity, amid the howlings of his drunken worshippers.

"Would you, then, never adapt anything Heathen to Christian use?"

I would not say so much, but would certainly avoid Heathen sculptures and emblems.

It is with pleasure that I recall what I have seen in some Pagan temples in Nubia—and, unless I am mistaken, also at Philæ in Egypt—where the idolatrous paintings on the walls had been daubed with Nile mud—obliterated, but not destroyed —by Christian worshippers, in order that their attention to their own service might not be distracted by Heathen blazonry.

With those long ago deceased Christians I have great sympathy; for painted windows are to me what, I suppose, painted walls were to them: they sometimes fascinate my imagination to the injury of devotion, and more frequently offend my taste.

Ancient Priestess of Isis.*   Modern Priest of Rome *

III.

THE EARLY CHURCH.

Part I.

THE corruption which Rome inherits began in the earliest days of the Church. As our Lord teaches, tares were from the first sown with the wheat. The prevalent idea of the purity of the early Church is a fiction: the Apostolic Church

---

* These illustrations, which form a striking parallel, represent an ancient Heathen priestess and a modern Roman priest, each with the aspersorium and aspergillum; that is, the holy water vessel and the sprinkling brush. The priestess is from a fine marble in the Capitol at Rome: the priest may be seen every day.

itself was not pure. And if that was not pure to which the Pentecostal effusion of the Spirit belonged, what purity can be subsequently looked for? See how the corruption was spreading even during the lifetime of the apostles. The Church of Galatia had turned away from the Gospel to the Law; the Colossians were scarcely in a better condition; the Corinthians were walking disorderly; the Hebrews were in a critical state. At Miletus the elders of the Ephesian Church were warned by Paul of "ravenous wolves," and told that ruin was imminent to their communion. Peter, James, and Jude give sad note, in their several epistles, of gross scandals which were then prevalent. And, last of all, the Lord's messages to the Seven Churches of Asia reveal deplorable corruption in their general condition.

This brings us down to about A.D. 96.

But if it went ill with the Church so far, things were much worse afterwards. By the rod of persecution the Christians were in some degree kept in the right path: but in the times of Constantine, when public persecution had ceased, worldliness and superstition openly took the lead. The effusion of the Spirit was small, and the standard of piety became proportionally low. Then priestly power and monkery asserted their sway, and Mariolatry began to come into prominence. And, while glorying in the faith of their martyred predecessors, the early Christians soon passed from venerating their memories to worshipping their bones. Then, as Jortin remarks:—"Itinerant monks, as pedlars, hawked their relics about the country, and their graves became the haunts of superstition. The Fathers of those times—Athanasius, Gregory Nazienzen, and others, but particularly Chrysostom with his popular eloquence—contributed to the utmost of their power to encourage the superstitious invocation of saints, the love of monkery, and the belief in miracles wrought by monks and relics. Some of these Fathers were valuable men; but this was the disease of their age, and they were not free from it. In the fourth century they usually introduced an irregular worship of saints on the following plea:—' Why should not we Christians show the same regard to our saints as the Pagans do to their heroes?' The transition from lawful to unlawful veneration was easily made. As the Pagans from honouring their heroes went on to deify them, so it was easy to see that, unless restrained, the Christians would conduct themselves in much the same manner towards their saints. And the Fathers gave the evil encouragement by their many indiscretions. Praying at the tombs of the martyrs was one of those fooleries which the Fathers should have restrained. What an idea did it give of the Almighty to weak Christians! As if He would show more favour to their petition because it was offered at a place where a good man lay buried!"—*Remarks on Ecclesiastical History*, Vol. iii., 7-17.

The same writer—he was Prebendary of St. Paul's and Archdeacon of London in the middle of the last century—in speaking of Justin Martyr, observes:—"Without detracting from the merits of this worthy man, truth and plain matter of fact extort from us that he and the rest of the Fathers are often poor and insufficient guides in things of judgment and criticism, and in the interpretation of the Scriptures; sometimes in points of morality also, and of doctrine."—Vol. ii., 163.

'So early, and so extensively, did Paganism begin to leaven the Church; and convenience, and also the course of events, forwarded the evil. For the Heathen temples and the Heathen courts of justice—the latter stately and convenient buildings termed *basilicas*, that is, royal structures—were naturally utilized as places of Christian worship. In the case of the second class of edifice the metamorphosis was especially easy. The *apse*, which the Heathen magistrate and his assessors were wont to occupy—he being seated on a lofty chair, and they on semicircular ascending grades of solid masonry—was now used by the bishop and his presbyters. There were rails—*cancelli*, whence the words *chancel* and *chancellor*—which separated the *apse* from the rest of the building. Close to these stood the Heathen *altar*, which gave place to the Christian communion-table. At the gates of the basilica—certainly at those of the temple—might have been the vessel for the *lustral water*, or water of purification, which remained as it was before, except that it was now called *holy water*. The images of the gods, if they were not removed, received new names, and, by a process of anointing and sprinkling, were turned into Christian saints. Sometimes, however, they were removed, and their places supplied by others less unsuitable. The hangings, draperies, and many of the ornaments, remained; the body of the building with its two galleries was left unaltered. These basilicas formed the pattern for our noblest churches, one of which, yet in existence at Bethlehem, is supposed to be the oldest Christian structure standing. The grandest in Europe is St. Paul's, outside Rome—one of those many wonderful buildings erected to captivate the imagination of man and powerfully assist in bringing him under the sway of superstition.

Enthroned in an edifice thus royal and splendid, the bishop became a person of the greatest importance, and his office was much coveted. Not infrequently his election was attended with bloodshed. As Gibbon (chap. xx.) says ;—" The interested views, the selfish and angry passions, the arts of perfidy and dissimulation, the secret corruption, the open and even bloody violence, which had formerly disgraced the freedom of election in the commonwealths of Greece and Rome, too often influenced the choice of the successors of the apostles." The historian is speaking of the era of Constantine, who died A.D. 337. The See of Rome, as being that of the capital, was of course the most coveted, and its bishops, who soon assumed a Heathen imperial title, that of Pontifex or Pontiff, naturally rose to the first distinction.

And so Paganism began to recover its power, and to prevail among the Christians themselves. "The gay and splendid appearance of the churches helped to allure the half-converts. New amusements made up for those which they had quitted. If they had been superstitious before, they might be so still. In the room of gods and goddesses they had saints male and female—lord and lady protectors—to whom they might pay their respects. Instead of sleeping in their former temples, they could slumber over the bones of the martyrs, and receive as good information and assistance as before. If they longed for miracles, prodigies, visions, omens, divinations, amulets and charms, they might be supplied."—*Jortin*, Vol. iii., 10.

In regard to the sleeping in the churches, we may remark that this is still practised at Jerusalem, in the church of the Holy Sepulchre, a night or more before "the holy fire." On one occasion I was much surprised to see a quantity of bedding in the church, and a number of both sexes waiting to occupy it. The sight was curious, but painful, and I was told that strange vows are made in connection with this ancient Heathen custom.

Du Choul (p. 319) says that in Pagan times the skins of victims which were part of the temple furniture formed the bedding. But he adds that, when Christianized, the custom became so abused that Constantine did away with such nocturnal devotions, *pour les insolences que l'on y faisoit.*

Something similar was, however, formerly carried on in St. Peter's at Rome, and continued even into the present century. At Easter a large cross was illuminated in the church, while the rest of the building was left in darkness. But all kinds of abominations compelled the discontinuance of the practice. Human nature, bad enough in the light, is still less to be trusted in darkness. However, when at Rome in 1852, I was told of something in St. Peter's even worse than this.

THURIFERS, OR INCENSE-BEARERS.
* Heathen. Christian.

IV.

THE EARLY CHURCH.

PART II.

IN the preceding chapter, allusion was made to the irregularities and violence which frequently disgraced the election of a bishop in the early times of the Church. "In the latter half of the fourth century," writes Dean Milman, "the streets

---

* The illustrations represent youthful incense-bearers, Pagan and Papal; the former from an engraving after the antique in Montfaucon's great work. Their duty was to attend upon the priest during the sacrifice, etc. An incense-box is seen in the hand of each, styled *acerra* by Pagan, and *navicello* by Papal, Rome. The Heathen official was called *camillus*: the Christian is named *thurifer* or *acolyte*. See Rich's *Dict*.

of Rome ran with blood during the contest of Damasus and Ursicinus for the bishopric of that city."

"One cannot say of Damasus, the successful combatant," remarks Archdeacon Jortin, "that he fought a good fight when he fought for his bishopric. His bravos, hired gladiators, and others, slew many of the opposite party; and great was the fury of the religious ruffians on both sides in this holy war. Pious times, and much to be honoured and envied!"

The historian Ammianus Marcellinus—an honest Pagan, as Gibbon calls him—relates that Juventius, the governor of Rome, was quite unable to put an end to these disorders, and was at last compelled by the violence of the Church factions to withdraw from the city. "Ultimately," continues the historian, " Damasus got the best of the strife by the strenuous efforts of his partisans. It is certain that on one day one hundred and thirty-seven dead bodies were found in the Basilica of Sicinius, which is a Christian Church." He adds that he does not marvel at the efforts which men put forth to obtain such a rank and power; "since, after they have succeeded, they will be secure for the future, being enriched by offerings from matrons—Damasus was called the 'ear-tickle of the ladies'—riding in carriages, dressing splendidly, and feasting luxuriously, so that their entertainments surpass even royal banquets." Strange contrast to the humble poverty of the apostles of Christ!

It was in A.D. 366 that Damasus fought for the Popedom, in the sixtieth year of his age. "But," says Jortin, "the strangest part of the story is that Damasus was a *saint*, and that miracles were wrought in his favour after his death!" The world will love its own, and here is an example of those whom it deifies! What matter, whether they be Heathen heroes or Christian saints?

Pope Damasus died towards the close of the fourth century,

and here is a bird's-eye view from Gibbon of what followed in the Church.

"If, in the beginning of the fifth century, Tertullian or Lactantius had been suddenly raised from the dead, to assist at the festival of some popular saint or martyr, they would have gazed with astonishment and indignation on the profane spectacle which had succeeded to the pure and spiritual worship of a Christian congregation. As soon as the doors of the church were thrown open, they must have been offended with the smoke of incense, the perfume of flowers, and the glare of lamps and tapers, which diffused, at noon-day, a gaudy, superfluous, and, in their opinion, a sacrilegious light. If they had approached the balustrade of the altar, they would have had to make their way through the prostrate crowd, consisting for the most part of strangers and pilgrims, who resorted to the city on the vigil of the feast; and who already felt the strong intoxication of fanaticism, and perhaps of wine. Their devout kisses were imprinted on the walls and pavement of the sacred edifice; and their fervent prayers were directed, whatever might be the language of their Church, to the bones, the blood, or the ashes, of the saint. . . . Whenever they undertook any distant or dangerous journey, they requested that the holy martyrs would be their guides and protectors on the road; and if they returned without having experienced any misfortune, they again hastened to the tombs of the martyrs to celebrate, with greatful thanksgivings, their obligations to the memory and relics of those heavenly patrons. The walls were hung round with symbols of the favours they had received; eyes, and hands, and feet, of gold and silver; and edifying pictures, which could not long escape the abuse of indiscreet or idolatrous devotion, represented the image, the attributes, and the miracles, of the tutelar saint."

Such was the semi-Pagan worship carried on in the Christian Church in the fifth century.

In the beginning of this age died St. Chrysostom, Bishop of Constantinople, who lived in the reign of Theodosius. He has left us copious and instructive details of the state of society in his capital and country at that period. In delineating its corruption, he also inveighs against the luxury of the times, and especially the dress of females, which he describes. He represents the stage as obscene and abominable, and tells us of rope-dancers, balancers, etc.; so that those who have read Kingsley's wonderful historic romance, "Hypatia," will at once perceive the source whence the author obtained some of his facts. Moreover, he censures the manner in which marriages were celebrated—the hymns which were sung in honour of Venus! the indecent plays which were exhibited to the guests, and the introduction of other abominations which were offensive, not to Christians only, but to the very Heathen themselves.

St. Cyril, Bishop of Alexandria in Egypt, comes a little after Chrysostom, and died A.D. 444. This saint was a remarkable man, and one who pushed his pretensions of priestly power to the utmost degree. His letters show the height to which the episcopal power aspired before the religion of Christ had become that of the Roman Empire. He demands implicit obedience for the priest of God, who is the sole infallible judge, or delegate of Christ, *Judex vice Christi.* "He was made bishop," says Jortin, "and made himself lord and master, of Alexandria." "He acted like a sovereign prince, and shut up all the Novatian churches, taking away their plate and furniture, and all the goods and chattels of their bishop."

At that time there were some forty thousand Jews residing in Alexandria. These had made an onslaught on the Christians, and it was thus that Cyril took his revenge. Without any magisterial sanction, he led a seditious multitude at dawn of day to destroy the synagogues, and succeeded in effecting his purpose. The Jews, taken by surprise and unarmed, were not able to resist; they were driven out of the city, and the pillage of their quarter rewarded the exertions of the *Christian* mob. Thus was Alexandria impoverished by the loss of a wealthy and industrious colony, which had been for centuries protected by special statutes.

But a yet darker crime is, it is to be feared, connected with Cyril's patriarchal chair. The Roman governor of Alexandria, Orestes, was attacked in his chariot and severely wounded by five hundred monks from the desert, the creatures of Cyril, from whose hands he was delivered by some loyal citizens. The ringleader of the monks, who was cruelly executed, was, though a rebel and assassin, treated as a martyr by Cyril, who buried him with grand solemnities, and highly eulogized him from the pulpit of the cathedral. Shortly afterwards something worse followed. Orestes and Cyril were at variance, and a rumour was abroad that their reconciliation was impeded by a person renowned, not merely in that city, but throughout the whole of civilized Europe. This was the celebrated Hypatia, whose statue in marble some of my readers may have seen in the last Paris *Exposition*. It is thus that Gibbon tells her dark story:—

"Daughter of Theon, the mathematician, she was initiated into her father's studies. Her learned comments have elucidated the geometry of Apollonius and Diophantus, and she publicly taught, both at Athens and Alexandria, the philosophy of Plato and of Aristotle. In the bloom of beauty, and in the maturity of wisdom, the modest maid refused her lovers and instructed her disciples. The persons most illustrious for their rank or merit were impatient to visit the female philosopher, and Cyril beheld with a jealous eye the gorgeous train of horses and slaves which crowded the door of her academy. . . . On a fatal day, in the holy season of Lent, Hypatia was torn from her chariot, stripped naked, dragged to the church, and inhumanly butchered by the hands of Peter the Reader, and a troop of savage and merciless fanatics: her flesh was scraped from her bones with sharp oyster-shells, which lay near, and her quivering limbs were delivered to the flames. The just progress of inquiry and punishment was stopped by seasonable gifts; but the murder of Hypatia has imprinted an indelible stain on the character and religion of Cyril of Alexandria." "At the mention of that injured name," adds Gibbon in a note, "I am pleased to observe a blush even on the cheek of Baronius."

Cyril professed his innocence; but since he would neither give up, nor even excommunicate, the murderers, we can draw but one inference.

The monks of Alexandria, with their patriarch Cyril, shared a Paganism which they held in common with that "rout that made the hideous roar," the murderers of the sweet-voiced Orpheus. They had indeed been baptized, but what difference was there in heart between them and the fierce Bacchantes who tore the poet's limbs asunder? Were not both monks and Thracian women Heathens alike?" "By their fruits ye shall know them."

And yet this Cyril was a saint!

A *camillus*, or Heathen acolyte, usually of noble birth, who acted as attendant to the priest at the altar. Copied from the Vatican Virgil.

V.

THE COMPROMISING SPIRIT OF THE EARLY CHURCH.

WE have sketched some of the corruptions of early Christianity; it is time to inquire to what causes they were mainly due. And the answer undoubtedly is—To the compromising spirit of the nominal Church.

"Rome," says Professor Blunt, "was under a temptation to mingle sacred and profane together. It did not, like Constantinople, rise at once a Christian capital. The Gospel was gradually introduced into it, and had to win its way by slow degrees through the ancient sympathies and inveterate habits of the Pagan city. It was a maxim with some of the early promoters of the Christian cause to do as little violence as possible to existing prejudices. They would run the risk of Barnabas being confounded with Jupiter, and Paul with Mercury. In the transition from Pagan to Papal Rome much of the old material was worked up. The Heathen temples became Christian churches; the altars of the gods, altars of the saints; the curtains, incense, tapers, votive tablets, remained the same; the aquaminarium was still the vessel for holy water; St. Peter stood at the gate instead of Cardea; St. Roque or St. Sebastian in the bedroom, instead of the "Phrygian Penates"; St. Nicholas was the sign of the vessel, instead of Castor and Pollux; the Matre Deûm became the Madonna; "alms pro Matre Deûm" became alms for the Madonna; the festival of the Mater Deûm, the festival of the Madonna, or *Lady Day;* the Hostia, or victim, was now the Host; the " Lugentes Campi," or dismal regions, Purgatory; the offerings to the Manes were masses for the dead."

Such is the testimony of Blunt, who adds in a note that the very name Purgatory is Heathen; since the annual Feast of Purification in February was called "Sacrum Purgatorium."

"This mode of acting," says Picart, in regard to the same subject, "was not intended to Paganize, but wisely to countermine Paganism, and as a counterpoise—*comme un contre-poids*—to parry the reproaches that the Pagans made against the Christians" (vol. i., p. 16).

"Wisely to countermine"! Such is the wisdom of this world. But "the wisdom of this world is foolishness with God" (1 Cor. iii. 19).

The following quotation, also from Picart, illustrates the principle, alluded to above, of doing no violence to sinful prejudices and habits; in other words, of doing evil that good may come. "In order to win the Pagans to Christ, instead of Pagan watchings and commemorations of their gods, the Christians rejoiced in vigils and anniversaries of their martyrs; and, to show that they had regard to the public prosperity, in place of those feasts in which the Heathen priests were wont to supplicate the gods for the welfare of their country—such as the *Ambarvalia, Robigalia*, etc.—they introduced rogations, litanies, and processions made with naked feet, invoking Christ instead of Jupiter" (vol. i., p. 26). And this, according to the writer, is the reason why "our fêtes and ceremonies have generally a Pagan origin."

Thus we trace what has been faithfully called the introduction of a baptized Heathenism. As Didron expresses it, "Christianity—his kind of Christianity—*found it necessary* to appropriate the images of Paganism, and to purify them with a Christian ideality."

Yes; and Mahomet also found the same necessity in introducing his false religion: nor is the reason difficult to discover in either case. Neither a depraved "Christianity," nor Islam, possessed an innate power that could grapple with and overcome the older idolatrous creeds : therefore both false systems were constrained to compromise. The tribes that were to be "Christianized" were allowed to transfer the peculiar worship of their old divinity to a patron saint of similar attributes. And, in much the same way, Mahomet also was forced to suit himself to circumstances, as the following remarks—copied from the *Times* of January 3rd, 1880—will show :—

"The old Sabean ceremonies and superstitions were so intimately connected with the social life of the Arabs that Mahomet was compelled to leave them almost as they were, contenting himself with forbidding a few of the most glaring and vicious abuses. Thus the mummeries of the Haji pilgrimage, with the visitation of the sacred mountains of Safa and Merwa, where two favourite idols used to stand ; the custom of pelting the Devil in the vale of Mina ; the sacrifices on the same spot ; the festival of the new moon, and a thousand other Pagan rites and observances, were left to temper the creed of the iconoclastic prophet."

In opposition to this time-serving complaisance on the part of false Christian and Mahometan, with what majesty does the uncompromising simplicity of the religion of Jesus stand forth, proclaiming in the ears of all men :—

"He that believeth on the Son hath everlasting life ; and he that believeth not the Son shall not see life ; but the wrath of God abideth on him" (John iii. 36).

VI.

FURTHER EVIDENCE TO THE COMPROMISING SPIRIT OF THE EARLY CHURCH.

IN further confirmation of the previous chapters on the early corruption of Christianity, we quote the following passage from Merivale's *Lectures on Early Church History*, in which the Dean gives his view of the Paganized condition of the Church in the fifth century—a period which many are wont to consider comparatively pure.

"But neither Leo—that is Leo the Great, Pope from A.D. 440 to A.D. 461—nor, I think, the contemporary doctors of the Church, seem to have had an adequate sense of the process by which the whole essence of Paganism was, throughout their age, constantly percolating the ritual of the Church, and the hearts of the Christian multitude. It is not to these teachers that we can look for a warning—

"'That the fasts prescribed by the Church had their parallel in the abstinence imposed by certain Pagan creeds;

"That the monachism which they extolled so warmly, and which spread so rapidly, was, in its origin, a purely Pagan institution, common to the religions of India, Thibet, and Syria;

"That the canonizing of saints and martyrs, the honours paid to them, and the trust reposed in them, were simply a revival of the old Pagan mythologies;

"'That the multiplication of ceremonies, together with processions, lights, incense, vestments, and votive offerings, was a mere

Pagan appeal to the senses, such as can never fail to enervate man's moral fibre;

"That, in short, the general aspect of Christian devotion was a faint, and rather frivolous, imitation of the old Pagan ritual.

"The working of true Christianity was never more faint among the masses; the approximation of Church usage to the manners and customs of Paganism never really closer.

"Surely we must complain that all this manifest evil was not, at this time, denounced by the teachers of the Christian Church; nay, that it was rather fostered and favoured by them."

A little further on he remarks :—

"The spirit of the old (Heathen) traditions had become to a great extent merged in the popular Christianity, and actually assimilated to it."

"The multitudes, half-Christian and half-Pagan, met together in those unhappy days to confuse the Feast of the Nativity with the Feast of the Saturnalia (in honour of Saturn); the Feast of the Purification with the Feast of the Lupercalia (in honour of Pan); and the Feast of Rogations with the Feast of the Ambarvalia (in honour of Ceres)."

Such is the opinion of Dean Merivale. We will now cite the testimony of a layman to the same effect, an extract from a well-known book, *Mathew's Diary of an Invalid*:—

"Amongst the antiquities of Rome you are shown the Temple of Romulus, built round the very house in which they say he lived. Need we go further to seek the prototype of the tale of the house of Loretto?

"The modern worship of saints is a revival of the old adoration paid to heroes and demigods.

"What are nuns with their vows of celibacy, but a new edition of the vestal virgins?

"What the tales of images falling from heaven, but a repetition of the old fable of the Palladium of Troy?

" Instead of tutelary gods, we find guardian angels.

" The canonization of a saint is but another term for the apotheosis of a hero.

" The processions are clearly copied from ancient patterns.

" The lustral water, and the incense of the Heathen temple, remain without alteration in the holy water and in the censer of the Church.

" The daily 'Sacrifice of the Mass' seems to be copied from the victim—hostia—of the Heathen ritual.

"The ceremonial of Isis to have been revived in the indecent emblems presented by women; *e.g.*, at Isernia, near Naples, up to the year 1790, as votive offerings at the shrine of S. Cosmo in that city.

" Nay, some would trace the Pope himself, with the triple crown on his head and the keys of heaven and hell in his pocket, to our old acquaintance Cerberus with his three heads, who keeps guard as the custos of Tartarus and Elysium.

" The very same piece of brass which the old Romans worshipped as Jupiter, with a new head on its shoulders—like an old friend with a new face—is now, in St. Peter's, adored with equal devotion by the modern Italians.

" And, as if they wished to make the resemblance as perfect as possible, they have, in imitation of his Pagan prototype, surrounded the tomb of the Apostle with a hundred ever-burning lights."

" Centum aras posuit, vigilemque sacraverat ignem."
Virg. Æn. iv. 200.

The writer further observes that " some traces of the old Heathen superstitions are indeed constantly peeping out from under their Roman Catholic disguises. We cannot so inoculate our old stock but that we shall relish by it. If anything could have improved the tree, it must have borne better fruit by being grafted with Christianity. But in many particulars, so far as Italy is concerned, all the change produced has been a mere change of name" (p. 90).

Just in the same strain Forsyth, a man well acquainted with Italy, and possessed of a fine classic taste, writes as follows:—

"I have found the statue of a god pared down into a Christian saint; a Heathen altar converted into a church box for the poor; a Bacchanalian vase officiating as a baptismal font; a Bacchanalian tripod supporting the holy water basin; the sarcophagus of an old Roman adored as a shrine full of relics; the brass columns of Jupiter Capitolinus now consecrated to the altar of the Blessed Sacrament; and the tomb of Agrippa turned into the tomb of a Pope."—Forsyth's *Italy*, p. 134.

And indeed all writers who are acquainted with antiquity—be they lay or clerical, Protestant or Papal, Italian or foreign—agree as to the Pagan origin of Rome's present usages and ceremonies. It is a palpable fact that, in very early times, the nominal Church made a compromise. She soon ceased to cry, "Come out from among them, and be ye separate; and touch not the unclean thing." There was no sound of the trumpet, no alarm of war, no protest, no extermination of idolatrous practices. A living Church in the midst of a sinful and adulterous generation must be an aggressive Church: but here all was compromise, polite assent, dilution, "the wine mingled with water." There was, just as there is now, a tacit consent to keep unpleasant subjects in the shade. There was peace when there should have been the shout of battle, and "Paganism was assimilated, not extirpated." "The leaders of the Church," says Merivale, "were afraid of any spiritual movement which should extend the limits of their dark outlook. They scouted the more spiritual reformers of the age, whom God will never suffer to be altogether wanting in His Church, and branded them as heretics, while they suppressed the testimony of their teaching."

How striking the likeness in the men of the present day to

the Christians of the fifth century; for the spirit of compromise is again abroad. And yet everything beyond St. Paul's "decently and in order," everything belonging to the old Heathen rites, such as gorgeous ceremonial, "high ritual," "stately worship,"—not one of these things belongs to the Gospel, not one is to be found in the New Testament, not one is countenanced by the teachings of our Lord and His apostles. All are but devices of the natural unregenerate heart of man, and have, therefore, appeared in all ages, and among all nations, whatever their religion might be.

Strange that those compromising priests of the early Church should not have been able to decipher the mind of Him, Whom they professed to own as God, by His direction given to His ancient people in circumstances very similar to their own. For the Israelites, like the early Christians, were set in the midst of an idolatrous people, and it is thus that they were commanded to deal with the abominations around them :—

"Ye shall utterly destroy all the places wherein the nations which ye shall possess served their gods, upon the high mountains, and upon the hills, and under every green tree: and ye shall overthrow their altars, and break their pillars, and burn their groves with fire; and ye shall hew down the graven images of their gods, and destroy the names of them out of that place" (Deut. xii. 2, 3).

But the teachers of the early Church could not resist the goodly Babylonish garment, and the shekels of silver, and the wedge of gold; they did not prayerfully consider God's hatred of everything idolatrous: for had they done so, Christianity would not have been handed down to us the jumble of Heathenism which it is.

Would that many clergymen in the Church of England would take warning from the mistake, and would earnestly study the Word of God with the view of ascertaining His mind upon this point: they would then no longer show that inclination toward the idolatrous Church of Rome which is now so painfully apparent.

"*Idolatrous* Church of Rome, did you say?" some might ask in surprise. Yes. On four counts at least Rome can be proved guilty of idolatry without any difficulty.

She worships graven and molten images, and to justify the idolatry frequently omits the second commandment in her catechisms, and divides the tenth into two, in order to make up the number.

She worships dead men and women, and angels.

She worships relics, especially pieces of the cross, to which she gives the highest kind of worship, called Latria.

She worships a piece of bread in the Mass, in that Sacrament which the Church of England, in her Thirty-ninth Article, designates as "a blasphemous fable."

On these four counts, then, without going further, we maintain that Rome is guilty of idolatry.

In our Protestant churches images are allowed by law for ornament, but not for worship. Unfortunately this permission opens the door for many abuses. For who shall say where ornament ends, and worship—that is, idolatry—begins? Or what true believer can read the denunciations of the Almighty against images, and all that is connected with them, and not exclaim,—"Perish images from Protestant churches!"?

The Moslem enters our places of worship, and says,—"These Christians are idolaters!"

The Jew looks into our churches, and cries,—"These Christians are idolaters!"

Both the one and the other execrate our Christianity as idolatry, and should we, for the sake of ornament, forsooth, cast this scandal and stone of offence in our brother's way? "Woe to that man," said the Lord of the Church, "by whom the offence cometh!"

In this respect, both the mosque of the Moslem, and the synagogue of the Jew, are more pure than the church of the Christian!

"Look," said a Polish Jew to his son, the latter, from whom I heard the story, being a recent convert to Christianity—"Look," said he, taking the youth to the window, and pointing to the image of a saint at the opposite corner of the street, "there is the idolatry by joining which you have degraded yourself, and dishonoured your ancestors."

The father, however, was mistaken: it was not to an idolatrous form of Christianity that the young man had become united.

"Look, look! aunt," said a little boy just come from India, as he entered an English parish church adorned with these legalized graven images, "Look at the idols!" The child in his simplicity took them for Siva, Vishnû, or other Heathen gods. One cannot help remembering to have read something about "little ones," and that it would be better for him who puts a stumbling-block in their way, if a millstone had been hanged about his neck, and he had been cast into the sea.

VII.

THE DARK AGES.

WE have already, in our third and fourth chapters, passed in review several facts illustrative of the early corruption and subsequent Paganizing of the Christian Church, from the times of the apostles to about A.D. 450. The subject is a painful one. But at a time when everything ancient—that is, post-apostolic—in Church matters is lauded and held up to imitation, it becomes a duty, however disagreeable it may be, to inquire what the truth really is. And hitherto our investigation has not strengthened our trust in antiquity. The extract from Gibbon's twenty-eighth chapter showed generally that Christian worship in the early part of the fifth century presented "a profane spectacle"; because it was to a great extent a mere reproduction of Pagan ceremonial. Then, again, the actions or writings of Damasus, Chrysostom, and Cyril, the bishops respectively of Rome, Constantinople, and Alexandria, prove that in those great centres—the capital cities of Roman Europe, Asia, and Africa—the state of religion was as corrupt as it could have been in the provinces. And what else could have been expected, seeing that two of the three saints, namely the Pope and the Patriarch, were, if not themselves men of blood, at least the abettors of murderers and assassins. The basilica of Sicinius at Rome, bespattered with the blood of the hundred and thirty-seven victims of ecclesiastical violence, and the great metropolitan church of Alexandria, desecrated by the ferocious murder of the gifted Hypatia, attest how little Christianity had subdued the Paganism of the age; while the writings of

Chrysostom give painful evidence to the same effect. Such, then, was the state of religion in the Church up to the middle of the fifth century.

Some brief notices of intermediate times may be useful, before we pass on to expose the gross darkness which was brooding upon Christendom when the light of the Reformation began to dawn upon it from the Word of God.

But was there no light through the long intervening period of gloom? Oh, yes! God did not leave Himself without witnesses. In the desert, in the monastery, in the city, here and there in dens and in caves of the earth, in the mountains of Piedmont, Dauphiné, and elsewhere, they might have been found; often destitute, afflicted, tormented, and yet the salt of the earth of whom the world was not worthy. Such were the secret ones of God; such were His elect, His faithful witnesses, who carried on the apostolic succession of the Spirit, and with whom was the fulfilment of the promise, " Lo! I am with you always, even unto the end of the world." But the sword of persecution, and the torture and flames of the Roman Inquisition—*the Holy Office*—cut off these holy ones in countless multitudes. Many of them were in the Church of Rome, but not of her: and of these not a few gradually learnt to look upon her as the woman sitting upon a scarlet-coloured beast, the mother of harlots and abominations, drunken with the blood of the saints. They testified against her idols and idolatries; and, in answer, she slew them. Very remarkable among the testimonies of the period is that of Dante, one of those who escaped the sword.

> " To you, St. John referred, O shepherds vile,
> When she, who sits on many waters, had
> Been seen with kings her person to defile—
> The same who with seven heads arose on earth,
> And wore ten horns to prove that power was hers
> Long as her husband had delight in worth.
> Your gods ye make of silver and of gold,
> And wherein differ from idolaters?" *Inferno*, xix. 106.

How terrible a comment have we upon the words "drunken with the blood of the saints" in the slaughter of the Vaudois, in A.D. 1686. Dr. Gilly informs us that, in the course of six months, out of a slender population, over twelve thousand were destroyed by imprisonment, fire, and sword,—

> "Slain by the bloody Piedmontese, who roll'd
> Mother and infant down the rock."

We will now adduce some evidence respecting the state of things in that period of the Church which is well called the Dark Ages.

Cardinal Baronius, the annalist and ready apologist of all Rome's evil deeds, thus describes it :—" It seemed as if Christ again slept a profound sleep in the ship of His Church, and there wanted disciples in the midst of the storm to awaken the Lord with their cries. . . . . They had thrust into St. Peter's chair, which was the throne of Christ, monstrous men, most debauched in their lives, abandoned in their morals, and in all respects abominable." (Quoted by Townsend in his *Accusations*, p. 103.)

"Against the Catholics," says Jortin, "their enemies alleged —'You have turned your love-feasts into Pagan sacrifices, and your martyrs into their idols, whom you serve with the very same honours. You appease the shades of the dead with wine (libations) and with funeral feasts. You celebrate the festivals of the Heathen, and their manners you retain without any alteration. Nothing distinguishes you from Pagans, except that you worship apart from them.'" The archdeacon adds, "In this there is falsehood and truth. Pagans had, with Paganism, begun to enter into the Church."

In regard to the appeasing of the dead with wine at their saints' festivals, this practice was considered good both for dead and living. As to the dead, "they thought they pleased the saints by pouring fragrant wine upon their tombs," after the manner of the Heathen. As to the living, they thought it good for themselves, and drank freely at the martyrs' graves. "Oh!" cries a saint of the time, "that they would offer with more sobriety; that they would not be quaffing wine within the sacred precincts!"

In the ninth century, Michael, the Emperor of the East, a foe to those images of which the Orthodox were so fond, in describing the worship of the Churches to the German Emperor Louis, says, "They sang before the images." This, however, is common enough now. Last Christmas I was at Arles and at Nismes, and heard young girls singing before an image of Mary in both places. It was at night, and the idols were beautifully and tastefully illuminated, while the other parts of the churches were in darkness. The effect was admirable, and the singing to the idols very sweet: but the virgins of Arles were more melodious in their songs than the virgins of Nismes. I have witnessed the same practice at Florence, and at Antwerp.

But let me say a word respecting the grand old church at Arles, to which we have just referred. Observe when you go there, reader, a curiosity—one of many—in the noble cloister of the cathedral; namely, the capital of one of the columns which represents the dream of the Magi. There they are, three little men all tucked up most comfortably in the same bed, and fast asleep. The old sacristan called my attention to this mediæval eccentricity. "*Voila!*" said he, "Monsieur perceives that they have their crowns on instead of night-caps!" And sure enough they had.

To return to the Emperor Michael. "Before the images," he says, "they sing, worship, and implore." Of course: but this, Heathenish as it is, we may see, alas! every day. What follows is, however, more startling. "Many dress the female figures in robes—a common practice still—and then make them stand godmothers to their children(!). They offer up to them the hair first cut off, just as the Heathen did. Some presbyters scraped the paint from the images, mixed it with the

THE DARK AGES.

DEIFICATION OF HEROES.

Apotheosis or Canonization Heathen.

Assumption Christian.

Eucharist, and gave it in the Communion. Others put the body of our Lord—that is, the bread—into the hand of the images, and made the communicants take it thence."—Jortin, vol. iv., p. 480. Such presbyters must have belonged to the genus wooden, as given by Boniface in a *bon mot* attributed to him. "Formerly," said he, "the Church had golden priests and wooden chalices; now she has wooden priests and golden chalices." Boniface was an Englishman known as "the Apostle of Germany," and, *although* he was canonized, seems to have been a true servant of Christ. He was Archbishop of Mentz, and, which is much more, a laborious missionary among the Pagans, who murdered him in the seventy-fifth year of his age, A.D. 755. "The day," said he, "for which I have long waited is come!" And so he departed in peace—a saint passing to his rest.

We observed that he was canonized. This process, an invention of the tenth century, was adapted from the custom of deifying heroes so common among the ancient Greeks and Romans. The illustrations on the preceding page will show the similarity of Heathen and Christian *apotheosis* or *assumption*. The first group is taken from a marble of the Empress Faustina at Rome, as given by Montfaucon; the second is from a Roman Catholic picture representing the *assumption* of our Lord's mother. The ceremony of canonization is very costly, for the fees demanded at Rome are many and large; but the result is that the canonized person becomes a saint.

I have before me a long alphabetical list, published at Naples in 1846, and entitled *Universal List of the Saints from the Beginning of the World to the Present Time*. It is impossible to number God's elect; the Lord alone knoweth them that are His, and they are a great multitude which no man can number. Yet this list may be perfectly correct; for Rome can count her own saints: but that is quite another matter.

VIII.

A DEVICE OF MAN FOR HIS OWN SALVATION.

THERE is in Scripture the record of an anxious inquirer who, nearly three thousand years ago, asked what· he could do to expiate his sins—how he could find peace for his soul. The answer was that the Lord required him to do justly, and to love mercy, and to walk humbly with his God. And so far as it went, this answer was good; though we, with our present light, would be able to refer such an inquirer at once to "the Lamb of God, Who taketh away the sins of the world."

Upon the conscience of this inquirer there was a burden of guilt so heavy that he would have made any sacrifice to be delivered from it. "Shall I," he cried, "give my firstborn for my transgression; the fruit of my body for the sin of my soul?"

And as it was with him, so throughout all generations it ever has been, is, and will be, with every conscience-stricken sinner. As soon as man feels a sense of sin, he will, if he be ignorant of the Atonement which Christ has made, manifest an earnest desire to find some way of expiating his iniquities, and of recommending himself to God. This is the religion of nature; and it is ever conspicuous in Heathenism, which is the outcome of nature.

As a rule, man is sure, sooner or later, to feel himself a transgressor; and, as a transgressor—if he be ignorant of the One Atonement—he seeks to make expiation for himself. Hence came self-inflicted tortures, scourgings, penance, privations, pilgrimages, and retirements to the hermitage or the cloister. And the universality of these religious practices—common, as they are, to all countries and all times—prove that they are no characteristic of particular races, tribes, or classes; but that they indicate a want felt by all humanity.

To meet this universal want, to calm the palpitating heart of anxious men, and to guide their steps into the way of salvation, God has given the glad tidings of His Word, which speaks peace through the sinners' Friend, the Lord Jesus Christ. And how stands the case? Man thinks he must do something to recommend himself to God. No, says the Scripture: for in the first place you *can do nothing* to recommend yourself; nor, again, is there need, since you are already recommended. Christ is your Saviour, and all that is to be done, or can be done, has been accomplished by Him. Your part is but to believe on Him: then His perfect atonement becomes effectual for you, and His wealth of righteousness is put to your account. "Believe in the Lord Jesus Christ, and thou shalt be saved."

Such, then, is God's simple and gracious method of salvation. This is *His* way of peace and holiness, and He declares that there is none other. Man, however, has many devices for the attainment of the same end, and we will now say a few words respecting one of these devices—that of self-inflicted privations and pains. Look at these scourges. One of them is Heathen —*ancient* Roman; the other is Christian—*modern* Roman. The former is from a marble in the Capitol Museum at Rome, and is figured in F. Righetti's great work (plate 130). The marble is very remarkable. It represents a priest of Cybele, an *archigallus* in full costume, with medals on his head and a picture hung round his neck, displaying the sacred *vitta* or garland, and bearing the *aspergillum*, or pot of holy water, and the whip which these priests of "the Great Mother" were wont to use upon themselves. This whip was a terrible instrument of torture, similar to the *flagellum*, or metal-loaded scourge, with which slaves were punished. The thongs, it will be noticed,

A DEVICE OF MAN FOR HIS OWN SALVATION. 43

are loaded with small squares: these are bones—pastern, or knuckle bones, *knucks*—of sheep, which must have inflicted a terrible punishment.

The other is from an original which I bought at Rome, in the Lent of 1852, at the church of the Flagellants. It is a severe instrument when applied to the bare back; its length is about two feet, and it is made of stout cord. There is a

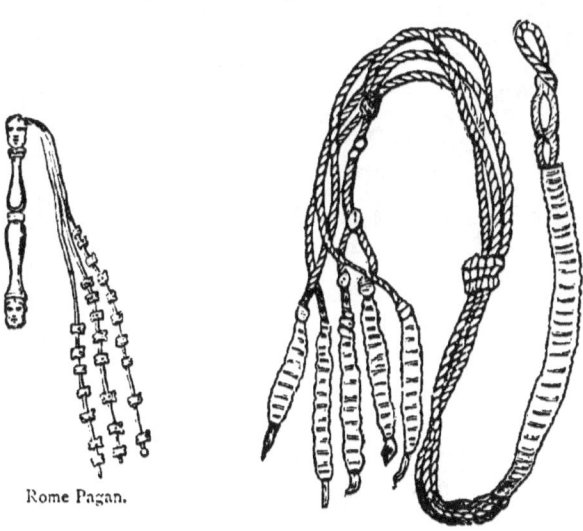

Rome Pagan.

Rome Papal.

peculiar way of using it which was once explained to me by a French ex-Trappist. The operator kneels down and strikes over his shoulders, right and left—over the right shoulder with a back-handed blow. This is done rapidly, according to the zeal of the flagellant; and, I need not say, with a very painful effect.

In the church at Rome the *disciplina* was at night, and was thus arranged. The monks assembled and sat in the choir, where I also sat with them. A few candles only were burning,

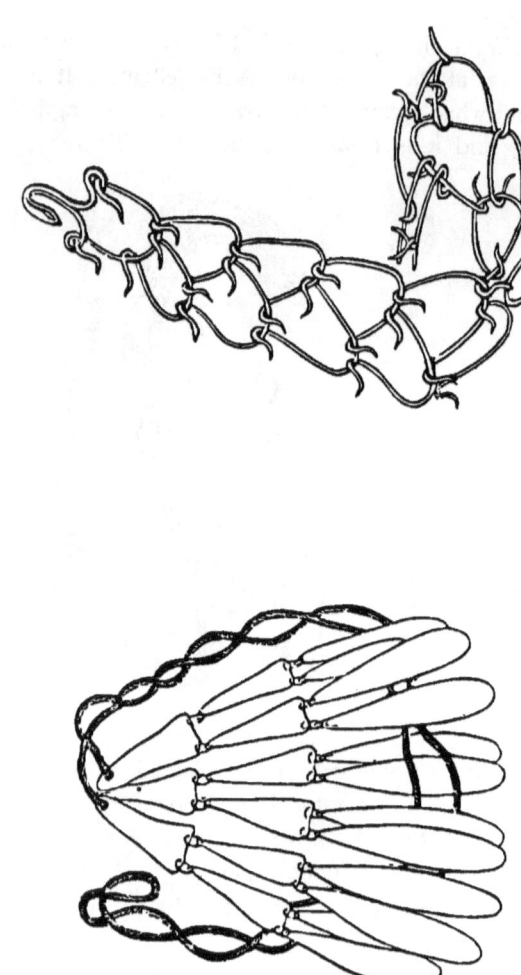

The illustration on the left represents a metal scourge which I bought some years ago at Rome. The second figure is another instrument of self-torture, the half of an iron wire belt with spikes, for wearing round the body: this also was brought from Rome.

"If in a sudden turn he felt
The pressure of his iron belt."

just so many as to enable the brother who handed round the scourges to see his way. All the candles except one were then extinguished, and by that feeble light I saw a little, while I heard much, of what was going on. The brethren—some of them at any rate, perhaps all—laid aside their garments and commenced the discipline. The church resounded with the strokes, but I heard no cries: all the monks were kneeling—some thirty or forty, perhaps—on the choir floor, opposite to each other. The exercise lasted some minutes; then the candles were relit, and we departed. A strange experience!

Ill-tempered people will say that the flagellants lashed the benches instead of themselves. I cannot tell. But the impression left upon my *mind* was that the discipline was real; while the impression left upon my *heart* was sad and painful. Every lash told me that "by His stripes" they were not healed; every reverberation echoing through the roof was a denial of the glad tidings of *free* salvation, for they by their pains and penalties were seeking to purchase it. They were as those Jews who, "going about to establish their own righteousness, did not submit themselves to the righteousness of God" (Rom. x. 3). While everything had been done for them by Another, they were seeking to do everything for themselves: they were stultifying the work of Christ, and raising up a righteousness in opposition and antagonism to His. Such is the whole monastic system. It is "another Gospel," a device of the natural man for saving himself.

Poor men! My heart bled for them, and I longed to see them delivered out of such Pagan darkness into the light of the glorious Gospel of Christ. For what real difference is there between the priests of Cybele, the Corybantes, or Galli, scourging themselves to appease their deity, and these flagellant monks? They were both alike in worshipping, not the God of Scripture, but a being of their own depraved and sensuous imagination; in following, not the guidance of God's Word, but the instincts of their own corrupt nature. In both cases the worship was Pagan; whether a pretence or a reality, it set forth the shedding of man's blood as the ransom for man's sin, and thereby ignored and trampled under foot the precious blood which was shed at Calvary.

The flagellant priests of Cybele were, like the modern monks who exercise the same vocation, ascetics; and they were well known in the same great city of Rome. Asceticism—a term derived from a Greek word which means *discipline*—together with monkery, had its origin, like most other superstitions, in the East. Thence it found its way to Rome and the West, at the time of the introduction of the worship of Cybele from Phrygia, if not earlier. There is a curious story respecting the conveyance of the miraculous image of Cybele to Rome, very similar to those which are told of other images of the same character. The ship which brought it from Phrygia ran aground in the mud at the entrance of the Tiber, and no power could move it, until, so runs the story, a young girl—whose character had been aspersed, poor thing—came, and, attaching her veil to the galley, drew it miraculously into the river. Such miracles are not uncommon in the region of superstition, whether of ancient or modern Heathenism. Have you, reader, been to Lourdes?

Besides the Corybantes, there were other monkish priests at Rome in early ages, such as those of Serapis the Egyptian Nile-god, so famed for the magnificence and glory of his worship.

The great "high place" of this divinity was Alexandria, where from an artificial mound rose the sumptuous temple erected either by Alexander or by the Ptolemy who immediately succeeded him. "There," says Milman, "all around the spacious level platform, rose the habitations of the priests and of the ascetics dedicated to the worship of the god. The temple was ascended by a hundred steps; and beneath were the dark chambers used for orgies which would not bear the light of day, and where the noblest and most beautiful women were sacrificed to the lust of the officials of the temple."—Milman, *Hist. of Christ.*, vol. iii., p. 68.

By the aid of torches I have visited some of these dark subterranean precincts. Their vastness, no less than the fine and delicate finish of all the huge stone-work of their formation, amazed me. And what obscurity, coupled with what hopelessness of escape! Fitting places, indeed, for evil men and for deeds of darkness.

Two instances have now been given of the early introduction of asceticism into Europe from the East. The practice seems, however, to have found its way among us at a still more remote period; for it was one of the earliest and most widespread manifestations of the corruption of pure and primitive religion.

In Chaldea, Thibet, China, Japan, and in India, priestly celibacy has been a custom from time immemorial, and the history of those countries bears copious testimony to the abominations which have flowed from it. In Athens there were sacred virgins bound to celibacy; and again in Scandinavia we hear of an order of nuns of noble family, whose duty it was to keep alive the sacred fire. The similar office of the Vestal Virgins at Rome, and the dreadful fate which awaited them in case of incontinency, are well known. In Peru, under the rule of the Incas, the same institution existed in the Virgins of the Sun. "These," says Prescott, "were young maidens dedicated to the service of the deity, who at a tender age were taken from their homes and introduced into convents, where they were placed under the care of certain elderly matrons, —*mamaconas*, that is, *Mother Priestesses*—who had grown grey within their walls." Their duty also was to keep watch over the sacred fire; and to be buried alive was, as in the case of the Roman Vestal, their dreadful doom if their frailty yielded to temptation. So, too, the incontinent nun of later times, when the mason had done his murderous work, found her living tomb in the wall of the convent.

One cannot but think of the scene in "Marmion," which depicts the end of poor Constance,—

> "Sister, let thy sorrows cease;"

and of the offending monk,—

> "Sinful brother, part in peace."

In 1852, travellers on their road to Rome were shown a skeleton so immured in a wall at Perugia. And Scott, in his notes to "Marmion," mentions that "among the ruins of the abbey of Coldingham were some years ago discovered the remains of a female skeleton, which, from the shape of the niche and position of the figure, seemed to be that of an immured nun."

Execrable system, which first dooms its victims to an enforced celibacy, and then with irresponsible power, and in secret tribunal, condemns them to the horrors of a terrible and lingering death if they yield to the instincts of outraged humanity! Yet such is the system which many among us would wish to see re-established in our own country!

IX.

CELIBATES AND SOLITARIES.

WHILE John the Baptist "came neither eating nor drinking," and made his home in the wilderness, our Lord "came eating and drinking," and dwelt among men. Taking advantage of this fact, His enemies were wont to say: "Behold, a man gluttonous, and a wine-bibber, a friend of publicans and sinners;" in other words, a sensualist and an associate of the profligate and the vile.

Now, by following the solitary and ascetic life of John, and declining the social life of Christ, the monastic system of Christendom declares its choice of the former and its rejection of the latter; shows its preference of the Law to the Gospel, of John to Jesus, of man to God. Monasticism is thus, from age to age, a permanent witness to the fact that the wisdom which is from beneath is opposed to the wisdom which is from above, that man's plan of salvation is diverse from God's.

Monasticism repudiates marriage; but it can find no Scriptural authority for such a course. The first celibate and the first solitary was Adam. But God said, "It is not good for man to be alone"; and so having formed Eve, He brought her to Adam to be his companion and his wife. Rome, on the contrary, affirms that the state of the solitary and the celibate is the nearest to perfection.

God says: "Increase and multiply." Rome builds monasteries, and forbids to marry.

God says: "I will, therefore, that the younger women marry, bear children, guide the house" (1 Tim. v. 14). Rome confines them within the gloomy walls of convents, and prohibits obedience to God's command.

And this the apostate Church does in the face of the fact that our Lord honoured wedlock by His presence and miraculous assistance at the marriage in Cana of Galilee—in the face of the prophecy, "Now the Spirit speaketh expressly, that in the latter times some shall depart from the faith . . . forbidding to marry"!

Indeed, so reckless is Rome of Divine authority that she pronounces the monastic life to be the perfection of Christianity—the highest of all spiritual attainments. She styles it "the religious life" *par excellence*; calls those who practise it "the religious"; and whether they be men or women, considers that they amass through their vows such a wealth of righteousness and merits that they can spare some for others who are not "religious" like themselves, and even for the souls in purgatory.

But now comes the question, Why is Rome thus opposed to marriage?

Because by means of celibacy she is enabled to detach from society, in all countries, a multitude of men and women whom she uses to forward her own selfish interests and intrigues to the detriment of society. Consider how vast a power she wields throughout the whole world in those myriads of monks and nuns who stand ever ready to do her bidding! Nay, how mighty an engine does she possess in that one department of the system, the confessional! Abolish celibacy, and you remove her chief support and stay. Who, then, can wonder at her earnest and impassioned appeals for its maintenance and extension?

But the question might be asked, Can you, then, perceive no good thing in connection with monasticism? I should be sorry to say so much as that. Nay, what chance would it have had in the world unless there had been some good mingled

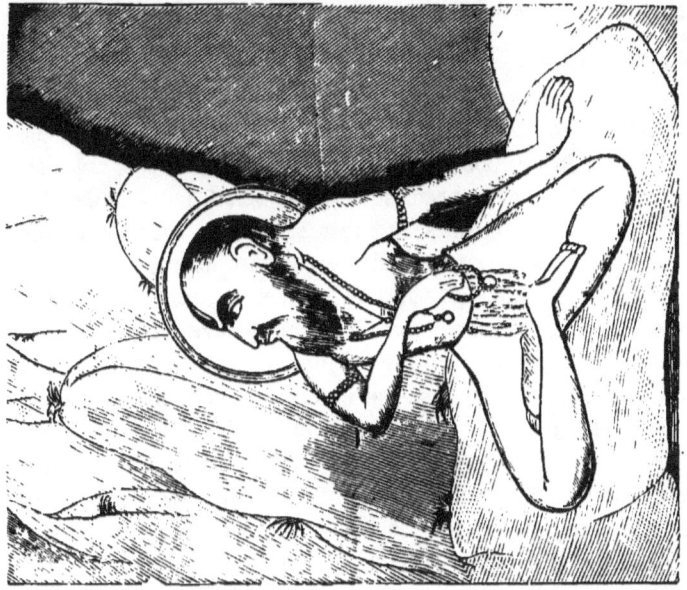

A Pagan Saint.

A Papal Saint.

with it? It must have had something whereby to allure the many excellent and honest individuals who have submitted themselves to it; and to those who, despite the influences brought to bear upon them, have rested, not on it, but on Christ, it may have been sometimes beneficial. Often, for example, amid the wars and massacres and anarchy of the Dark Ages, cloister life provided an asylum for the persecuted, the weary, the hopeless, and the ruined. And, to men and women of a certain temperament, it must have presented great attractions, promising as it did—and not always without some fulfilment of the promise—a quiet and comfortable home, the society, perhaps, of spiritual and intellectual companions, opportunities for retirement, study, and devotion, time for the cultivation of the contemplative life, and an absence of gnawing cares and of many of the temptations of the world.

But after all has been said, nothing can countervail the truth of God. For the monastic life is, as we have seen, unlawful: it is opposed both by the example of Christ and by the precepts of His Word; it is a retrogression from the liberty of the Gospel to the bondage of the Law, from faith to works. Besides which the system of monastic vows is sinful, and the forcible detention of its victim through all the long years of life soon becomes intolerable. The cloister, if you will; celibacy, if you will; but no vows. God will have us to preserve our liberty. "Be not entangled again with the yoke of bondage," is His command: and how terrible a yoke have multitudes found these vows to be! No; however well-intentioned, however useful it may have been at the first, the whole system is wrong; and the vow should be broken as soon as the conscience, through the Word of God, is convinced that it is sinful.

But monks and solitary ascetics are by no means confined to the Romish Church. On the preceding page are representations of two anchorites; the one Christian, the other Pagan; the one ancient, the other modern; the one from Europe, the other from Asia. Both of them are inhabitants of the desert: both are in a state of nudity, disgusting and pitiable objects: both have their beads, which are more necessary to them than clothing: both are holy men in the estimation of their co-religionists, and bear the name of saints.

The first picture represents St. Giles, and is adapted from Mrs. Jameson's *Monastic Orders*. The second is taken from a series of drawings "illustrating Hindoo Mythology," which were lately lent to the South Kensington Museum by Colonel Ouseley. The use of the chaplets, rosaries, or beads, which may be seen in both pictures, is one of the many Heathen practices which have been imported into Christianity.

I might add a description of two other such saints—Mohammedans, and held in the highest veneration—from my own personal observation. It was in Egypt that I saw them; the one was walking in the neighbourhood of a town; the other, whom I will describe, was seated near the Nile in Upper Egypt, not far from a village where he had lived—so I was told—for fourteen years. Both of these men were perfectly naked.

Observing one day a number of people assembled at some distance, I inquired what was going on, and, on being told that a saint was the attraction, went to see him. I found the holy man surrounded by about thirty men and women who had their eyes fixed admiringly upon him as he sat upon the ground, undraped—in the conventional language of art—and presenting a disgusting appearance. His body was much covered with hair of a reddish colour, while the hair of his head was like the wool of sheep; his skin, scorched by the fierce sun, was scorbutic and scarlet; his person was large and fat—these ascetics are well supplied with food by the people; and his countenance was sensual in the extreme. Such was the unclothed and unwashed creature, dignified by the name of saint, which I saw in the country where, in times long past, Simon the Stylite, and other ascetics *his predecessors*, had in their ignorance degraded and bestialized our common humanity.

The crowd of admirers which surrounded him were kissing his hand; while the women touched his filthy flesh and then kissed their finger, hoping thereby to receive some virtue in regard to progeny. Even our dragoman, as well as some of the ship's company, did the same as the others. The former I rebuked for so doing, because I knew him to be a Syrian Christian. "I beg your pardon, sir," said he, "I kissed my thumb."

Kissed his thumb! I remember, when a child in Devonshire, hearing just the same thing said of a man who had been sworn on the Testament in a court of justice. "No; he did not kiss the book, he kissed his thumb." And so his oath was invalid!

Men are alike in all parts of the world: the astute Syrian and the Devonian clown have the same nature, and the same tendency to resort to subterfuge. And, because this is the case, all men have, if left to themselves, one religion, that of their common nature. Look at the two saints represented above, the European and the Indian, the Christian and the Heathen: what difference is there between them? Then compare them with the saint of the Nile. Is not he, too, of precisely the same type? European, Asiatic, and African, differing as they do in nationality, language, colour, habits, and faith, are yet, as unregenerate men, one in spirit; and, being ignorant of God's Word, carry out, each in his peculiar creed, the leading instincts of natural religion. Our own fathers were no better; and had not the light of the gospel shone into our hearts, we should be like them. "But for the grace of God, there goes John Bradford," as that good man said when he saw a criminal being led to execution.

X.

MONKS AND MONASTERIES.

WE will now take a brief glance at the history of Monkery. As we have before observed, it is of Pagan and very early origin. "It maintained its authority among all the older religions of the remoter East," says Milman (*Hist. of Christ.*, ii. 35). It was introduced into Europe from Asia, and was commonly practised in various nations long before the Christian era. It was also found to be existing in America when that continent was discovered. Thus, the system was by no means new or peculiar when it was introduced into the Church: it was merely the adaptation of an old custom, which had been for centuries connected with the worship of the Heathen gods.

It seems to have first crept into the Church in the following manner: In earlier times, the Christians were cruelly persecuted, and many of them fled, as well they might, into the wilderness, and there supported life in whatever way they could.

They must have lived in somewhat the same way as the Heathen hermits did, and probably gave many hints to those who came after them. But a little later, in the reign of Constantine, the persecutions ceased, and a period of rest followed; bringing with it, however, a corruption so frightful and so universal, that numbers of pious men were more alarmed at the profligacy and wickedness of the world than they would have been at its hostility; and so, ignorant alike of what was due to their God, to their families, and to their fellow-men, they abandoned their station and their duties, and fled to join the hermits in the desert. Then a rage for celibacy and asceticism set in. Marriage was reprobated, and true chastity was said to be confined to the unmarried state; while those who had already entered into wedlock were taught that, if they would attain to a high degree of holiness, they must thenceforth lead separate lives. Many obeyed these teachings, receiving the traditions of men rather than the Word of God. Thus, the wilderness became peopled with anchorites, who soon began to devote themselves, like the Indian Fakirs, to the most terrible penances. It is stated that there were over 100,000 of these unfortunates in Egypt alone, in the fourth century. Many of them were deeply in earnest; but they were ignorant of God's Word—the only source of light; and so they thought to appease and please Him by their sufferings, in accordance with that religion of nature which belongs to all of us, and springs from an instinctive consciousness of guilt.

As the celibates and solitaries of the desert multiplied, they began to form themselves into societies, and so, after a while, the monastic system was developed.

Then different religious orders arose, the most important of which was the Benedictine, so called from its founder Benedict, who was born in Italy, A.D. 480. He was a most remarkable man, and, as Sir James Stephen remarks, "A profound genius, of extensive learning, and in the very first rank of legislators." The fraternity which he founded, with its numerous branches ramifying in all directions, exercised for centuries a vast influence over Europe, in theology, literature, agriculture, and other matters. And, unlawful and faulty as monasticism is, nevertheless, in those early days, before its corruption had passed all bounds, it certainly did confer great benefits upon the surrounding barbarism and savagery of Europe. When almost everything besides was vile, monkery, then in its prime, was better.

Moving a little lower down the stream of time, we come, in

the thirteenth century, to those wonderful institutions, the Mendicant Orders, which were also by their vows opposed to the Gospel. These were the Franciscans, Dominicans, Augustines, and Carmelites—the latter deriving their name from Mount Carmel, in Palestine.

In regard to the two former, it was in the year A.D. 1216 that, without previous concert, Dominick the Spaniard, and Francis of Assisi the Italian, met at Rome. The first of these men was a fierce zealot, the other an amiable enthusiast; but both of them were wholly devoted to the Papacy, and they had each conceived a new order of things by which to aid the Pope in crushing heresy, in checking the uprisings of the human mind, just awakening, as it then was, to the Gospel after its long and deep slumber. Pope Innocent III. approved of their schemes, and the two men bade each other farewell, and departed from Rome "to divide," as Sir James Stephen says, "the world between them." Well and rapidly did they succeed. The ferocity of the followers of the one, acting through the medium of the terrible Inquisition, and the gentleness of those of the other, which everywhere provided access for them to the homes of the people, combined to make their work effectual and complete.

By a play on their name, the Dominicans were called Dominicanes, the Lord's dogs, and the emblem of the community was a dog with a firebrand in his mouth—uncleanness, ferocity, and fire! No one can dispute the aptness of the device; for how terrible were the fires kindled by that brand in Spain, the Netherlands, Italy, Sardinia, India, and other places!

As to St. Francis, violent proceedings were not congenial to his mind; he was too amiable and gentle. He dealt in visions, revelations, and such things; nay, he would even preach to the birds and the fishes, and one of his sermons to the former is still extant. "Yet," says Sir James Stephen, "he would draw up codes and canons with the precision of a notary."

There is no doubt that by his influence, and that of his followers, he greatly assisted in extinguishing the light of the Reformation. A portrait by Sassetta represents him as trampling upon the emblems of various vices; and, among other things, upon a printing press—the type, in monkish estimation, of heresy.

Later, and immediately upon the Reformation, came the Jesuits, whose founder, Ignatius Loyola, a Spanish soldier, died in A.D. 1556. It was mainly through the address, talents, courage, and intrigues, of the members of this indefatigable organization that the Papacy recovered so much of the ground which it had previously lost. For, as Lord Macaulay observes, "during the first half-century after the commencement of the Reformation, the current of feeling in the countries on this side of the Alps and of the Pyrenees ran impetuously towards the new doctrines. Then the tide turned, and rushed as fiercely in the opposite direction. . . . It is difficult to say whether the violence of the first blow or of the recoil was the greater."—*Essay on Ranke's History of the Popes.*

But the means used to bring about this "Catholic revival" were very diverse. "The great effort," says Michelet, "of the ultramontane reaction about the year 1600 was at the Alps, in Switzerland and Savoy. The work was going on bravely on each side of the mountains, only the means were far from being the same; they showed on either side a totally different countenance—here the face of an angel, there the look of a wild beast; the latter physiognomy was against the poor Vaudois in Piedmont. In Savoy, and towards Geneva, they put on the angelic expression, not being able to employ any other than gentle means against populations sheltered by treaties, and who would have been protected against violence by the lances of Switzerland."

We will not, however, pursue the history of these orders any further; but wish to say a few words respecting the Benedictine monastery of St. Alban, an essay on which is included in one of the volumes of Froude's recent work, entitled *Short Studies on Great Subjects.*

Among some old English records, which are now in the course of publication under the authority of the Master of the Rolls, are *The Annals of the Abbey of St. Alban*, the "wealthiest and most brilliant of all the religious houses of Great Britain." These annals were collected by the historian Walsingham, who, having been himself a monk of the abbey, may probably be trusted not to give what he would consider a bad character to his *Alma Mater*. His details are very amusing and instructive.

According to tradition, St. Alban was the protomartyr of Britain. He was a Roman citizen, and is said to have been put to death during the Diocletianic persecution (A.D. 303) for sheltering his friend Amphibolus, a deacon. In his honour, and over the sumptuous shrine—a part of which is still existing —supposed to contain his remains, and another shrine said to be that of his friend, the present noble church was erected.

But did these persons ever exist? Or has all this great architectural display of shrines, monastery, and church, this acquirement of lands and other possessions, a purely fictitious origin, and is it merely due to the tricks of ignorant or designing priests?

I cannot tell. But there is no authority but tradition, and we know how unreliable that is. The whole story is extremely uncertain, and one of the latest authorities, a contributor to *Smith's Dictionary of Christian Biography*, writes, " *St. Alban, if ever he existed;*" while in reference to Amphibolus he adds, " *This is a twelfth century fiction.*" The name Amphibolus is Greek, and in that language signifies a cloak : there are those who think that this good Amphibolus is nothing more than the saint's *cloak!*

Why not? The mistake would be no more unlikely than that which gave rise to the fable of St. Oreste, whose monastery may be found on the mountain anciently called Soracte. You,

perhaps, know the story. Horace says of the old mountain:—
"Vides ut alta stet nive candidum Soracte" ("Thou seest
how deep with snow Soracte stands"). The name is now softened
into S. Oresti, with the S separated, which is the Italian method
of writing "Saint." And in this manner a new saint, one of
very many, has been added to the Roman calendar, and a
monastery has been erected in his honour upon the mountain
which gave him birth and name. There the mythical Church-
god is now taking the place of the old Heathen god Apollo,
of whom Virgil writes, "*Sancti custos Soractis Apollo*" ("Apollo,
guardian of holy Soracte").—Virg., *Æn*. xi. 785.

St. Viar, a Spanish saint, has a similar parentage. An
ancient stone fragment was found with the letters S. VIAR
inscribed upon it. "A saint!" they cry, and his fame is spread
abroad. The antiquaries, however, read the fragment otherwise, and science laughed at superstition. The letters are
old Roman characters, and, if complete, would have read,
PrefectuS VIARum; that is, in plain English, *Overseer of
roads!* The stone was a portion of an inscription in honour
of some Roman official connected with the highways. Such
is the story of St. Viar, and there are others of the saintly
brotherhood who might be shown to have as strange an origin.

But to return to the great church and monastery of St. Alban.
It was founded A.D. 793, by a murderer, the Saxon king
Offa, a descendant from Odin, who thought thereby to atone
for his crime. And the then Pope, Adrian I., himself as
ignorant as Offa, confirmed him in his error by giving him
license to found a monastery, "*in tuorum peccatorum remis-
sionem*"—"for the remission of your sins."

Of course there were the usual miracles leading to the dis-
closure of the spot where the relics of the saint were to be found.
And after their discovery they were placed in a magnificent
shrine adorned with gold and jewels of such great value that a
gallery, or loft—which you may yet see—was erected close to it

for the watchers who guarded its treasures by day and by night. If you visit it, do not forget to notice the curious stair of blocks of ancient oak. In the shrine itself, and under it, you will observe certain holes. These—the *Guide to the Abbey* tells us—"were possibly intended for the admission of diseased limbs, or of cloths to be applied to them, which, placed beneath the martyr, might derive thereby some special virtue."

Much the same thing is done to-day at the famous tomb of St. Antony in Padua. I have myself seen people rubbing their heads up and down on the tomb, in the hope that some of the goodness of the saint's dry bones might *somehow* get through the thick stone to them. It was a pitiful and sorrowful sight.

But how were the relics of St. Alban discovered? Heaven lent its aid, and somebody had a dream; in consequence of which, bishops, monks, and priests were seen moving towards the appointed spot in long procession, carrying banners, and chanting hymns. "Suddenly lightning flashed out of the sky, and struck the ground before their feet. Then, *terram percutiunt* —they strike the earth; and the bones of the saint were found entire, and placed in a *loculus*, or box—*Anglicé*, locker—inlaid with gold and set with sapphires."

This is Papal Rome's manner of procedure in such cases, and it is easy to show that she has borrowed it from Paganism. How like, for instance, is the story of St. Alban to that of the finding of the relics of Theseus as narrated by Plutarch. When the Athenian Cimon was searching for these remains, it is said that he espied an eagle breaking up the earth with its beak and talons. He recognised this as a Divine omen, and, like Offa and his ecclesiastics, at once began to dig. Of course he found; and the bones of the *Hero* were received at Athens with as much gladness as those of the *Saint* at St. Alban's.

But we may carry out the parallel a little further. The Pagans erected a magnificent temple called the Theseum over the relics of the *Hero*, while over those of the *Saint* the Christians built a noble church which they named St. Alban's. And yet again, the Pagans celebrated the "invention" of the bones of their god by setting apart a day in honour of the event: the Christians, following them to the letter, commemorated their discovery in the same manner. Whether it be dealing with heroes or with saints, the religion of nature is, in its objects and manifestations, always the same.

St. Alban did not always remain in his box. Once upon a time he manifested himself in the shades of evening to a monk who was reciting his office in the church. A discussion was being carried on in those days touching the identity of the contents of the locker, and the monk was among the doubters. But suddenly the shrine which contained it burst open, and an awful form strode out of the obscurity, and stood before the prostrate unbeliever. "*Ecce, ego Albanus!*" "Behold, I am Albanus! Didst thou not see me issue from my tomb?" "Yea, Lord and Martyr," replied the monk. Whereupon the blessed St. Alban went back into his locker—*Beatus Albanus rediit in loculum.*

The community of St. Alban's, like all other religious communities, was best in its earliest days. Wealth, and those invariable concomitants of wealth, luxury and idleness, worked its ruin. That which at first showed so fair, became so foul that its ill odour reached to Rome, "and shocked even the tolerant worldliness of the much-enduring Pope." He, Innocent VIII., enjoined Cardinal Morton to visit St. Alban's and report upon it. The original of the report is now in Lambeth Palace, and in it the Cardinal states that "the brethren of the abbey were living in filth and lasciviousness with the nuns of the dependent sisterhoods, the prioress of the adjoining nunnery of Pray setting the example by living in unrebuked adultery with one of the monks." There is much more to the same effect, "the details of which cannot be quoted even in Latin," says Froude, and with which I should be sorry to defile this book.

Alas that our rulers in State and Church should have lately selected a place so desecrated by pollution for the seat of a Protestant bishop! "The only reason for this arrangement of the new diocese—which is inconvenient, and opposed to the wishes of a majority both of clergy and of laity—is, so far as I can see, the ecclesiastical fancy to revive the memory of St. Alban." So writes to me a friend for many years an incumbent in South London, which is now a part of the newly-arranged diocese.

"To revive the memory" of one who probably never existed! Such is the present tendency to superstition in high places in the Church! Such is the outcome of the "spiritual revival," falsely so called, of the last thirty years. A *spiritual* revival in the Church of England I utterly deny; an *ecclesiastical* revival, hostile to what is spiritual, and delighting in services, ceremonies, dresses, processions, congresses, priests, bishops—provided they are favourable to it—and ecclesiasticism generally, I admit. St. Alban's is a "consecrated place," which, in the eyes of many, renders it sanctified. Froude declares that it is stained by every crime, even to the sin of Sodom, and was in the olden time "a nest of fornication, the very aisles of the church being defiled with the abominable orgies of incestuous monks and nuns."

Froude thus concludes his essay: "There is a talk now of restoring St. Alban's. We are affecting penitence for the vandalism of our Puritan forefathers, and are anxious to atone for it. 'Cursed is he that rebuildeth Jericho!'"

XI.

THE SUPERSTITION AND IMMORALITY OF MEDIÆVALISM.

SINCE there are so many who desire to restore the priestly and monkish dominion of the Middle Ages, it is most important that we should understand what it was. We will, therefore, endeavour to get a few more glimpses of the religion and morality of that period. The following remarks of Hallam are instructive:

"In that singular Polytheism, which had been grafted on Christianity, nothing was so conspicuous as the belief of perpetual miracles. . . . Successive ages of ignorance swelled the delusion to such an enormous pitch, that it was as difficult to trace, we may say without exaggeration, the real religion of the Gospel in the popular belief of the laity, as the real history of Charlemagne in the romance of "Turpin." It must not be supposed that these absurdities were produced, as well as nourished, by ignorance. In most cases they were the work of deliberate imposture. Every cathedral or monastery had its tutelar saint; and every saint his legend, fabricated in order to enrich the churches under his protection by exaggerating his virtues, his miracles, and consequently his power of serving those who paid liberally for his patronage.

"That the exclusive worship of saints, under the guidance of an artful, though illiterate, priesthood, degraded the understanding, and begot a stupid credulity and fanaticism, is sufficiently evident. But it was also so managed as to loosen the bonds of religion and pervert the standard of morality. . . . They—the saints—appeared only as perpetual intercessors, so good-natured and so powerful, that a sinner was more emphatically foolish than he is usually represented, if he failed to secure himself against any bad consequences. For a little attention to the saints, and especially to the Virgin, with due liberality to their servants, had saved, he would be told, so many of the most atrocious delinquents, that he might equitably presume upon similar luck in his own case.

"This monstrous superstition grew to its height in the twelfth century."—*Middle Ages* (1860), vol. iii., pp. 298—300.

In a note Hallam gives some examples of the stories used by the monks, from which we extract the following :—

"At the Monastery of St. Peter, near Cologne, lived a monk perfectly dissolute and irreligious, but very devout towards the apostle. Unluckily he died suddenly without confession. The fiends came as usual to seize his soul. St. Peter, vexed at losing so faithful a votary, besought God to admit the monk into Paradise. His prayer was refused ; and though the whole body of saints, apostles, angels, and martyrs joined at his request to make interest, it was of no avail. In this extremity he had recourse to the Mother of God. ' Fair lady,' he said, ' my monk is lost if you do not interfere for him.' . . . The Queen-mother assented, and followed by all the virgins, moved towards her Son."

"The rest," says our author, "may be easily conjectured." And he adds, "Compare the gross stupidity, or rather the atrocious impiety of this tale, with the pure theism of the *Arabian Nights*, and judge whether the Deity was better worshipped at Cologne or at Bagdad."

We will quote one other story from the same source, in which "the Virgin takes the shape of a nun, who had eloped from the convent, and performs her duties ten years, till, tired of a libertine life, she returns unsuspected. This was in consideration of her never having omitted to say an "Ave" as she passed the Virgin's image."

These and other examples are taken, Hallam tells us, from a collection of "religious tales, by which the monks endeavoured to withdraw the people from romances of chivalry." Certainly this was casting out Satan by means of Satan.

Of a similar tendency is the story of St. Kentigern, who figures in the armorial bearings of the city of Glasgow. It is furnished to me by my friend Mr. Macgeorge, and is taken from his *Armorial Insignia of the City of Glasgow* (Glasgow, 1866).

"The fish with the ring in his mouth in the ancient seals of the Bishopric of Glasgow, refers to the story of St. Kentigern and the lost ring of the Queen of King Cadzan. It is given in the office for the day of the saint in the Breviary of Aberdeen.

"The Queen, enamoured of a certain knight, gave him a ring which the king had before presented to her. The king, aware of her unfaithfulness, got it from the knight, and, after throwing it into the Clyde, demanded it from the queen, threatening her with death if it were not produced. Having sent her maid to the knight, and failed to recover the ring, the queen despatched a messenger to Kentigern, telling him everything, and promising the most condign penance. The saint, taking compassion on her, sent a monk to the river to angle, directing him to bring alive the first fish he might take. This being done, the saint took from the mouth of the fish, which was a salmon, the ring, and sent it to the queen, who restored it to the king, and thus saved her life."

The crest of the city of Glasgow, adopted from this vile story, is the saint vested as a bishop. On the shield is a salmon on its back, holding up to the saint a ring in its mouth; the supporters are two salmon, each with a ring in its mouth. The whole fable is represented in the seal of Bishop Wyschard

—made about A.D. 1271. The legend to the seal, on which are figured the saint, the king, and the queen—but not the knight—briefly tells the story:—"*Rex furit: Hæc plorat: Patet aurum: Dum sanctus orat.*" That is, in English, "The king rages: she laments: the ring turns up: while the saint is praying."

The hymn appointed for the *more solemn altar service* of the saint's day thus sums up the story:—

> "Mœcha mærens confortatur,
> Regi reconciliatur,
> Dum in fluctu qui jactatur
> Piscis profert annulum."

Which, perhaps, may be freely rendered :—

> "Saint queen and knight an evil union make
> With monk, who, with a hook, the fish doth take.
> The adulterous queen is by the saint consoled,
> Who kindly cloaks her guilt, and brings the tell-tale gold."

The moral tone of this Scotch saintly story is not, it must be confessed, higher than that of the two which have preceded it. And even in the present day the Church of Rome seems to have the same low estimate of her gods.

Some years ago, Ali Pasha, at that time governor of Egypt, presented the Pope with some pillars of oriental alabaster for the magnificent Basilica of St. Paul, which was then in process of reconstruction. They were designed by the architect to support the Baldachino, or canopy of the high altar, in which position the reader may now find them. In the winter of 1852 I was in Rome, and went to see them. They were lying on the ground at the time, ready for erection, and splendid monoliths they were. As I stood, with a group of friends, looking at and admiring them, the old *Custode*, who was exhibiting them, remarked, "I am sure the Virgin will never allow those columns to be erected to the honour of St. Paul."

"But why?" we asked. "Oh, she will be jealous," was the reply; "she will want them for herself."

Thus calmly did the votary attribute the vile passion of envy to his goddess. One is carried back to Homer and the courts of Olympus, to the gods the greater and the gods the less, to their squabbles, envies, intrigues, and uncleanness: and one is moved to ask,—What difference is there between gods Heathen and gods ecclesiastical; between the Pantheon of Olympus and the Pantheon of the Church?

The courteous intimacy implied in the chivalrous phrase attributed in our first story to St. Peter, when he addresses the Virgin as "Fair lady," reminds me of an Irish fact—not story—illustrative of the great familiarity existing between the gods and their ministers.

I can vouch for its authenticity, having received it from two independent quarters; and one of my informants, an Irish archdeacon who knew the persons concerned, has furnished me with their names.

A Roman Catholic priest, Father James O'M. of B——, while taking a friendly glass with some of his brethren, was summoned to attend a parishioner—a woman in child-bed at the point of death. The priest dismissed the messenger with a promise of speedy attendance, but at the entreaty of his friends, jolly fellow that he was, he stayed to take another and another glass of punch. More than once was the messenger sent away with the same assurance. Again he appeared, not, however, for the same reason as before, but to inform the priest that his presence was not now needed, since the poor woman had just passed away, without having received the last Sacrament of the Church—Extreme Unction, the priest's passport to Paradise. At first the priest was so agitated by the anger of his parishioner, and so ashamed of his own neglect, that he forgot the power he possessed over the invisible world. But, on recovering his presence of mind, he told the man that there was no cause for alarm in regard to the departed, since he could make it all right. Then, calling for a piece of paper, he wrote a few lines, and screwing the paper tightly together, desired the man to place it in the mouth of the corpse. At the same time he charged him on no account to allow the paper to be opened, or the charm would vanish and the soul be ruined.

The man went off satisfied, and so far all was well. But unfortunately the curiosity of the doctor was excited, and he felt a great desire to see what Father James had written on the screw of paper. Accordingly he persuaded the nurse, and at a convenient moment she secretly withdrew the paper, and brought it to him.

"The words written on the paper," says the archdeacon in his letter to me, "were these: 'Dear Saint Peter, please admit the bearer—she is a parishioner of mine;' and I think there was something added about being late, owing to company. Dr. H. saw the paper, and often told the story to the late bishop, Mr. L.: and many a laugh Mr. L. and myself have had over Father James and St. Peter!"

However, the Irish priest had only followed the example of no less a man than St. Gregory, called "the Great," of whom Mrs. Jameson, in her *Sacred and Legendary Art* (vol. i., p. 323), relates the subjoined story.

A monk under the excommunication of Gregory had died unabsolved, and when the saint heard of it he was filled with horror; but at the same time was by no means without resource.

"He wrote upon a parchment a prayer and a form of absolution, and gave it to one of his deacons, desiring him to go to the grave of the deceased and read it there."

The charm—which seems to have been valid only if used in a particular place, that is, at the grave—was successful; for "on the following night, the monk appeared in a vision, and revealed to the saint his release from torment."

The following modern instances from the East, for the

correctness of which I am able to vouch, are not inapt illustrations of this kind of superstition.

A priest of the Greek Church was importuned to go to a sick person, and being at play was unwilling to do so. "There," said he, taking off his cap and giving it to the messenger, "place that on the head of the sick man, and it will answer all the purpose." The messenger went away well-contented!

An indolent bishop of the same Church, too lazy to go to a distant ordination at which a part of his duty was to breathe on the candidates, adopted this expedient. Having procured a couple of bladders and filled them with his breath, he despatched them to the ordination, directing that puffs from them should be blown upon the heads of the candidates.

Such are a few specimens of mediævalism as it was, as it is still in many parts, and as some would have it to be again in Protestant England—"which peril, Heaven forefend!"

Before closing this chapter, let us glance for a moment at the applicability of Hallam's remark on saint-worship to the examples we have quoted. "It was also so managed," said the historian, "as to loosen the bonds of religion and pervert the standard of morality."

In the first instance, the profligate monk of Cologne dies in his sins and irrepentant. Yet, because he has a friend at court, and through favour of the Queen of Heaven, he escapes punishment.

The Virgin, for ten years, takes the place and duties in the convent of the dissolute nun, and for what purpose? That the latter may live an abandoned life, undetected, as long as she pleases. And, when she is tired of it, the Virgin puts her back again into the convent, and enables her to re-appear among her former companions as a chaste woman, nobody having the least suspicion of what she had been doing. She thus receives from her heavenly patroness the power to hoodwink the conventual authorities, and the privilege of being able to spend the rest of her days in peace and lying hypocrisy!

In the third, St. Kentigern is exhibited as a patron of vice.

In the fourth, the old *Custode* of St. Paul's attributes envy of the meanest kind to the Virgin, without a suspicion that he is injuring her character.

In the fifth, the moral and religious tendency of Father James' story is in every respect deplorable.

In the sixth, St. Gregory is proved to be Father James' precedent and authority, both in magic art and in pious fraud.

Lastly, in the seventh and eighth instances, the conjuring-cap of the card-playing Greek priest, and the bladders of the idle Greek bishop—but of what use is it to make remarks on such a tricky and amulet-kind of religion?

There can be no question as to the truth of Hallam's saying. Saint-worship does indeed loosen the bonds of religion and pervert the standard of morality. And saint-worship ever has been, and still is, prominent in the religion of Rome.

XII.

CHARMS AS USED IN THE PAGAN WORLD.

Part I.

FROM the earliest times to the present hour the use of charms or amulets has been universal. The strange power of fascination which belongs to them is due, I conceive, to the fact that the natural mind, being ignorant of God, must have some object of veneration or superstition. Hence the nations which have become enlightened by the teaching of the Bible have, in a greater or less degree, cast off such follies; while the Church of Rome has retained them, together with many other Pagan usages and customs, merely superadding a drapery of Christianity. For she throws something, indeed, over the nakedness of her Heathenism; but it is a veil so transparent that no practised eye is needed to detect the Gentilism which lies beneath.

The following extract is interesting.

"It is curious to note in Rome how many a modern superstition has its root in an ancient one, and how tenaciously custom still clings to the old localities. On the Capitoline hill, the bronze She-wolf was once worshipped, as the wooden Bambino is now. It stood in the Temple of Romulus, and thither the ancient Romans used to carry children to be cured of their diseases by touching it. On the supposed site of the temple now stands the church dedicated to St. Teodoro. Though names must have changed, and the temple has vanished, and church after church has here decayed and been rebuilt, the old superstition remains, and the common people, at certain periods, still bring their sick children to the saint, that he may heal them with his touch."—*Roba di Roma :* quoted in Hare's *Walks in Rome*, vol. i., p. 223.

We implied above that Romanism has not so much adopted as continued Heathen usages. And such is indeed the fact. Though called by the preaching of the Gospel to cast off Heathenism, she still carried it with her in her profession of Christianity, and made Christ, so to speak, a con-templar god —or, fellow in the temple—with "gods many and lords many." She forced the, in one sense, unsocial religion of Christ into Heathen company, somewhat as the Emperor Alexander Severus introduced the statue of Jesus among the deities of his *Lararium*, or private chapel.

This will be shown as we proceed; but, as an illustration of her general spirit, I will here quote an inscription from an altar in the cathedral at Luca. It is given in C. S. Bird's *Romanism* (Hatchards, 1851), and runs as follows :—" Christo Liberatori, ac Diis Tutelaribus ; " that is, " To Christ the Deliverer, and to the Guardian Deities," the latter being those saints who specially preside over Luca. The Heathenism of this will be apparent to those who know that the titles here given to the gods and heroes of the Church Pantheon are identical with those given by the ancient Romans to their gods and heroes.

The Lares have been already mentioned; they were little images representing the household gods, and were universally used as charms. " To what extent they were employed in this capacity," says Blunt, " may be guessed from the number of small antique figures still existing—formed of bronze, ivory, bone, and other materials—bored, and evidently intended to be worn about the neck.

" In like manner, to this day, there is scarcely an individual of the lower classes in Italy, or Sicily, who is not provided with an image, or print, of a favourite Madonna or Saint, suspended from the neck.

"I remember a shop at Trepani, in Sicily, where the principal stock consisted of figures of the Virgin of that place, carved in bone, about an inch in length, and actually having no perceptible difference from those in use among the Romans eighteen hundred, or two thousand, years ago."—*Vestiges*, p. 40.

In 1877, the writer of this book bought one of these charms in Rome; it was made of bone, and perforated so as to be worn round the neck of a woman; being, in fact, a charm for children. He gave it to the British Museum, since it was of such a character that he did not care to keep it. Museums are the proper depositories of such things, where they become lasting witnesses of the foulness of Heathenism, and of the truth of such statements as those in the first chapter of Romans, and similar Scriptures.

In Dyer's *Pompeii*, p. 446, there is an engraving of a necklace taken from a box which was found in the hand of a female skeleton at Pompeii. The poor owner was evidently fleeing with her little treasure when she was overwhelmed by the outburst from the mountain. She seems to have been a worshipper of Isis, since her necklace is composed of no less than thirty-five pieces, all of which are consecrated to the goddess and her belongings. Thirty-five charms, and yet unavailing to ward off her doom! Two of them are of the same character as the one deposited by the writer in the British Museum.

In the museum of the late Sir Richard Colt Sloane, at Stourhead—and also in the British Museum—are some *phalli*, which he obtained in 1719 at the cathedral of Isernia, near Naples, where *they had been offered ex voto!* So that, up to that time, at least, the worship of the obscene god Priapus seems to have been continued in Isernia under Roman Catholic direction.

But before we can compare the modern usages of Roman superstition with early days, we must know something of the Pagan doctrines and practices in regard to charms, and to this end we will now devote a few pages.

The following translation from the eighth Eclogue of Virgil will exhibit the popular ideas respecting charms some thirty or forty years before the birth of Christ. The rendering is that which was given in the *Fortnightly Review*, vol. xxii., p. 87.

> "Bring forth water, and wind round this altar a soft woollen fillet.
> Richest of vervain and strongest of frankincense burn on the altar.
> These be the magic rites whereby the cold heart of a husband
> Fain would I seek to entrance. 'Tis but the charm that is wanting;
> Back to his home from the city, my charms, draw the wandering Daphnis!

> "Charms have the power to draw down the truant moon from the heavens.
> Circe by charms transformed the trusty band of Ulysses.
> Crushed by the force of charms the cold snake lies dead in the meadow.
> Back to his home from the city, my charms, draw the wandering Daphnis!

> "Like as this image of clay grows hard, and the waxen one liquid
> Under the self-same fire, so let my love work upon Daphnis.
> Sprinkle the cakes, and light up the crackling laurel with sulphur.
> Daphnis burns me, and I burn this laurel, and wish it were Daphnis.
> Back to his home from the city, my charms, draw the wandering Daphnis!

> "See how the quivering flames have laid hold of the horns of the altar!
> Now, while I dally, it burst forth unbid! Be the sign a good omen!
> Something is certainly there! and Hylax barks on the threshold!
> Shall we believe it? Or is it a dream from the brain of a lover?
> Stay, my charms! From the city he comes, the wandering Daphnis!"

But after all, the testimony of Virgil is comparatively modern. Here is evidence of an earlier date. In the Swiss Lake of Brienne are the remains of a prehistoric Lacustrine village; and there human skulls have been found, submerged in the lake, with round pieces cut out of them "for use as amulets." Bits of infants' skulls were once used for this purpose, and were "put inside the heads of the dead to protect them from evil beings in the world of spirits. The same custom prevailed among the American Indians of Michigan, and in the South of

France, in Sweden, Germany, and Austria."—The *Times*, Nov. 16th, 1878. Charms, then, were known even in the prehistoric period, and when we come into historic times, they may be traced in every country. Ancient Egypt bears witness to their use. Examine the mummies in the British Museum, and you will find them fortified with amulets. I have counted as many as twenty upon one mummy.

Assyria also, in her recently discovered literary treasures, brings the same fact to light. The talismanic principle is to be seen in her very careful arrangement of lucky and unlucky days; and her monarchs wore talismans upon their persons, as their disinterred statues reveal.

Again, in Persia, similar customs prevailed; for we read that Haman (B.C. 520) was casting lots for a whole year before he could hit upon a *lucky day* for the destruction of Mordecai and his nation.—Esth. iii. 7.

In Asia Minor, we have—say ten centuries before Christ—the Palladium of Troy, an image of the goddess Pallas considered to be a charm of such power that until it was removed the city could not be taken. So Ulysses and Diomedes, as the story runs, contrived to steal it. Again, at Ephesus, the figure of Diana, "the image that fell down from Jupiter" (Acts xix. 35), was also a talisman.

Passing from Asia into Europe, we find, some seven centuries before Christ, the wondrous *Ancile* in the palace of the second king of Rome, that shield "not there conveyed by mortal hands," the sure pledge of empire. To protect the treasure from theft on the part of such rogues as Ulysses, "fertile in counsel," and his not very respectable friends, Numa caused eleven other shields to be made exactly similar to the *Ancile*, and committed the whole twelve to the twelve *Salii*, or leaping priests of Mars.

While in Dresden, in 1879, I saw, in the Museum on the other side of the Elbe, a good illustration of the first line quoted above from Virgil, " Wind round this altar a soft woollen fillet." It is "a triangular pedestal of a candelabrum in Pentelican marble."

On it are three sculptures in low relief, very arresting. In the first of them Hercules, bad fellow, steals a tripod ; and Apollo pursues him. A pretty pair !

In the second, which contains the illustration, a priest with flowing hair and long cloak, and a young priestess in a Doric robe, are consecrating a torch, perhaps for a torch race : both are standing on tip-toe, in accordance with the ancient custom of officiating priests. A bowl is set to catch what may fall from the torch, and both torch and bowl are bound round with fillets. But another feature of the picture interested me more than the illustration of Virgil, because it exhibited a modern priestly act to which I may again refer. This was the very peculiar position of the fingers of the consecrating persons in holding the fillets. " The priest with his right hand, the priestess with both hands, touch the torch *in a sacred manner*, holding up the third, fourth, and fifth fingers, the thumb and forefinger being crossed (priore digito in erectum pollicem residente)."

In the third picture, we have again both priest and priestess ; but the latter alone is in the act of consecrating a tripod, with the same peculiar arrangement of the fingers and thumb of the right hand.

XIII.

CHARMS AS USED IN THE PAGAN WORLD.

Part II.

AS we move on down the stream of time, the number and variety of amulets and charms increases. We will now notice a few of them, and may begin with the charm which was worn by all, or nearly all, of the Roman youth. This—it was not of a very delicate character—was enclosed within a small globe of metal or leather called the *bulla*, and was hung round the neck, just as in the present day the Neapolitan or Spanish peasant wears his charm.

Then, again, *bells*, when jingled, were considered by the ancient Romans to act as a powerful charm for the driving away of evil Genii. See *Rich's Dic.*, p. 666.

"tunsaque concrepat æra,
Et rogat ut tectis exeat umbra suis"

Ovid, *Fasti*, v. 4.

"The bells he jingles, and requests the shade
That speedy exit from his roof be made."

This superstition still prevails in Italy. "Why are the church bells making that noise?" said an inquirer to a peasant of that country. The answer was, "Per cacciare il Diavolo, Signore"—"To chase away the Devil, Sir."

Bells were very common among the Romans. In the Museum at Naples are several from Pompeii. The writer has an old Roman bell which he obtained at Perugia: its shape is nearly square; it is made of bronze with an iron clapper, and is fairly sonorous. It stands three or four inches high, and may, perhaps, have been worn by cattle.

Lustral, or *Holy water*, was also used by the Heathen as a charm for the purification of persons, of houses, and of temples. At the gate of the Pagan temple stood a vessel filled with it for the use, as in modern Roman Catholic churches, of those who entered. At funerals, too, the Heathen used this charm just as their Church successors do now. So Virgil (*Æn.* vi. 229-31), in describing the obsequies of Misenus, says of Æneas :—

> "From branch of olive thrice the holy dew
> Of *lustral water* sprinkling on the crew,
> The men he purified."

The use of *candles* at funerals is another Heathen custom, though now adopted by the Roman Church. Rich (*Art. Candela*) proves this from Varro, and gives an illustration from a sepulchral marble at Padua.

On leaving home for a journey, a Roman would repeat some *verse* or *incantation*, as a protection from evil.

For the same purpose he would also habitually carry some small *image*, or other

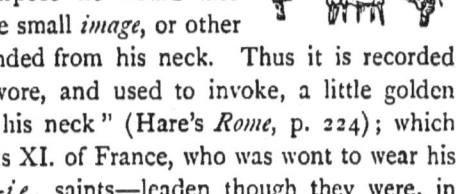

sacred object, suspended from his neck. Thus it is recorded of Sylla that "he wore, and used to invoke, a little golden Apollo hung round his neck" (Hare's *Rome*, p. 224); which reminds one of Louis XI. of France, who was wont to wear his "gods protectors"—*i.e.*, saints—leaden though they were, in his hat!

A magic property was also imputed by the Romans to *coral*,

a branch of which was thought to be eminently efficacious in affording health and protection to infants. See Blunt's *Vestiges*, chap. x., where Pliny is quoted and mentioned as having been "most industrious in recording the charms of his own time."

Did you ever, reader, drive from Perugia to Assisi; or from the station on the Ferrara and Bologna line to Cento, to see the Guercinos in that little town? (As regards the pictures of the illustrious artist, however, to examine which was my sole object in visiting the town, I confess I was disappointed.) Well, then, you may have noticed that the road to each of the two places abounds in charms. "What are all those slender wooden *crosses* stuck in the fields?" I asked my rustic companions in the public carriage. "What are they for?" "To drive away the devil, and evil spirits; and the pictures of saints you see in the trees are, Signore, for the same purpose."

Two thousand years ago, for the same purpose, there used to be suspended in the fields—what? Masks of Bacchus! Now crosses and pictures of saints have taken their place. And not only in Italy: for I have seen the same charms in the fields north of Munich.

Of the Heathen usage, the suspension of *oscilla*, or little masks, there was a good illustration in the Exhibition of the Royal Academy of 1879. It was in a small and charming picture of a *Pomona Festival* by Alma Tadema. In the British Museum one of these faces of Bacchus is preserved with the ring attached to it by which it used to be suspended.

Another talisman of Heathen Rome is the *lightning of Jupiter*, which is represented on the opposite page, from a medal of Augustus.

I give this from Du Choul, who informs us that "the Heathen—*les Gentils*—held it in singular estimation, . . . believing that after it had been consecrated by the Chief Pontiff —for the consecration of such things by a priest belongs as much to Heathendom as to Christendom—it preserved from tempests, and possessed a certain virtue."—*La Religion des Anciens Romains*, p. 286. The "S. C." on the medal is, I believe, for *Senatûs consulto*—" by decree of the Senate."

To pass on to more modern times, since the next chapter will treat of the ages intervening, we quote the following in regard to Heathen America.

"The Spanish missionaries in the fifteenth century were amazed to find the *cross* as devoutly worshipped there as by themselves. It is not generally known that the cross is originally and properly a Heathen emblem, perhaps the most ancient and

most universal of any throughout the world, east or west, north or south. The Spaniards found it everywhere in America, and made of every material. It figured on the vestments of priests, and was worn as an amulet by the people. . . . It was believed among the inhabitants both of north and south to be endued with power to restrain evil spirits."—*The Pre-Christian Cross*, *Edin. Review*, Jan. 1870.

Here, again, is something respecting China, taken from Picart's *History of all Religions*, vol. ii., p. 214.

"Navaretti informs us that the Chinese, after sacrificing to Confucius, carry home what remains of the sacrifice, which is given especially to the children, in hope that it will make them become great men." In other words, the *consecrated elements* are expected to act as a charm.

An artillery officer, related to myself, told me that, in the late Chinese war, he was present when a Tartar, badly wounded, was brought in as a prisoner. Though the poor fellow expected little mercy, his great anxiety was, not for his own safety, but for that of something which he wore suspended round his neck —his charm. This, and terror lest it should be taken from him, seemed to occupy all his thoughts.

Lately there appeared in some English journals a piece of advice to distressed Chinese, copied from a Chinese newspaper. Certain wags had been making free with some native tails by removing them from the heads of the proprietors. The result was a general feeling of insecurity and alarm; and how did the journalist endeavour to allay it? By suggesting a charm! Meet these foreign devils, said he, thus :—Fold such a paper in such a manner, carry it on your person, and your tail is safe.

The kind of charm referred to—that is, *written paper*—is also very common among the followers of Islam. I have by me several specimens which I obtained from one of the crew of the Nile boat, a Hadji, or pilgrim who had been to Mecca, and so, according to Mohammedan ideas, had become a holy man. He wore them on his person. They are of leather, about two inches square, and contain bits of paper.

Fifteen hundred years ago the learned Heathen author Quintus Sammonicus recommended the same kind of amulet. Letters were to be written in a peculiar form upon several pieces, and "then," said he, "tie them together, and hang them by a linen thread to the neck of the patient."

In the *Graphic* of February 22nd, 1879, appeared an illustration by their artist in Affghanistan, the subject of which was ' Camels passing under the Koran." The explanation given is as follows :—" Returning from pasture, camels are driven every Thursday evening—their Saturday night—under the Koran, which, placed in a turban, is suspended between two lances. The drivers are most particular to see that every camel passes under the book. It is a charm against sickness and other evils."

The *evil eye* is well known as a charm of malignity which must be met with more potent charms. It was lately stated in the *Athenæum*, in reference to Holman Hunt the painter, that " his models in Jerusalem had all forsaken him, having taken it into their heads that they were under the influence of the charm."

I have myself had a similar experience in the same country. On the high lands of Benjamin, at Jeremiah's town, Anathoth—a wretched desolate place, where, however, there is a fine Roman pavement—I was looking compassionately upon a sick sheep. The owner at once became very angry, because, as our Dragoman told me, he considered that my evil eye injuriously affected his property.

A recent number of the *Jewish Chronicle*, in giving an account of the inauguration of the religious head of a sect of Jews at Jerusalem, informs us that the new dignitary was protected from the evil eye by hands dipped in the blood of a sheep just slaughtered, the mark of the ten fingers being imprinted on his door. The *Chronicle* also states that at Tangier a red hand, painted outside a door, is a favourite charm for the same purpose.

The belief that some had power to injure by their look was as prevalent among the ancient Greeks and Romans as among the superstitious of modern times ; and the evil eye is frequently alluded to by the Classical writers ; as, for instance, in the following verse of Virgil (*Ecl.* iii. 103):

" Nescio quis teneros oculus mihi fascinat agnos."
" Some unknown eye does fascinate my lambs."

Various amulets were used to avert its influence, the most

common of these being the *phallus*—the *turpicula res* of Varro —hung round the necks of children. See Smith's *Dict. Ant.*, Art. *Fascinum*.

An Irish correspondent of mine writes to me as follows:— "The Church has continued these charms, of which some are decent, some the contrary; and many of them are, or were, placed in churches. I am told that several taken from old churches are in the museum at Dublin. They are statues of naked women which were formerly placed over the entrance doors of the buildings as lucky objects." If the eye rested on them the first thing in the morning, it was supposed that a person would be free from bad luck for the rest of the day. They were called *Shela-na-gigs*.

What the *Shela* were to the outside, that St. Christopher is to the inside of the church, his decent and respectable figure being often painted on the wall opposite the door, to catch the eye of the worshipper as he enters, "for good luck." Hence the old distich, the original Latin of which I regret that I have mislaid:—

> "Betimes to see St. Christoph is good luck:
> That day shall see thee by no evil struck."

Lastly, *Fetish*, so common in Africa, is a widely-spread charm, constituting the whole religion of many peoples. In *Macmillan's Magazine* for July, 1878, we are informed by Max Müller that "the Portuguese mariners first gave the name of Fit-igos, *i.e.*, Fetish, to the ornaments worn by the Negroes of the Gold Coast, because they themselves were perfectly familiar with the Fici-tigo (*sic*) or amulet." Indeed, since they all carried crosses or beads blessed by their priests they were themselves, in a sense, fetish worshippers.

Ample evidence has now been laid before the reader to show the antiquity, universality, and continuity in the human family, of the use of charms; to prove that, belonging, as it does, to all nations and all times, its universal development manifests a universal principle inherent in the human race; that principle being the kind of superstitious *reverence* which forms so large a part of the Religion of Nature.

In the following pages we propose to demonstrate how fully this principle is recognized and sanctioned in the Church of Rome.

XIV.

USE OF CHARMS IN THE CHURCH OF ROME.

Part I.

OUR sphere is now more limited than in the two previous chapters: we have to consider the use of charms in the Church of Rome.

In speaking above of "the lightning of Jupiter," we quoted Du Choul, as testifying to the great power attributed to it by the ancient Romans. And, from the same author, we gave a cut of the charm as imprinted upon a medal of Augustus.

We now subjoin a representation of a modern charm, equally

potent, taken from another learned Roman Catholic author quoted in Picart. It is the Agnus Dei, and forms a good pendant to Du Choul's "lightning of Jupiter."

The Agnus Dei, that is, Lamb of God, is "a medal made of wax mixed with oil and balm," on which is stamped "The Lamb and Flag," the well-known device of that once powerful and profligate order of monk-warriors, the Templars. Together with "The Saint Petershead," "The Salutation," and one or two similar subjects, it yet figures among us as the sign of a public-house.

From Du Choul we have already learnt in how great estimation the Romans held "the lightning of Jupiter," as a protection against tempests, and as possessing "a certain virtue." He also tells us (p. 285) that "the little Agnus Dei when blessed, and bells when consecrated, obtain virtue, the one to drive away tempests, the other to expel evil spirits."

The "little Agnus," then, takes in the Church the place and efficacy of "the lightning of Jupiter," so far as the weather is concerned; while the bells, able even in Ovid's time to fray the ghosts, are equally potent in the spirit world.

Here are influences exerted upon the natural and the supernatural! But why are the bells, and not the Agnus, supposed to be capable of the hardest work?

Perhaps on the score of the length of their pedigree; for the bells were originally well-known Heathens, though they are now baptized Christians. You are doubtless aware that bells are baptized. But the Agnus only appeared in comparatively recent times, to take the place of the Heathen "lightning of Jupiter," which could not be baptized. So the bells keep their own: they are now in the Church just what they were thousands of years ago in Heathendom, whereas the Agnus is only an interloper, lately come into fashion.

To the passage quoted above, Du Choul adds:—"In like manner, salt and water—that is, holy water—by means of *benediction and exorcism* obtain *force and virtue* to chase away evil spirits"—the same power as that which is attributed to the bells.

But how very strange that salt-and-water should be able "to chase away evil spirits!" Is this anywhere mentioned in Scripture?

Scripture! No. But who supposes that Church ways and doings have any necessary connection with Scripture? Nay, the priest, the charmer, and the charms—these are more to the point; these are the powers which put virtue into "the salt and water," into the "benediction and exorcism;" that which avails is the incantation, the "Double, double, toil and trouble."

> "When in Salamanca's cave
> Him listed his magic wand to wave,
> The bells would ring in Notre Dame."

And there is nothing which the priest cannot do. Of late years, since A.D. 1215, he has even taken to assert that he can turn a morsel of bread into God Himself! He does it—so he says—every day, though his senses and ours declare the falsehood of the assertion.

But to return to the Agnus Dei. If the Heathen Pontifex Maximus could by consecration infuse such power into his charm, "the lightning of Jupiter," we may well suppose that the consecration of his successor, the Church Pontifex, would bestow no less virtue upon the Agnus Dei. The following doggrel verses, a literal translation of the old French in Picart, will leave us in no doubt upon this head. They were sent by Pope Urban V. to the Greek emperor, to explain to him the value of an Agnus Dei, in order that he might properly appreciate three with which the Pope at the same time presented him.

> "Thunder it chases,
> Sin it effaces,
> From fire it saves,
> And flood when it raves.
> Sudden death shuns it,
> Devils revere it,
> Enemies fear it.

> Far from danger are set
> Both children and mother
> Who to make it are met.
> Where good is found,
> It makes it abound.
> Big pieces or small
> Are alike good to all."

So the spell of the Pope is even more efficacious than that of the Heathen. And after all, the Agnus must be as potent as the bells, and more so still; for, "sin it effaces."

But how subservient to the priesthood must the laity have been, that the former could dare, in the person of their chief and in the name of religion, to palm off such barefaced lies upon the world! What an illustration of the ancient saying, "The people wills to be deceived. Deceived they shall be."

Modern Heathenism also has its parallel to the Agnus. The following account of what has lately happened in Thibet is taken from the *Illustrated Missionary News*, 1879.

"A priest of Laboul had died, one who would, the people considered, be reckoned among the gods. So, after having burnt his body, they mingled the ashes with clay, from which small medallions were made, distributed everywhere, and kept in sacred places."

Thus, the customs of Heathenism, ancient and modern, "the lightning of Jupiter," and the medallions of Buddha, form with the Agnus of Papal Rome a trio alike illustrative of the natural religion, which is the basis of them all. Neither in Rome nor in either of the other false systems is there any power to rise from the grossness of sense to the spirituality of faith. The unregenerate man can deal only with the tangible and the sensuous; beyond this he has no perceptions, no capacity of reception. "Can a man enter a second time into his mother's womb, and be born?" "Show us the Father." "Except I shall see in His hands the print of the nails, and put my finger into the print of the nails, and thrust my hand into His side, I will not believe."

XV.

USE OF CHARMS IN THE CHURCH OF ROME.

PART II.

WE will now adduce a few more instances of the use of amulets.

Just as Sylla, the Dictator (d. B.C. 68), consulted a little Apollo hung round his neck, so Pope Gregory XIV. (A.D. 1590) put his trust in a figure of St. Philip Neri, "by which image he believed that his life was saved in an earthquake at Beneventum."—Hare's *Rome*, vol. ii., p. 168.

In Spain, during the age of chivalry, a knight was not allowed to enter the lists until he had made a declaration that he had no relic or charm upon him. Ford, in his *Handbook for Spain*, informs us that even now, few Spanish soldiers go into action without such a preservative; that the Duchess of Abrantes hung the Virgin del Pilar round the neck of her favourite bull-fighter, who escaped in consequence; and that Jose, his own guide, attributed his frequent escapes from danger to an image of the Virgin which never quitted his shaggy breast.

Spanish robbers, Ford adds, have always been "remarkably good Roman Catholics." They, too, wear their charms; while "Italian banditti always wear a silver heart of the Madonna."—Vol. ii., p. 192.

In the *Times* of Sept. 21st, 1879, the Naples correspondent wrote as follows:

"'The fanatics, who are the observers of the superstitions

practised in Naples, are those who supply the most abundant materials for the police courts. Crime and superstition go hand-in-hand. The brigands who were taken red-handed in this province were invariably found to have rosaries and relics around their necks."

I remember a painful example of this confidence in amulets at Devonport a few years ago, in a case in which it would not have been expected. It was that of an aged and well-known clergyman, who on his death-bed held a consecrated medal with the greatest tenacity.

"Mary," said a Protestant minister to a sick convert from Romanism, "what are you doing?" She had been fumbling with something under the bedclothes while he was reading the Scriptures, and made no reply to the question. It was, however, repeated, and at last the truth came out in the shape of some medals, and other consecrated toys, which she had been keeping about her. "And must I give them up?" she said in a pitiful voice. "Yes," he replied, "Christ will not share your heart with idols."

But this case is surpassed by that of two educated English ladies of my acquaintance who were not satisfied unless they had a crucifix in their bed—I suppose as a charm!

The following story, which I heard from an Indian judge, is a good instance of the trust which superstitious minds put in these charms. About forty years ago, my friend stayed at Rome on his way to the East, and presented a letter of introduction to Bishop Baggs, honorary chaplain to the Pope. He had frequent intercourse with the bishop, who evinced great anxiety to win him to "the true faith," and on one occasion said, "Will you wear this medal for nine days, while I and others pray for your conversion?" Some virtue in the medal was to dispose him to conversion; but it did not, and he remains a good Protestant up to the present time.

The following extract from Sterling's *Cloister Life of*

Charles V. illustrates the influence of charms over a great mind.

"Towards eight in the evening," his chronicler relates, "Charles asked if the consecrated tapers were ready. 'The time is come,' said he, 'bring in the candle and the crucifix.' These were cherished relics which he had long kept in readiness for the supreme hour. The one was a taper from Our Lady's shrine at Monserrat; the other a crucifix which had been taken from the dead hand of his wife at Toledo. He received them eagerly from the Archbishop, Carronza, the Primate. . . . On his bosom was placed the crucifix of the Empress, and at the head of the bed hung a beautiful picture of our blessed Lady."

So died the great Emperor!

The lamented Prince Napoleon had—as a Roman Catholic soldier commonly would—a charm upon him when he was killed by the Zulus. It was a medal of the Madonna; and a London newspaper stated that the Zulus would not detach it from his neck, because they believe that "charms," if removed from the last wearer, bring his luck with them.

It is recorded that the Duke of Monmouth, when taken prisoner at Sedgemoor, was found to have similarly fortified himself with several charms tied about his body; while his "table book"—purchased in this century at a book-stall in Paris, and now in the British Museum—is filled with songs, recipes, prayers, and charms. But all did not avail to save him from defeat and the block.

A good story connected with our subject is told by a correspondent of the *Times* in a letter dated Rome, May 26th, 1879. It relates to one of the then newly-made Cardinals, Monsignor Pie, the well-known Bishop of Poitiers—the man who denounced Napoleon III. as Pontius Pilate, was most active in recruiting the Antibes Legion for the Papal army, and supported Pio Nono in his most ultramontane measures. Here it is.

"An amusing story is told of Pie's having ordered a grand funeral mass for a Pontifical Zouave who was supposed to have fallen at Castel Fidardo—of his having extolled in glowing language the exalted virtues and heroism of the defunct, whom all should strive to imitate; while the man himself was in the church, attending his own funeral ceremony.

"At the end of the service, however, the man was arrested as a runaway debtor, to the scandal of all good Catholics.

"To escape from his creditors he had taken service in the Papal army; had fallen, shamming death, at the first encounter, and to get clear off after the battle was over, had changed clothes and passports with an officer of his own regiment, who had been killed. He had been cunning enough to leave the officer's scapular on the body, and to put the beads into the pocket of, and the decorations upon the breast of, his own jacket in which he had dressed the corpse.

"These things, found on the body of a private soldier, were taken as undoubted proofs of his virtues and valour. According to the passport, the defunct was a native of Poitiers, Pie's diocese, and when the news of so edifying a death reached him, he thought the occasion too valuable not to be improved —with the result as above.

"And the result was also improved by the Liberals, who published an account of the affair in double columns. In the one was the discourse delivered by Monsignor Pie; in the other the police report of the martyr's antecedents and shortcomings!"

We have before seen that several famous cities were in ancient times supposed to be preserved by charms such as the *Palladium* and the *Ancile*. Just in the same manner the images and relics of saints are the security of cities now. Thus, there is an annual procession on the fifth of September at Pegli, near Genoa, in honour of St. Rosalia; because in A.D. 1667 she protected the place from a prevailing pestilence.

In a church near Nice a lady once drew my attention to an ugly little image of the Virgin, which she told me had saved the town from cholera. She quite believed it, poor thing, and I well remember the energy of her statement. I had previously asked her if the tawdry little goddess was miraculous: "*Molto miraculoso*, Signore," was her reply.

We have already seen that the *Bulla*—there is a fine specimen in gold in the Vatican Etruscan Museum—contained the charm which blessed the children of Heathen Rome; a parallel may be found in these days.

"What, madam," said I to a French lady, "permit me to ask, is that object hung round the neck of your infant?"

"That, sir," she replied, "is a medal blessed by the priest, to keep the child from harm."

So the Heathen usage is continued in the Christian custom.

The coral charm, before alluded to, acts precisely the same part now as it did in old Rome, "affording health and protection to children." So wrote Pliny, and so his people still believe, and even now protect their children with coral against evil spirits.

Did you, reader, ever observe how the old painters often deck even the Holy Child Jesus with this Heathen talisman? We give a specimen above, after a picture by Pinturicchio, in the National Gallery. The four detached ornaments belong to the Child Jesus in other pictures—by Lippi, Crivelli, and others—also in the National Gallery. See pp. 37, 88, 151, 270, and 330, of the authorised catalogue, 1876.

Seven examples may, I think, be found in the gallery.

Sometimes the charm is attached to a coral necklace, and bracelets of the same material are occasionally added.

Nor is this amulet represented only on canvas. Among the bronzes in the South Kensington Museum it may be seen in bronze on the necks of a pair of children—seventeenth century —a Child Jesus and a Cupid. What a union!

We have already remarked that a superstitious Pagan blessed himself on leaving home, by some form of incantation thrice repeated. The worshipper of Papal times blesses himself by signing the cross three times.

The use of Lustral, or Holy Water, by the ancients has also been noticed. They applied it to the purification of houses, as well as persons, and even in this they are still followed. "The modern Italians," says Blunt, "use holy water as a charm. All their rooms are annually sprinkled with it."—*Vestiges*, p. 172. The writer has himself witnessed this ceremony in Florence at Easter.

Modern holy water is mixed with salt; how very ancient and Pagan this custom is, the following rendering from Theocritus (xxiv. 95-7) will show:

> "With sulphur let the house be purified;
> Then, from a full urn, sprinkle on the floor
> Pure water, mixed with salt, from side to side;
> For so the holy custom doth provide."

I conclude the chapter with a specimen of the unlimited popular belief in this charm. It is quoted from a letter which appeared in a Roman Catholic journal, from one who is entrusted, apparently, with the care of Irish émigrants.

"A storm was raging, when an old woman sent for me. I

went to her. She said she had a bottle of holy water, and that if I sprinkled the ship with it, it might still the storm. I complied with her request; after which she desired me to throw the bottle into the sea, so that it might calm the rage of the angry waters."

Christ using His cross as a charm to break open the gates of Hell, in order that He might bring forth the Old Testament saints, with Adam and Eve at their head. From a French miniature of the thirteenth century.

XVI.

USE OF CHARMS IN THE CHURCH OF ROME.

PART III.

WE have stated that, in Pagan China, the remains of a sacrifice to Confucius are carried away and given to children as a talisman, "to make them become great men." A few instances will now be cited of the uses to which the consecrated wafer filched from "the Sacrifice of the Mass" is applied in Christendom, by way of a charm.

The following are from Picart. "Sometimes," he says, "it is used as a love-charm, or philtre, both for honourable purposes, and by priests in dishonest love. Here is an example of the former.

"'A woman of Ancona,' says the Monk Bassius, 'with an unfaithful husband, reserved part of the wafer in her mouth, took it home, and then made it into a philtre to win back his love.'"

Very much like the passage of Virgil quoted in a former chapter—

"Back to his home from the city, my charms, draw the wandering Daphnis."

Again; we find, also from Bassius, that the wafer has been used as a bee-charm. The bees belonging to a certain woman were barren; so one day she did not swallow the Host at the Communion, and, "after taking it out of her mouth, placed it in one of her hives."

It will also serve as a garden-charm. A young girl of the

Isle of St. Nicholas had a garden which was eaten up by caterpillars. So she, like the others, hides the wafer in her mouth, and then, "breaking it into morsels, sows it broadcast among the vegetables."

Again; "a woman of virtue and of piety," whose son Accacius was born blind, cured him by a poultice made of this charmed bread.

But the wafer can develop still more extraordinary powers. It was the custom, Deacon Amaliri, of Metz, informs us, to bury the dead with a wafer laid on the stomach; and this, he adds, was done in the case of St. Cuthbert. Now, there was a certain man so wicked that when, after his decease, attempts were made to bury him, his dead body was twice cast out by the earth. His relations were distressed and perplexed, and appealed for advice to no less a person than St. Benedict. The saint directed them to use the charm just described, and gave them a wafer for the purpose with his own hand—*de la propre main*. This treatment proved successful, and the corpse was comfortably settled in its grave.—*Picart*, xi. 49-65.

Picart considers that the custom of burying with a wafer is a relic of Paganism, and that the wafer on the stomach was substituted for the coin which used to be put into the mouth of the corpse for the purpose of paying Charon's fee.

In the Twenty-eighth Article of the Church of England it is affirmed "that Transubstantiation hath given occasion to many superstitions." If any of us have not hitherto realized the force of this, we can hardly fail to do so after considering the quotations just given.

To one believing in Transubstantiation, the desire to have the Host buried with him is surely most natural and proper. It certainly would be my wish had I faith in the doctrine; for how comforting the idea of having God with one's flesh in the grave!

Yes, and that, too, of having Him certainly with us in life.

CHARMS IN THE CHURCH OF ROME. 99

The large Wafer used in the Mass.

The small Wafer given in the Communion to the people.

Were I a believer of the type of the woman of Ancona, or the girl of St. Nicholas' Isle, I fear I should long ago have yielded to sore temptation, just as they did, to effect such a purpose; and would wear the filched wafer ever round my neck. I entirely sympathize, *not* with their theft, but with the cravings of their humanity.

Of the caterpillars we will not say much: the girl, though sincere, must have been idle; or why did she not pick them off with her fingers? But the wife of Ancona—conceive! To be able by means so simple to restore the love of her "wandering Daphnis"!

The *quantity* of bread given to the recipient in the Sacrament has also been a cause of superstition: for the Church of Rome uses a large and a small wafer, figures of which may be seen on the previous page.

"Pride," says Picart, "leads some laics to desire to communicate with the large wafer—*grande Hostie*—in order to distinguish themselves from those—*pour se distinguer des autres*—who have only the small one." And he describes the manner in which the Sieur of Schlosperg, in the Tyrol, was punished by God for this sin, the pavement of the church yawning at his feet to swallow him up. St. Theresa, too, he says, avowed that she was glad to receive a great wafer; and so others, piously but ignorantly, "in order to obtain more abundant grace—*en vue de recevoir des graces plus abondantes.*"

Well, poor things, who blames them? I am sure I do not: it would have been the same with me but for the grace of God through the Reformation. We are all alike enwrapt in nature's night until the Word of God shines into our dark heart.

Another powerful amulet, among Heathens and Christians alike, is the *Cross.*

Here is what *The Poor Man's Catechism* teaches in regard to it. "This sacred sign is a means of preserving us from evil spirits, which disappear at its sight." How impudent a statement, when we remember some of the scenes in which the cross or crucifix has been prominent!

An engraving illustrating this charm, and intended for the instruction of young people, is sold in Paris. It depicts a child calling his good angel to succour him against a serpent which crawls towards him. In the child's hand is a cross, and the angel says, " Carry that sign before thee in confidence, and the serpent will be powerless at thy feet." How well this "Catholic" print agrees with another verse of the passage quoted above from Virgil's Eclogue :—

" Crushed by the force of charms the cold snake lies dead in the meadow."

The following from *Picart* (i. 102) is curious.

In Toulouse there is a considerable portion of the cross, which is exhibited twice in the year. At those times it is steeped in water, and the water is afterwards given to the sick, who find it a great comfort—*qui s'en trouvent extrêmement soulagés.*

Among some of the Heathen inhabitants of America the cross is, according to the testimony of the Spanish missionaries, used as an amulet, and called "the wood of health" (*Edinburgh Review*, Jan. 1870). It appears, therefore, to be good for health by way of an infusion in France, and as a solid in America!

But of the universal prevalence of the cross as a Pagan charm we say no more here, because the subject has been already treated in an illustrated work by the present writer, entitled *The Cross: Heathen and Christian*, and published by Messrs. Seeley.

The *scapular* and the *rosary* are also powerful charms. Of the efficacy of the latter the following story—from Ford's *Handbook for Spain*, vol. ii., p. 192—is an example.

" A robber, shot by a traveller, was buried. His comrades passing by, sometime afterwards, heard his voice. They opened the grave, and found him alive and unhurt; for when he was killed he had a rosary round his neck, and consequently, St. Dominic—its inventor—was enabled to intercede with the Virgin on his behalf."

A saving efficacy is supposed to reside in a *Monk's dress*, and I am told that it is still usual in Spain for sick persons to have one put on in order that they may die in it. "A monk," says *Picart* (vol. i., p. 181), "imagines that he exhales from his body corpuscles, or particles, of piety, and that if a dying man be covered with his holy garb, these particles will go straight to the heart of the latter. Thus, as regards dignity, the Monk can always *put his dress on a par with Baptism and with the Passion of Christ.*"

From what follows—extracted from the *Daily News*, March 25th, 1879—it will be seen that a similar virtue is supposed to proceed from the bodies of Heathen Monks even in the present day.

"The Phongees, priest-monks in Burmah, have great influence. There are whole districts in Mandalay devoted to Phongee monasteries. A Phongee has no bother about anything at all. He is forbidden to have any money, nor does he want it: he wears a bright yellow garment. People bring him his food—rice from this admirer, or from that. His life is celibate: he is not supposed to let his eyes rest upon a woman, but has a quiet knack of giving a sly glance out of the corners of them. He never goes hungry, and when he dies, has a funeral the pageant of which may last for days. When dead, he is plunged into a *cask of honey;* and, after such a time as may be sufficient to allow the virtues of him—'corpuscles of piety'—to pass into the honey, he is fished out, and pious people greedily consume the honey."

So closely is the monachism of Heathendom allied to that of Churchdom; so clearly do they exhibit their common origin in the Religion of Nature.

Homer tells us of the wonder-working cestus, or girdle, of Venus—

> "The broidered cestus wrought with every charm
> To win the heart."

Like it is the *girdle* of the Virgin of Tortosa in Spain. "It was brought from Heaven by herself in A.D. 1178, and became the Palladium of the city. Like the Bambino Jesu of the Ara-Cœli at Rome, it is also particularly invoked by women in child-birth."—Ford's *Handbook for Spain*, vol. ii., p. 160.

Lucky and unlucky days, as in the already quoted case of Haman, were much regarded by the Heathen. In the Assyrian monuments great stress is laid on them; and reference to them may be found also in the Classical authors. "Days," says Aulus Gellius (v. 9), "of ill-repute for their bad omen, and forbidden, are termed superstitious, on which one must neither perform religious rites nor begin any new undertaking." Christianity puts all days except the Lord's day on a level: but superstition ever resists this, and exalts one day above another to the bane of the Church of Christ. "How turn ye again to the weak and beggarly elements, whereunto ye desire again to be in bondage? Ye observe days" (Gal. iv. 9, 10).

Numerous are the Saints' days of Rome; and it is sad to know that our bishops and clergy are pressing the observance of them upon us, as well as that of the forty days of Lent. Neither of these, so far as I can understand, suit that "liberty wherewith Christ hath made us free." What is Lent but a "yoke of bondage?" Its observance may be traced among Heathens ancient and modern: long fasts and oft-repeated prayers are ever characteristic of the Religion of Nature.

XVII.

THE CONSECRATION OF HOLY FIRE AND HOLY WATER.

WHENCE comes the holy fire which one sees ever burning in Roman Catholic churches?

Having this morning—"Holy Saturday," April 12th, 1879—witnessed its generation by the priests, just outside the gate of the large church at Mentone, I am able to tell.

Saturday in "holy week" is a great day for Church ceremonies, especially for those which are connected with "holy fire" and "holy water."

The week has been, of course, ceremonious and sombre. Last Sunday the blessing of palms and branches took place: the ceremony was performed in the church with "holy water" manufactured a year ago. As I was going to the Protestant place of worship on that day, I met with a number of people carrying home consecrated palms, in order to place them in their houses, and use them as charms. Of two persons who bore them, I asked their use. "For charms," was the reply—*Contre les mauvais esprits, et pour chasser le Diable.*" These palms, like the holy fire and water, are renewed at the same time every year. The old ones are burned: and with the ashes, my informant tells me, he made the sign of the cross on his forehead on Ash Wednesday. So at Rome, on the same occasion, and with similar material, I have seen the Pope in grand state charming the Cardinals as they knelt before him.

There are many other sights in this week, such as the table set out for the Supper, the washing of the pilgrims' feet, and the procession, on the night of Good Friday, of the dead

Christ. This is a figure as large as life, and shocking to look upon. It is placed upon a bier, and, accompanied with lights and music and chanting, it is carried through the town upon men's shoulders from church to church. For a while it is deposited in a public place on its illuminated catafalque, and then it is borne back in procession to its pretended tomb in the church. Such is the manner in which I have seen the ceremony performed.

Subjoined is a list of the usual doings in Roman Catholic countries during Passion week; it is extracted from the *Monaco Journal*, April, 1879.

Offices De La Semaine-Sainte A La Cathédrale.

6. *Avril. Dimanche des Rameaux.*
Bénédiction des palmes faite par Mgr. l'Evêque. Procession. Grand'Messe, à laquelle Sa Grandeur assistera en cappa. Chant de la Passion.

L'après-midi.—Vêpres, Sermon, Salut.

MERCREDI SAINT.

Trois heures et demie.—Office des Ténèbres.

JEUDI SAINT.

Sept heures du Matin.—Communion générale, donnée par Sa Grandeur.

Matin.—Grand'Messe Pontificale. Bénédiction des Saintes Huiles. Procession au Reposoir. Lavement des pieds par Mgr. l'Evêque.

L'après-midi.—Office des Ténèbres.

Du soir.—Procession de la Confrèrie des Penitents. Sermon à la Cathédrale.

VENDREDI SAINT.

Matin.—Chant de la Passion. Adoration de la Croix. Procession du Reposoir. Messe des Présanctifiés.

Après-midi.—Les trois heures d'agonie avec chants. Sermons suivis de l'Office des Ténèbres.

Huit heures du soir.—Procession du Christ mort de l'église des Penitents à la Cathédrale. Sermon. Chant du "Stabat Mater."

Samedi Saint.

Huit heures et demie du Matin.—Bénédiction du Feu. Chant des Prophéties. Bénédiction des Fonts. Grand'Messe Pontificale.

We said that the week has been sombre : but its oppressiveness will presently be relieved by an Easter outburst of enjoyment and dissipation—a natural reaction after the enforced, and therefore unscriptural, observance of Lent. Since Thursday even the bells, always so offensively noisy in advertizing the Clergy and their doings, have been silent. In some places —as, for instance, in Malta—the people are called together during these days by the clapping of boards, a process which I have also witnessed at the Armenian monastery in Jerusalem. But, at any rate, the silence is frequently broken by the rattling of Judas' bones—a statement which may fairly require some explanation.

Well, the said bones are pieces of wood, used as a sort of castanet, which the boys rattle in the streets more or less throughout Lent. This is one way in which the people show their piety, by rattling the supposed bones of the traitor: while, at the end of Lent, they belabour his image with clubs, and afterwards burn it. In the same manner one may sometimes see the effigy of Judas burned amid execrations, at this time of the year, on board the Portuguese ships in the London Docks. Truly there are strange ways of expressing piety !

But we will now watch the ceremony of the blessing of the fire. Just outside the door of the church, on the right side and on the upper step, is a little heap of shavings and fircones ; and many children in picturesque dresses are standing near to see the sight. Immediately within the door a lectern has been placed, and the service-book is laid upon it ; so that everything is now ready for the ceremony.

Soon after nine o'clock, a company of priests, handsomely dressed, with acolytes, etc., march in procession from within to the door. They bring with them a censer, a vessel of holy water with a sprinkler, and a plate upon which are laid some small candles, a piece of incense, an apparatus for striking a light, and four lemon-coloured and lemon-like balls. There is some trouble in producing the light, since the Papacy will have nothing to do with the "lucifers" of the nineteenth century, and rigidly adheres to the old flint-and-steel as appointed by her rubric.

So there is a long pause, while the priest is contending with his difficulties. At length, however, the light is obtained in the orthodox way, the shavings and fircones are kindled, and from them the incense in the censer, and also the candles. Now follows a brief office in the porch, and the candles, objects in the plate, etc., together with the fire itself, are all sprinkled with holy water—that is, with the old holy water consecrated a twelvemonth ago. Now a procession is formed, and as it slowly advances up the church, those who compose it chant, and, at stated intervals, fall on their knees, until in this manner they reach the altar, where some candles, which have been previously extinguished, are relighted with the newly-obtained fire.

Such was the ceremony, and very Heathen and wizard it seemed. Picart gives an engraving of it, but no explanation. Foye's *Romish Rites* furnishes the following additional particulars, among others.—That the priest blesses the new fire in front of the church, then blesses five grains of incense to be put into the wax taper, and sprinkles them with holy water; and also that three candles, previously blessed, and fixed on a triangle elevated upon a cane, are lighted at intervals.

Later, in the same morning, the water ceremony is performed; but this takes place within the church. I extract from Foye the following particulars in regard to it.

It appears that there are three kinds of holy water, two of which are used for the consecration of churches.

Of these two, the first is considered to be inferior, since nothing but salt is used in its preparation—"salt exorcised for the salvation of those that believe." It serves for sprinkling the building.

The other is made up by a mixture of salt, ashes, and wine —all blessed, of course. This appears to be the holier of the two, and is used for the consecration of the altar.

The third class of holy water, that which is referred to above as being consecrated on "Holy Saturday," is used for baptisms during the following year; and also, as I gather, for sprinkling generally.

In its preparation—amid many exorcisms of devils and evil spirits, and forms of prayer—the following ceremonies are observed.

The priest divides the water in the font, with his hand, in the shape of a cross.

In exorcising the water, he touches it with his hand.

In blessing it, he thrice makes over it the sign of the cross.

In dividing it, he pours it towards the four quarters of heaven.

He breathes thrice into it in the form of a cross.

He lets down the great Paschal candle a little into it, and says, "The might of the Holy Ghost descend into this fountain-plenitude"—*In hanc plenitudinem fontis.*

Then he takes the candle from the water, and again merges it more deeply, saying the same words as before, but in a higher tone.

The third time he plunges it to the bottom, again repeating the formula with a still louder voice.

Then blowing—*sufflans*—thrice into the water in the form of the Greek letter *Psi*, he says, "Impregnate with regenerating efficacy the whole substance of this water;" and so takes the candle out of the font.

Besides these doings, various oils are poured into the

water, and mixed with the hand; and, still more strange, *spittle* is mingled with it, as I have once seen with my own eyes in the grand Baptistry at St. John Lateran in Rome!

"*The might of the Holy Ghost descend into this fountain-plenitude, and impregnate with regenerating efficacy the whole substance of this water.*"

Such is the spell. Exorcisms first chase all evil spirits from the water, then incantations and charms—dividings, oils, crossings, breathings, candle-plungings, and other things—cause the might of the Holy Ghost to descend and impregnate the water with regenerating efficacy. It is no longer ordinary water, such as that wherein the eunuch or Cornelius and his friends were baptized; but, by the power of charms, it has become an ecclesiastical compound, and those to whom it is administered are made new creatures and regenerate, not—so far as I understand—because they are brought by faith to Christ, but through the mere application of the fluid impregnated with virtue by an ecclesiastical process. And the only man who can make and apply this "Elixir of Life"—of eternal life!—is the priest.

To the Law and to the Testimony, and how cruel a deception is this system of magic detected to be. It is not the water of Baptism which regenerates, but the Word of God implanted in us by His Spirit. Hear the evidence:—

"Of His own will begat He us with the Word of truth" (James i. 18).

"Being born again, not of corruptible seed, but of incorruptible, by the Word of God which liveth and abideth for ever" (1 Peter i. 23).

"That He might sanctify and cleanse it—the Church—with the washing of water *by* the Word" (Eph. v. 26).

XVIII.

THE FEAST OF THE PURIFICATION, OR CANDLEMAS.

THE Feast of the Purification, or Candlemas, was, as Picart tells us, substituted for the Heathen festival called Ambarvalia; in which processions were made through the fields, and a sacrifice was offered for purification. At the same time it also took the place of the nocturnal perambulations with lighted torches, which commemorated the wanderings of Ceres, when she traversed the country in search of her daughter Proserpine, whom Pluto had carried off.

In the early ages of the Church, it could not but be noticed that these Roman feasts were the causes of much debauchery, and consequently Christian Pontiffs were anxious to do away with them. It was, however, thought necessary to give the people some equivalent; and, with this view, the second day of February was devoted to the Feast of the Purification. It was called Candlemas, and the torches and wax tapers, formerly carried about in honour of Ceres, were now connected with the Holy Virgin; while the people were permitted to indulge in the diversions and pleasures which such occasions never failed to inspire. See *Picart*, vol. i., p. 163.

Thus Ceres went out, and Mary came in; torches disappeared, and candles succeeded.

In Sicily, a similar transformation was effected, but with the difference that there Agatha, the patron saint of Catania, and not Mary, was substituted for the Heathen goddess Ceres.

The following extract will show that Picart is not alone in his opinion respecting the design of these adaptations, which were as common as they were ruinous to the purity of Christianity.

"Theophylact, Patriarch of Constantinople, with a design of weaning men from Heathen ceremonies, particularly those of Bacchus, substituted Christian festivals partaking of a similar spirit of licentiousness, which led to a still further adoption of rites more or less imitated from the Pagans."—Chambers' *Book of Days*, Jan. 14.

Judaism, Gnosticism, and Heathenism—these from the first were the tares sown with the wheat.

During his stay in Sicily, Professor Blunt witnessed the festival of St. Agatha, and was much struck with its correspondence to that of Ceres. He mentions, among other things, the fact that the day of observance, February 2nd, is the same; and also that, according to the testimony of Ovid, the fête of Ceres commenced with a horse-race, at which the Town Council were present, which is also the custom at St. Agatha's festival.

Candles and torches of an enormous size used to be dedicated to the "Bona Dea." Similar offerings are now presented to the saint, and in a similar manner.

The goddess was borne to her temple upon a splendid throne, and in great state; the saint is conveyed to her cathedral with equal pomp, and on a silver throne.

Ovid tells us that at the Eleusinia, or festival of Ceres, all were draped in white, and at the feast of St. Agatha, the favourite colour is also white.

To the programme of each of the festivals there is appended a grand procession, during the progress of which the ancient cry to the goddess was, "Hail, Ceres!" while "Viva, Sta. Agatha!" is the modern greeting addressed to the saint. And it is certainly remarkable that the day of the modern procession coincides with that of the ancient, both of them being the fourth day of the festival.

Lastly, in the matter of relics the goddess resembled the saint; for the relics of the former were deposited in a holy basket, which was conveyed in a consecrated cart; while those of the latter are placed in a sacred chest, and carried in a sacred car. Goddess and saint, basket and chest, cart and car—how exact the parallel between ancient and modern Heathenism!

Relics have ever been objects of reverence in Heathen worship. According to Varro, the original sow which verified an augury to Æneas was preserved by the priests at Lavinium —a somewhat strange fancy! To the bones of Theseus, which were laid up at Athens, we have already referred. Men have always had a passion for such things: what has been, is; and what is, will be.

The relics of St. Agatha, as Blunt tells us, are her veil—by means of which the eruptions of Mount Etna have been more than once stayed, if you are disposed to believe it—her foot, and her breast. According to the legend, both her breasts were cut off; where the other is I do not know, but how much better if such things were buried out of sight. These relics are generally to be seen in her pictures, so that one can easily recognize her. I shall never forget the look of contempt which a painter, who was copying something in a gallery at Florence, gave me when I pointed to St. Agatha, and said, "Who, pray sir, is that saint?" Much more polite was the treatment I received at Naples, from an artist of whom I inquired the name of the painter of the Virgin, in copying which he was busily engaged. He not only told me the name, but added the undesired information, "And the original, sir, was his mistress."

While staying at Orvieto, in South Italy, in the May of 1879, I was much struck with the very pleasing effect of a procession which had assembled to perform some such ceremony as that of the ancient Ambarvalia. Led by the clergy of the cathedral, beneath the spacious roof of which it had been marshalled, and composed of various guilds of the town in their many-coloured costumes, its distant appearance was charming. First traversing the streets of the town, it then emerged into the country, passing through vineyards, cornfields, pastures, and woodlands, with streaming banners long drawn out. As it wound round the rocks of that magnificent scenery, and went in and out among the olive-trees, the sight was certainly delightful. But what was the use of it? Heathenism and processions have, indeed, always kept company; but where in the New Testament do we read of such a thing in association with Christianity?

Among the many remarkable pictures at the Luxembourg, there is one which well illustrates our subject. It depicts an imitation of the Heathen ceremony of Ambarvalia. The priest, with his attendants, is seen carrying the Host, as he winds his way through the cornfields in spring, and blesses them with holy water and other mystic rites. It is difficult to realize that the subject is " Christian," and not Heathen.

XIX.

THE IMAGES OF THE GODS.

MANY are the objects of worship to which the heart of man has turned aside from God. Among these are the heavenly bodies (Job xxxi. 26-28), the brute creation (Rom. i. 23), fire, the generative principle, the productive principle, the frame of nature, and fetish. But there is also another and very prevalent kind of idolatry; that is, the worship of dead men—ancestors, heroes and heroines, gods and goddesses, and saints male and female.

·This is hero-worship; and is called Demonolatry, or the worship of the spirits of dead men who, by ecclesiastical authority, whether Christian or Heathen, have been canonized, and are thus supposed to have become qualified recipients of public worship.

But of these—since they are invisible, and the nature of man desires something which can be laid hold of by the senses—tangible representations have been made in the form of images and pictures.

"Images," says the Roman Catholic writer in *Picart*, "are nearly as ancient as worship itself; and no wonder, since their origin is due to the weakness of humanity. Man could not long fix his attention on purely spiritual objects, and, therefore, insensibly turned to the material, and tried, so to speak, to render the object of worship palpable.

"It is true that the use of these signs becomes dangerous. Formerly God was obliged to forbid it to the Jews: the Christians, however"—mark the writer's irony—"thought that they might without risk imitate their predecessors, the Heathen.

"Serenus, Bishop of Marseilles, in order to preserve the new converts from the guilt of idolatry, destroyed the images in his diocese. But St. Gregory, the Pope (d. 604), ordered them to be restored, considering that pastoral instruction would correct the grossest of popular errors."—*Picart*, vol. i., chap. 3.

Fallacious and ruinous idea, too clearly manifested by the prevalence and endurance of idolatry in Christendom! I suppose Gregory thought as did a traveller of the last century, who, after remarking upon the difficulty of teaching an illiterate peasant to comprehend an immaterial and invisible God, adds, "But set up before him the figure of a fine woman, with a beautiful child in her arms—the most interesting object in nature—and tell him she can procure him everything he wants; he knows perfectly well what he is about, feels himself animated by the object, and prays to her with all his might."—Bridone's *Tour*, vol. i., p. 163.

"The ancient Heathen also, long before the introduction of Christianity, attributed the power of working miracles to the images of their gods and heroes. Livy, that ingenious Pagan fabulist, adorned his pages with an infinity of miracles and prodigies, among which are several relating to images. And Cicero—not one of the credulous—often mentions religious marvels; as, for instance, the sweating of statues. He assures us that the statue of Apollo at Cumae perspired, as also that of Victory at Capua."—*Picart*.

And such things are still believed, as we may easily discover from well-known instances of sweating saints and winking Virgins. Here is an example from the *Report of the Syrian Schools at Beyrout*, 1876. "The priests publicly announced that, on a certain day, the image of the Virgin would perspire; and that all must come and dip their fingers in the perspiration, and make the sign of the cross."

In May, 1876, I was at Clermont Ferard, the capital of Auvergne, in France, and upon entering a shop close to the famous Sanctuary of Nôtre Dame du Port, found myself confronting a *grisette* who was selling prints and images of this same Lady of the Port.

"But tell me, Ma'm'selle, tell me, pray," said I, "is the image in the church yonder really miraculous?"

"Certainly it is, Monsieur. It has performed many—many miracles."

She, too, believed the lie, poor thing. So I went to see the idol; and lo! there it was, a mean diminutive little thing, but painted of course by St. Luke, as most of these images were, if you will only be good enough to believe what you are told. It was placed above the altar, in a crypt brilliantly lighted with candles, adorned with many votive offerings, and at the time occupied by a crowd of worshippers; for the Fête of the image was then going on. The sight was touching; for all seemed, and many no doubt were, much in earnest.

One incident specially affected me. A young servant girl, brimming over, no doubt, with love of the image, offered a rosary, and Sœur Marie, an habituée of the church, mounting some steps and kneeling upon the altar, hung the little gift round the idol's neck.

Dear child! no doubt she gave the tiny offering with all her heart: but, oh! that that heart had been drawn to Christ instead of to the senseless image! Then her adoring love would have been worship, and not idolatry.

In the Museum of the Capitol at Rome, there is another girl, portrayed in marble—not French, but Roman; not modern, but ancient; not a worshipper of the image of Mary, but of the image of Hygeia, the goddess of health, to whom, as you see in the cut on the opposite page, she is presenting the usual offering of cakes.

She lives now but in marble. Yet once she, too, was warm

with life, and her heart beat with emotions like that of the
French girl. How similar their circumstances! Each of them
had a patroness, revered her image, would have kissed it with

lively feeling, and sought to gain favours from it. Both of
them offered gifts, the most acceptable they could procure;
the one the rosary, the other the cakes. The Roman girl did

so for the restoration of her health; the French maiden for the success, it may be, of a love-affair, or, perhaps, for prosperity in some little "commerce" which she was meditating.

Here then are two girls equally, we will say, well-intentioned, pious, and devout, yet the one is called a Christian, and the other a Heathen. Nay; it is not so. In the particular acts of worship of which we have been speaking both girls were alike Heathen: for both performed a Heathen rite, and both bowed down to a graven image. Such things are idolatry; and it matters little whether they be done in the temple of the goddess Mary at Clermont, or before the image of the goddess Hygeia in the temple of Æsculapius at Rome.

A great contrast to the pretty Heathen votary and her goddess is a wooden idol, about six inches high, and painted in blue, red, and yellow, which people venerate at Le Puy, the capital of the volcanic region of Auvergne in the centre of France. It is a black Virgin, and is represented on page 119.

I visited Auvergne, in the August of 1861, to examine the remarkable church-architecture of the district, and then obtained a portrait of this beauty. How hot it was that summer!—the thermometer in the carriage at 93°—it should have been a good vintage.

But, to return to the Black Virgin, I am thoroughly puzzled in regard to the attractiveness of ugliness; for in England, alas! we have an artistic school devoted to it. How often do we see children enamoured of their very ugliest doll; and certainly in the churches the most hideous images, and this Black Virgin of Le Puy among them, are generally the most popular. There is an instance of this at Dijon, and I have a vivid remembrance of a little ugly deformity in Rome, brought—so they say—from Jerusalem. It may be found in the church just outside the city gate, below the Vatican palace; and the last time I was there, a lovely basket of camellias, the offering of Pio Nono, lay before the image.

THE IMAGES OF THE GODS. 119

Evidently beauty is no necessity to an object of adoration; for the black deformities abound in France and Italy. And could there be anything more offensive than the *volto sacro*, or "sacred countenance," of our Lord at Luca? How frightful, again, are the gods worshipped by the Heathen of modern

times. And even the idols of the old Etruscans, a people of taste, are, as we see them on their monuments, often not merely ugly, but ridiculous. The attraction of ugliness certainly is a puzzle.

The Black Virgin of Le Puy is actually called the Mother of God! "Mother of God!" exclaimed John Knox, when, during his captivity in France, they presented to him a similar image to kiss, "Mother of God! Why, it is only a painted board!"

My beauty, too, is, as you may infer from the woodcut, only a painted board. Together with the rest of its kind, it probably originated in a Byzantine type. "Those artists," says Cardinal Wiseman, "occupied the field for centuries in Italy, and degraded the types of sacred art under revolting forms."

However, the revolting forms still retain their hold upon the masses; or, in other words, upon the depraved taste of idolatrous hearts.

Addressing a priest in the stately cathedral of Cologne, I asked, "Why, sir, do you allow in this noble building a thing so contemptible, and so unsuited to the place, as that doll?" My question referred to a gaudy image of the Virgin in a glass case.

" Sir," he replied, "the people like it, and we do not refuse them."

Yes, "My people love to have it so!" But who will answer the question which follows:—"What will ye do in the end thereof?"

XX.

THE IMAGE OF ST. PETER AT ROME.

WE will now turn from Nôtre Dame du Port, and the Black Virgin of Le Puy, to an image more renowned than either of them—the bronze statue of St. Peter, in the great temple called after his name, at Rome. On the next page you will see a picture of it, ugly and vulgar as it is celebrated.

How often have I seated myself before it, and watched, with painful interest, its devout worshippers, while every passer-by was careful to show his veneration for the ugly idol! The scene is an exact repetition of the acts of Heathen ancestors, some two thousand years ago, as described in the lines of Lucretius—

> "So oft the crowd respectful, as they pass,
> Salute and touch the consecrated brass."

But what is "the consecrated brass" in this case? It seems pretty generally agreed that the image, in whole or in part, was re-cast from the bronze of a statue of Jupiter. The author of *Il Vaticano Illustrato*—see Tavola 75—observes that Torrigio, who wrote of it in the eighth century, believed it to have been executed in the fifth century, by order of Leo the Great.

"This metal," he says, "which previously served for a false divinity, now serves for a sacred and devout use. It is thus that the Church of Jesus Christ converts the remains of superstition and error to a better cause; for whereas, before, the metal only exposed human madness, and the folly of the Gentiles, the Church now exhibits it as a monument of faith and devotion.

"On the apostle's foot are imprinted the kisses of the people who assemble there to obtain *the indulgences* granted by the Roman Pontiff.

"Remembering that the bronze from which the statue of the Prince of the Apostles was formed was, in remote times,

an ornament of the Capitol, we will add a few words on the object presented to us.

"Jupiter Capitolinus was so named from the temple of the god on the Capitoline Hill. In one hand he held the thunder, in the other a javelin. He was covered with a purple robe similar to that of the Roman emperors.

"In the Vatican Basilica, on various annual solemnities, it is also the custom to clothe the statue of St. Peter in full pontifical dress, and so to present it for the worship of the faithful, rich with gold and gems."

Thus far our author. Here, then, we have successively on

the two hills, the Capitoline and the Vatican, two great gods—the one belonging to ancient, the other to modern, Rome; the one Pagan, the other Papal; the one identified with the Empire by the imperial mantle, the other made one with the Papacy by the tiara and pontifical robes.

Jove and Peter are their names: each of them has his hill, his dome, and his throne: each is a dumb idol of brass or bronze: to each belongs gorgeous array, incense is offered to both of them, and they alike receive the adoration and kisses of prostrate multitudes.

Wherein do the two gods differ? If we are to look only to outward appearance, certainly the earlier statue of Jupiter, with its Greek inspiration, has some power to attract, whereas the stolid stupidity of its inartistic Roman successor repels even to loathing. But which am I to worship, the Capitoline or the Vatican Jove?

Call up some ancient Roman from the dead, show him the "Christian" worship at St. Peter's, and ask him what he thinks. He would at once reply that Rome has not changed her gods, and he would tell the truth.

But Rome is wise enough to meet the times, and, while she retains the old worship, she retains it under modified forms. She has baptized her ancient gods, and they have come out with new names, in new dresses, in new temples, and with a new cult suited to the age. Of course: but the substance is always the same; it is but the form that varies.

The religion of the seven-hilled city is still the religion of Numa, of Tarquin, of the consuls, and of the Cæsars; the old gods are still there, but with changed names, and with Christ and His human mother adopted among them. The Capitoline Jove has moved to the Vatican, but is still the chief of the gods in Rome's Pantheon, though he now holds keys in the place of the thunderbolts, and on festive days is clad in pontifical vestments instead of the imperial mantle.

Name, place, form, attributes, garments—all these change; but the substance, the perpetual brass, never!

XXI.

THE ADORATION OF IMAGES BY KISSING.

WHILE I was walking in Antwerp cathedral, some years ago, my attention was arrested by a man who was very devoutly and affectionately kissing the recumbent figure of a saint. He did this in a most orderly and systematic manner, first from top to toe, and then from heel to head, completely covering the idol with lines of kisses.

Picart (vol. i., p. 13) thus refers to this strange custom of ancient and modern Heathenism.

"Another ceremony common among idolaters is kissing the objects which they venerate. They kiss their idols, addressing them in soft and tender language, holding them by the knees, and offering them fruits and flowers.

"Influenced by a like superstition, the Mohammedan pilgrims kiss a certain black stone at Mecca. And the modern Indian and American idolaters observe a similar custom.

"With us, the priest kisses the altar, the cross, the relics, the thurible, the paten, and the chalice. And again the priest's own hand is kissed.

"But when the devotees cannot embrace the object of their adoration, they kiss their own hands, and thus send their kisses to the gods. This act of devotion is most common among the Spanish and Portuguese, who make the form of the cross with the first finger and thumb, and then kiss the hand in honour of the image from which they are separated by distance."

In writing on the same subject, Blunt observes—"At

present nothing meets the eye more frequently than the wood of a crucifix deeply worn by the lips of the devout. Nay, I have seen the waxen image of a saint duly provided with a bronze foot to prevent attrition; and the toe of the statue of St. Peter formed out of the metal of an old Jupiter Capitolinus, in the great church of the same saint at Rome, is worn perfectly bright.

"It appears also, from Cicero, that the mouth and chin of the image of Hercules at Agrigentum in Sicily were polished in the same way. 'In that temple,' says he, 'there is a bronze statue of Hercules, than which it would not be easy to find anything more beautiful. Its mouth and chin are slightly worn away, because the people, in their prayers and thanksgivings, are not only in the habit of worshipping, but also of kissing it.'

"Lucretius, again, tells us that, in his day (d. B.C. 55), the hands of the idols were apt to suffer in a similar manner.

> "Then, near the doors, the reverend statues stand,
> Worn down, and polished, in the outstretched hand.
> So oft the crowd respectful, as they pass,
> Salute and touch the consecrated brass."

"Where it may be remarked, that the people offered this salutation in passing, as they entered or quitted the temples; the very custom actually existing at this day."

In the writer's work, *The Cross: Heathen and Christian*, p. 83, will be found an illustration and description of the bronze crucifix at the Mamertine Prison, in Rome, the face of which is entirely worn away by the kisses of the people. This crucifix forms a suitable pendant to Cicero's Hercules— the one adored at the present time in Rome, the other formerly worshipped in Sicily. Intervening centuries have not changed the worship: it is of the same kind, whether offered to Jesus or to Hercules. It is the outgoing, the sincere affection, of the unregenerate heart towards forbidden idols—the religion of nature, unrestrained, uninstructed by grace, and directly opposed to revelation.

The bronze of the rude idol in St. Peter's at Rome is brightly polished by the kissings and rubbings of the worshippers: the Pope himself kisses it when he visits the Basilica. There is a picture of this statue in the work of Ciacconius (4 vols. fol., Rome, 1677), together with the following information.

"Cardinal Baronius (d. 1607) was the first to introduce its worship: for, going daily to St. Peter's, he placed his head under its feet, devoutly kissing them and saying, '*Pax et obedientia*.' Which laudable custom others followed, to the wearing away of the brass of the statue."

In the church, Sopra Minerva, near the Pantheon, the foot of Michael Angelo's marble statue of Christ has been worn by kisses, and is protected by a bronze sandal: needlessly so now, however; for it has no worshippers. There is, strange to say, a fashion in worship as in other things. And at Rome, the worship of Christ—I speak with reverence and sorrow—has gone out of fashion, and a goddess has taken the place of God. It is Mary, and not Jesus, who reigns there.

If you doubt this, sit for a while, as I have done, before the statue just mentioned—or any other statue of the "Man of sorrows"—and observe how many worshippers you have to record. Then go to the Augustino, and stay a while before the famous image of Mary in that church. Write the sum of the multitude of her adorers, and you will see that, if He has units, she has hundreds for each of them.

Often have I sat contemplating the scene in the latter church, which is very remarkable, and very sad. The sick, the sorry, the careworn, the afflicted, and the earnest, resort thither: and can you wonder? For the statue they believe to be miraculous; and she whom it represents is their divinity.

As I sat before the image, and the suppliants defiled

between it and me, I used to imagine myself in the Rome of eighteen hundred years ago, occupying a seat in the temple of the healing god Æsculapius.

And just as in his temple there *were*, so in Mary's church there *are*, votive offerings suspended on the walls around, and votive pictures, too, declaratory of healings wrought, and of favours received.

Then there is the mysterious holy oil, which supplies the ever-burning light, and is good for anointing—mighty to heal. The deaf and the blind anoint themselves with it; and I have watched mothers blessing the eyes, ears, and members of their babes with its potent touch. Awful in the sight of these worshippers is the idol of superhuman size, and gemmed and bedecked with gold and silver. The people bow before it, kiss the dust, as I can testify, in their profound reverence. The foot of the image has been partly kissed away by the devotees, and the marble is now protected with bronze.

Strange and sad scenes of genuine Heathenism have I, at various times, seen enacted before that idol. If, reader, you desire to investigate the worship of the Roman people, go to the church of S. Augustino, and, if possible, on a fête day. Till you have visited either this, or some similar place of materialistic worship—there are many such in Rome—you can scarcely realize the identity of Pagan with Papal Rome.

How exclusively and continually has adoration by kissing characterized false worship.

Two hundred years before Christ, men kissed the beard of Hercules at Agrigentum.

Six hundred years before that period, apostate Israel had turned to the Egyptian god Apis, and the rule of worship was—" Let the men that sacrifice kiss the calves " (Hos. xiii. 2).

A century earlier, and Israel was bowing the knee to Baal, and adoring with kisses the blood-stained idol of Phœnicia. (1 Kings xix. 18).

Thus, in the multitudinous kisses which are daily bestowed upon images in Rome, and wherever Rome is obeyed, we cannot but recognize a continuance of the old world's idolatry. The only change is that the images of Jesus and Mary are substituted for those of Hercules and Apis; so that we have a new edition of the old religion in a Church binding.

It may, however, be urged that the modern images are miraculous.

Well, that is just what Livy and most other ancient authors assure us was the case with the statues of the gods in their days.

Bas-relief on Arch of Titus representing that Emperor's deification

XXII.

THE CLOTHING OF IMAGES.

WE have already referred to the clothing of images; and any one who has visited Roman Catholic churches on the Continent will have seen statues of the Virgin dressed in splendid robes, and decked with gold, precious stones, and pearls.

The Duke de Montpensier was, some little time ago, lauded in the *Tablet*, because he had presented the Virgin with a magnificent dress of tissue of gold trimmed with white lace, and with a silver crown; and a similar act of piety is recorded of the dissolute Queen of Spain.

Yet this, too, is imitated from the old Pagan worship, in the sacred ceremonies of which the clothing of the gods occupied an important place.

Thus, when Hecuba, the Trojan queen, was about to lead the penitential procession through the streets of Troy to the temple of Pallas, she received the following direction:—

> "Bring your gifts; and on the knees
> Of fair-haired Pallas place the fairest robe
> In all the house, the amplest, best esteemed."

The royal lady obeyed, and

> "Her fragrant chamber sought, wherein were stor'd
> Rich garments, by Sidonian women work'd,
> Whom god-like Paris had from Sidon brought,
> Sailing the broad sea o'er, the selfsame path
> By which the high-born Helen he convey'd.
> Of these, the richest in embroidery,
> The amplest, and the brightest, as a star

THE CLOTHING OF IMAGES.   131

Refulgent, plac'd with care beneath the rest,
The Queen her offering bore to Pallas' shrine :
She went, and with her many an ancient dame.
But when the shrine they reach'd on Ilium's height,
Theano, fair of face, the gates unlock'd,
Daughter of Cisseus, sage Antenor's wife,
By Trojans nam'd at Pallas' shrine to serve.
They with deep moans to Pallas raised their hands;
But fair Theano took the robe, and plac'd
On Pallas' knees."

See Homer's *Iliad*, vi. 269-311.

This extract establishes the antiquity of the custom beyond question, and points as clearly to its unchristian origin.

The statue of St. Peter in its ordinary dress I have already introduced to the reader. Above is the same idol as it appears, in the nave of the grand Basilica, in full dress on a fête day.

The second woodcut, given below, represents the Heathen goddess Cybele, the wife of Saturn, the Idæan mother, also clothed in her best dress.

She was usually called the mother of the gods, and this figure is taken from Montfaucon (tome i., part i., p. 19). In point of dress, she certainly forms a good pendant to the

Christian saint. But from whence did she derive her very singular costume with its striking ecclesiasticism? Evidently from the same source as that from which Roman Catholic ecclesiastical dress came. And if the reader will take the trouble to examine the Assyrian and Babylonian antiquities in the British Museum, he will probably come to a conclusion as to what that source was.

XXIII.

THE MOTHER AND CHILD.

WE must not dismiss the subject of the images of the gods without saying a few words respecting the most famous and universal of all—that of the Mother and Child.

If we examine old pictures of the Madonna, or Madonna and Child, in the National Gallery, we cannot but be struck with the fact that she is rarely, if ever, made to resemble a Jewish woman; but is of fair complexion, with blue eyes and golden hair. At first an easy explanation seems to offer itself. Of course the painters naturally sought their models among the beautiful women of their own country. But when we reflect that these painters were for the most part Italians or Spaniards, such a suggestion only increases the perplexity, and confirms whatever suspicion we may have previously entertained, that there is some distinct reason for so general a practice.

The fact is that here again we have pure Paganism under a Christian name. The so-called Virgin Mary and Infant Jesus are nothing more nor less than the yellow-haired Aphrodite and Eros of the Greeks—the Venus and Cupid of the Romans. Under the disguise of Mary, there is still being carried on the worship of the goddess of nature—of her who, with a mere variation of name and appearance to suit the peculiar race of her votaries, has ever been the chief object of veneration to Pagan peoples. She is the Mylitta, or "great goddess," of the Assyrians and Babylonians, the Astarte of the Phœnicians, the Isis of the Egyptians, the Diana of the Ephesians. Her shrines may be found in India: the Jesuit Missionaries were astonished when they met with her in Thibet, China, and Japan: she was known to the Aztecs of Mexico. There is, perhaps, no part of the world in which some traces of her may not be detected.

She seems to have made her formal entrance into the Church through some miserable compromise at the first Council of Nice. Hosius and the orthodox party found that they would be outnumbered by the Arians, and, therefore, invited the Egyptians to come to the rescue, offering to condone their worship of Isis on condition that she should thenceforth be called the Virgin Mary. Consequently we find the Melchite section at the Council of Nice holding that there were three Persons in the Trinity—*the Father, the Virgin Mary, and the Messiah their Son!* " And thus," says Newman, in his *Development*, p. 405, "the Arian controversy opened a question which it did not settle. It discovered a new sphere, if we may so speak, in the realms of light, to which the Church had not yet assigned its inhabitant. . . . Thus there was 'a wonder in Heaven'! A throne was seen far above all created powers, mediatorial, intercessory, a title archetypal, a crown bright as the Morning Star, a glory issuing from the eternal throne, robes pure as the heavens, and a sceptre over all. And who was the predestined heir of this majesty? Who was that Wisdom, and what was her name? 'The mother of fair love, and fear, and holy hope,' 'exalted like a palm-tree in Engeddi, and a rose-plant in Jericho,' 'created from the beginning before the world,' in God's counsels, 'and in Jerusalem was her power'! The vision is found in the Apocalypse, a woman clothed with the sun, and the moon under her feet, and upon her head a crown of twelve stars. The votaries of Mary do not exceed the true faith, unless the blasphemers of her Son come up to it. The Church of Rome is not idolatrous, unless Arianism is orthodoxy."

Such is the triumphant strain of an English Cardinal over

PLATE I.

HEATHEN.

1. The Egyptian Venus.
2. The Mexican.
3. The Indian.
4. The Cyprian.
5. The Assyrian.
6. The Chinese.

CHRISTIAN.

7. Madonna and Child.

PLATE II.

1. Mary suckling her Infant.
2. Lactuary for milk of Mary.
3. Lieb-Frauen-Milch.
4. Indian Venus and Babe.
5. Isis and Horus. Horus was the son of Isis, whose name was changed to Jesus when his mother became the Virgin Mary, about the time of the first Council of Nice. Though Isis was a mother, the ancient Egyptians believed in her perpetual virginity; and King, in his *Gnostics and Their Remains*, describes a sard in his collection representing her standing before her husband Serapis, with the legend, ἡ κυρία Ἴσις ἁγνή, "Immaculate is our lady Isis." Here, then, we have the source from whence the doctrine of the Immaculate Conception was derived. There is no hint of such a thing in the Scriptures, but there is in Egyptian Paganism. Several other things, supposed to be Christian, come from these Egyptian deities, and among them the I.H.S. so prominent in churches. This device was copied from Egyptian altars, where it stood for the initials of the Pagan Trinity—Isis, Horus, and Serapis.
6. The Milky Way.
7. The Hindoo goddess Siva—Nature—standing on a sea of milk pressed from her own bosom.
8. Diana—Nature—mother and feeder of all.
9. The Milk Cave of Bethlehem, formed in white chalk. "The friars," says Mr. Stephens, "sometimes show a grotto where they say the Virgin took refuge from a shower of rain, and her milk overflowed; and now there is a faith among the people that, if a woman to whom nature has denied the power of nursing her children comes to this grotto, and prays before the altar, the fountain of life will be opened to her. Nor was the virtue of the place confined to those who should resort there in person; for the friars having prayed for, had obtained, a delegation of the Virgin's power; and a small portion of white powder from the rock, swallowed in a little water, would be equally efficacious to women having faith!"—Gadsby's *Wanderings*.

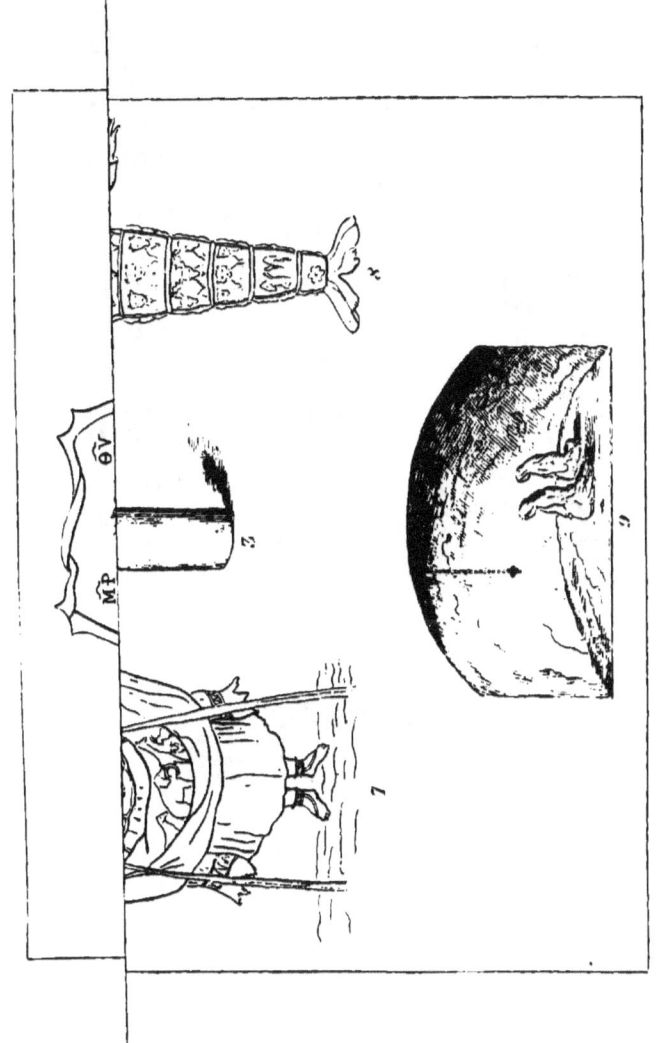

the work of those who opened the flood gates of corruption upon the Church. Once admitted, the Pagan goddess, under her false name, soon became the popular favourite, and was quickly allowed to take her seat as Queen of Heaven within the Church, just as she had previously done without its pale.

As soon as we understand her origin and real nature, we are no longer liable to that bewilderment which was recently expressed by the reviewer of a London newspaper at the fact that infidels like Strauss and Comte worked round, in spite of their apparent antagonism, to the same conclusion as Cardinal Manning—to the worship of a young woman, of about thirty years of age, with a child.

Our plates (I. and II.) will illustrate this worship, and give some idea of its universality.

 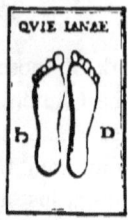

XXIV.

VOTIVE OFFERINGS.

AMONG the many Pagan usages in connection with the images of the gods was that of suspending, in their shrines, offerings which had been vowed in times of distress or anxiety. If the trouble had been disease, a model of the limb, or part of the body, affected would be set up as a testimony to the healing power of the god. If his interference had been—as was supposed—successfully entreated for sick animals, or for the safe return of a ship, figures of the creatures or of the vessels would be hung up, and so on.

This practice has been largely adopted by the Church of Rome, as the cuts will show. They are figures of votive offerings for the most part collected and presented to the Bristol Museum by the author: the material of the antiques is terra-cotta, and that of the moderns white metal, both being coarse in their structure. They are arranged in two divisions, the first consisting of Pagan, and the second of Roman Catholic offerings: and they are numbered in pairs, so as to illustrate each other (see Plate III.).

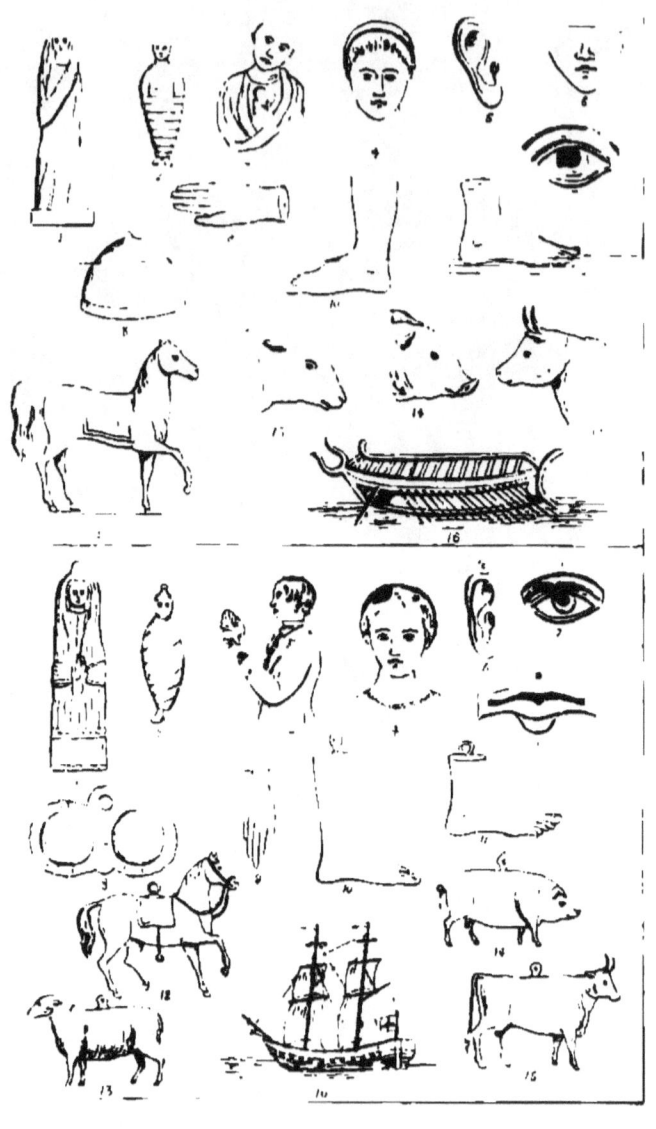

PLATE III.

PAGAN.

1. Ancient Roman lady, possibly offered after deliverance from death.
2. A baby.
3. Roman citizen devoting his heart to Pan.
4. Female head.
5. An ear in terra-cotta.
6. Part of face.
7. An eye.
8. Woman's breast, life-size.
9. Hand, life-size.
10. Leg.

11. Foot.
12. Horse.
13. Sheep, in terra-cotta.
14. Pig.
15. Cow.
16. Ship.

ROMAN CATHOLIC.

1. Portuguese lady. Each of these is about two inches high.
2. A Bambino. Eleven inches high purchased by me at Rome.
3. A youth making a similar offering.
4. Female head.
5. An ear in silver.
6. Part of face in white metal.
7. An eye.
8. Woman's breasts, life-size.
9. Hand, life-size.
10. Leg, in wax. In this case I saw the patient in the shop explaining to the artist where the sore had been
11. Foot.
12. Horse.
13. Sheep, in silver.
14. Pig.
15. Cow.
16. Ship.

Iris with Nimbus.

XXV.

THE NIMBUS.

EVERYONE has noticed the disc of light, or luminous circle, which, in ecclesiastical pictures, usually surrounds the head of the Virgin Mary, or of a saint, as well as that of Christ. It is called the nimbus, or sometimes, the aureola; although the technical meaning of the latter term is restricted to the oval or circular halo which surrounds the whole body of a saint.

It is often supposed to be an exclusively Christian symbol, indicative of divinity or holiness: but such an illusion is quickly dispelled by a little research. For it appears in representations of the gods and goddesses of Babylon, of Greece and Rome, and even of India and China. A passage of Virgil—*Æn.* xii. 162-4—will give us some clue to its meaning.

In describing Latinus, the poet says:—

> " Cui tempora circum
> Aurati bis sex radii fulgentia cingunt,
> Solis avi specimen."

> " Twelve golden beams around his temples play,
> To mark his lineage from the god of day."

It appears, therefore, that the nimbus is the symbol of the sun-deity, or denotes some connection with him. Hence Apollo is often represented with it. And in a well-known painting, found in Pompeii, of the scene between Ulysses and Circe, the head of the latter is surrounded by a luminous circle, because she was the daughter of the Sun. But in course of time, this ornament seems to have been given to any deity: for the Latin commentator Servius, in interpreting Virgil's description of Pallas,

"Nimbo effulgens et Gorgone sæva,"

explains nimbus as "the luminous fluid which encircles the heads of the gods."

In earlier times, however, the meaning of the symbol was more confined, and doubtless another expression of it is to be found in the circular tonsure of priests and monks. To how early a period of the world's history this custom dates back, we may judge by the fact that God warned the Israelitish priests against it, by the mouth of Moses, in the words, "They shall not make baldness upon their head" (Lev. xxi. 5). It was, therefore, no doubt practised by the Egyptian priests in those days, as we know it to have been by the Chaldean, and may be traced in many parts of the world. For instance, more than five hundred years before Christ, Buddha shaved his head, and commanded the tonsure to his followers. And again, Herodotus, when writing of the Arabs, about four and a half centuries before Christ, says, "They have but these two gods, to wit, Bacchus and Urania (that is to say, the sun and moon), and they say that, in their mode of cutting the hair, they follow Bacchus. Now their practice is to cut it in a ring away from the temples" (iii. 8). The same custom was common to the priests of Osiris and Isis, and also to those of Pagan Rome. In fact it may be traced from Egypt and Babylon, through all the great Pagan systems, down to Papal Rome.

But to understand its full significance, we must remember

that in the obscene nature-worship which is at the bottom of all false religions, the sun—and also the kindred element of fire—is the male emblem, and consequently the meaning of his sign was extended in such a way as we cannot here describe. A feminine emblem, used in connection with it, was what is now called the pallium. This was often adorned with crosses, but not in remembrance of Christ, however convenient it may sometimes be to give such an explanation: for these were phallic crosses. And it is high time that Christians should understand a fact of which sceptics have been long talking and writing, namely, that the cross was the central symbol of all ancient Paganism. What it represents must remain untold: but it was probably made the medium of our Lord's death through the crafty devices of the Wicked One, into whose hands He was for a while delivered, with a view to the future corruption of Christianity, and the carrying on under its name of all the abominations of the Heathen.

Earth is, indeed, set thick with snares, and teems with temptations and enticements from the simplicity of the faith. "But the wisdom that is from above, is first pure;" and "blessed is the man that endureth temptation: for when he hath been approved, he shall receive the crown of life, which the Lord promised to them that love Him."

Derived as it was from the Pagans, the nimbus is not of frequent occurrence in Christian representations during the times of persecution—the first three centuries, and part of the fourth. Nor is it often found in the Catacombs, as a competent authority, M. Didron, informs us. But as soon as unrestrained corruption set in, this Heathen symbol was openly adopted by the Church, and began to appear upon the heads of her deities, angels, and saints, as well as upon those of Jupiter, Apollo, Mercury, and the Heathen Emperors. From that time to this it became so general that it is unnecessary to give examples here, though one or two will be found, in company with their Pagan models, in the large plate at the end of the chapter.

We select, however, three pictures from Didron, and one from our own collection, to illustrate less known uses of the symbol.

The first is that of a Persian king, whose head is surrounded by a pyramidal flamboyant nimbus.

This figure seems to prove the truth of Didron's observation, that in the East the nimbus is not merely an attribute of holiness, but "a characteristic of physical energy, no less than of moral strength; of civic or political power, as well as of religious authority." Presently we may, perhaps, be able to show how this comes about.

That which surrounds the head of the king is, doubtless, a flame—sun and fire worship are closely connected—and we may compare Virgil's *lambere flamma comas*.

In the South Kensington Museum, I have noticed several Indian miniatures with similar adornment. And at the present moment a Chinese saint or goddess—figured below—with fine circular nimbus, looks down upon me benevolently from my own study walls.

The next illustration is somewhat startling. It is taken from a Byzantine miniature of the tenth century, and "represents Satan standing before Job, who is seated sadly upon the ruins of his house. The demon is nimbed, and holds in his hand a brazier wherewith to set on fire the habitations he has overthrown."

But probably Satan has a better right to the nimbus than any one; for, in his character of Prince of this World and of the Power of the Air, he seems, under the name of the Sun-god, to have been the real object of worship from the earliest times down to the modern Yezidis, who still venerate him as Sheik Shems, or the Lord Sun. His name Satan becomes Sheitan in Chaldee, and in Greek is changed into Titan, a name applied to one of the race of giants who rebelled against the gods, and also to the Sun-god. For more on this subject see *Earth's Earliest Ages* (Hodder and Stoughton), chap. iii.

If, then, the nimbus originally belonged to the Prince of this World, it is easy to understand how it became a symbol of all that he gives, and was used as a characteristic of

physical energy and of civil and political power, as well as of authority in certain religious systems.

After what has been said, our fourth illustration, from a miniature of the twelfth century, will follow naturally.

"It represents," says M. Didron, "the seven-headed monster of the Apocalypse, the leopard with claws like a bear. His heads have a nimbus of blue, and one—that in the centre, the smallest in reality, but unquestionably the greatest in its

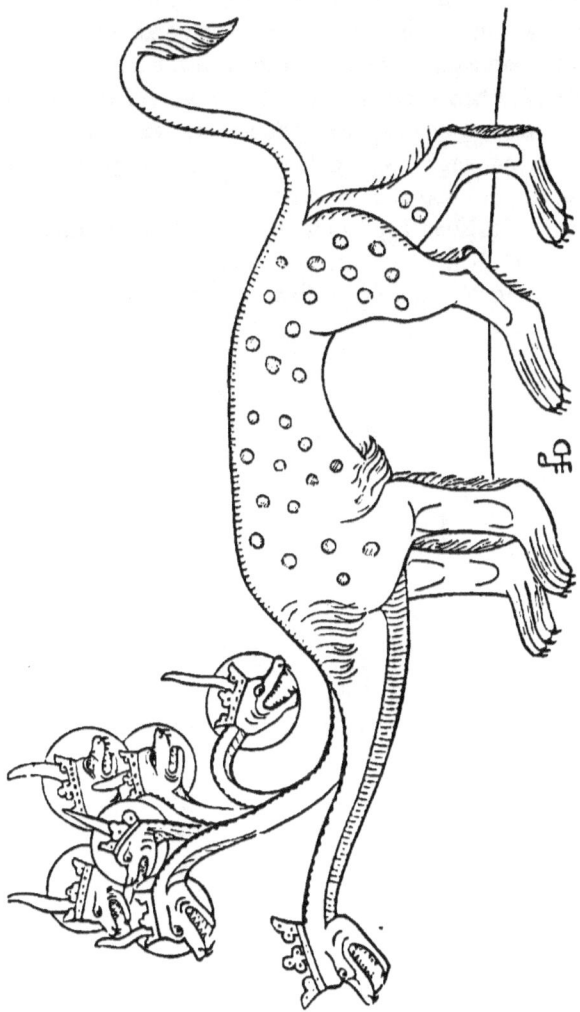

hierarchical importance, and sovereign of the others—has a crimson nimbus of the colour of fire. One of the heads is without a nimbus; it is undoubtedly intended for that which, as we are told in the Apocalypse, was wounded to death."

In the large plate, the illustrations on the left, numbered 1 to 6, are Heathen examples of the nimbus. No. 1 is the god Pan; No. 2, Nemesis, the goddess of Retribution; No. 3, a Heathen emperor; No. 4, the Moon; No. 5, the Sun; and No. 6, the Hindoo deity Siva.

Of the Christian figures on the right, No. 1 is a monk; No. 2, a saint; No. 3, a Christian empress; No. 4, a Christian queen; and No. 5, a figure from St. Peter's at Rome.

XXVI.

MARKS OF THE GODS.

WE have already mentioned the Mamertine Prison. This curious relic of antiquity was originally constructed by Servius Tullius, after whom it was called the Tullianum. It is supposed to be the most ancient building in Rome—a fact which may, perhaps, be allowed to excuse us if we digress for a few moments to describe it, before speaking of the miracles said to have been wrought by St. Peter within its gloomy walls.

It is a dark and horrible place of Oriental pattern—like some prisons in Asia which date back to a time earlier than the founding of Rome—and was used for the confinement and execution of State prisoners. Among its victims we may mention Jugurtha, king of Mauritania, starved to death by Marius; the brave Gaul Vercingetorix, killed by order of Julius Cæsar; and the accomplices of Catiline, strangled at the bidding of Cicero, who went forth and announced their death to the people by the emphatic word, "Vixerunt!" "They have lived!" The remains of the stairs which he ascended are still to be seen: they were called the "Scalæ Gemoniæ," or "Steps of Sighs," with which we may compare the "Bridge of Sighs" at Venice.

Originally there were three prisons, one above the other; the upper of which, now destroyed, was above ground, and admitted light and air to the prisoners. Immediately beneath this was the middle cell, which was underground, the only access to it being by a man-hole from above. This was the *carcer interior*, the inner or lowest prison; and those who were confined in it were in darkness and in chains. Underneath this again was the *Carnificina*, or place of torture and execution, represented—but not well, since it is made to seem too spacious—in the cut.

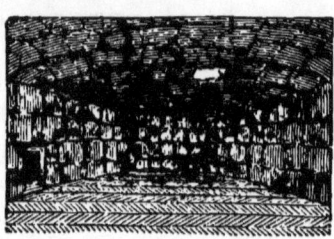

The vault is small, in the shape of a beehive, and perfectly dark. The condemned was let down into it by a rope, through the aperture, or man-hole, in the ceiling, through which also his body was dragged up again by an iron hook—*uncus*—after the execution. The small doorway on the left hand, though ancient, does not belong to the original construction; it gives admission to a low subterranean gallery, now filled with rubbish, but which takes a direction towards the Tiber, and was, perhaps, used for carrying the dead bodies to the river, when they were not dragged out of the prison for exposure on the Gemonian stairs. In speaking of these prisons in his day—B.C. 35—Sallust says that "the filth, stench, and darkness were terrible."

Their arrangement reminds one somewhat of the Castle of Chillon, on the Lake Leman; where there is first the Hall of Justice(!), then the Chamber of Torture, and, lastly, the hatch through which the bodies of the guilty or innocent, as the case might be, were shot into the calm waters below. Nor was Chillon without its *oubliette*, whence some fifty years ago, together with bones and other *débris*, there was taken out the high-heeled shoe of one who had been a lady of quality.

What ages of blood were those, in which men planned their dwellings with a deliberate intention to murder!

At Herculaneum, a similar prison to the Mamertine has been discovered with the three parts entire: it would seem, therefore, that this was the usual arrangement of such places in ancient Italy.

But we must now go on to the two miracles attributed to St. Peter: for although it cannot be proved—and indeed, with the evidence in our possession, is improbable—that he ever was at Rome, tradition, nevertheless, affirms that he suffered imprisonment in the dungeon of the Mamertine.

The first of the wonders is an intaglio, or indentation, made by his head when, as recorded in the inscription, it was dashed by the "*shirri*," or police, against the rock. The second is a fountain which, in answer to his prayer, sprang up miraculously to supply water for the baptism of the gaolers whom he had converted.

In regard to the intaglio, the profile is, as may be seen by the cut at the end of the chapter, exceedingly rude, and is probably a natural or accidental indentation in the tufa-rock, helped out by the chisel. It is on the right side of the *modern* stone stair as you descend, and the Custode, in passing down, puts his candle within the grating, and so exhibits this manifest imposture.

The origin assigned to the fountain is equally fabulous: its spring is, perhaps, as old as the present condition of the earth. At any rate it is mentioned by Plutarch as existing in Jugurtha's time, that is, more than a hundred and fifty years before the date of Peter's incarceration, if such an incarceration ever took place.

Both of these lying wonders are, then, easily refuted—the first, because in ancient times there were no stairs from which Peter's head could have been dashed against the wall; the second, by Plutarch's testimony to the prior existence of the fountain.

Let it not, however, be supposed for a moment that St. Peter has the monopoly of wonderful springs at Rome: there are no less than three which are attributed to St. Paul. These may be found in a locality near the city, where the latter apostle is said to have been beheaded, and from them the place takes its name of Trè Fontani, or Three Fountains.

The story is that the head of St. Paul, when severed from his body, made three rebounds, and that three fountains sprang up miraculously to mark the sacred spots. "In proof of the truth of the miracle," says Hare, "it is asserted that the water of the first fountain is still warm; that of the second, tepid; and that of the third, cold!"

Unfortunately for the credit of the story, the whole place is so spongy that fountains are to be seen on all sides. Nay, upon entering the church I saw the water, even there, collected in little trenches round the pillars. See Hare's remarks upon the humidity of the place in his *Walks in Rome*.

But I noticed one good thing at the Trè Fontani, the Eucalyptus, or blue gum-tree of Australia, which has been planted for some years, and, although it does not show so fine a growth as in the Riviera of Nice, is, nevertheless, exercising a most healthful influence upon that malarious and fever-stricken spot. This fact has been recognised by the Italian government, and a grant of land was made to the Trappist Monastery on condition that a certain number of the healing trees should be planted every year.

In 1877 a resident monk told me that, since the trees had been established, he and his brethren were able to sleep in the monastery even in unhealthy seasons, which they could not do previously; so great had been the salubrious effect exercised by the trees on the malaria-poisoned air. He added that they were also accustomed to drink a decoction made from the leaves of the Eucalyptus, which, when bruised, emit a resinous odour.

We scarcely need to add that there are many wonderful springs in the mythology of the Romish Church besides those of Peter and Paul. And among others, St. Alban, the traditional, but probably—as we have already shown—fabulous, proto-martyr of England, has the reputation of having called up a spring for the more selfish purpose of satisfying his own thirst. See Froude's essay on the Abbey which bears this saint's name.

But, leaving the Romish Church, we find that stories of marks of the gods impressed upon rocks, like that of St. Peter's profile in the Mamertine, and fables of miraculous fountains, are common to all false religions and systems, and seem to possess a powerful attraction for the heart of the natural man.

The "Mountain of the Holy Foot," in Ceylon, is a good illustration of this statement. It received its name from the supposed impression of a gigantic foot on a stone at its summit, to which multitudes of pilgrims wend their way for the purpose of worshipping the holy mark.

This mark was affirmed by the Brahmans to be the footstep of Siva, and by the Buddhists to be that of Buddha, when he strode across the ocean on his journey to Siam. The Gnostics, again, attributed it to Ieu, the Mohammedans declared it to be the print of Adam's foot—whence the mountain is known as Adam's Peak—"whilst the Portuguese were divided between the conflicting claims of St. Thomas and the eunuch of Candace, Queen of Ethiopia." Here, then, we have the authorities of no less than five great religious systems agreeing in their recognition of the sacredness of the same mark, and differing only in regard to the particular divine person to whom it should be assigned. What an instance of the unity of principle in error!

Another example of these lying wonders, an impression five feet in length, may be seen in the South Sea Islands' department of the British Museum. But a still better illustration was given in the *Daily News* of November 9th, 1878.

Hoosan Abdul, a town known as far back as the time of Alexander the Great, lies near the Grand Trunk Road from Lahore to Peshawur. Here the Great Mogul Akbar, the illustrious Emperor of Delhi, had a palace; now the neighbourhood is occupied by a British camp.

The place is famous for a sacred tank, formed by a miraculous spring issuing from beneath a miraculous mark in the rock—a combination of wonders precisely similar to the mark and fountain of St. Peter in the Mamertine. The story given by the *Daily News* correspondent runs as follows:—

"It appears that the Sikh apostle, coming one day thirsty and foot-sore to the bottom of the hill—crowned even then by the still more ancient shrine of the Mussulman saint Baba Wali—ventured to demand from the spirit of the earlier ascetic the hospitality of a cup of water. But the good Mohammedan, scandalised even in his grave by such a request from the founder of a new sect among the infidels, ungenerously replied by flinging at his head a massive stone, some dozen tons in weight, which might fairly justify the American phrase of 'putting a rock at him.' Baba Nanak, equal to the occasion, fielded the rock, and, laying it gently on the ground, left the indelible impression of his fingers upon its solid surface. Of course a spring at once gushed forth to satisfy the apostle's necessities, and the stream which it afforded flows on to this day as proof positive of the miracle.

"But the irreverent Mohammedans declare that this handmark was really cut by a certain Mussulman stone-mason of Hoosan Abdul for his own amusement."

Such is an Eastern church-fable, to which the Western church-myth bears a close affinity. Both of them evidently came from the Father of Lies, and they combine to demonstrate the fact that, in the matter of fable and the marvellous

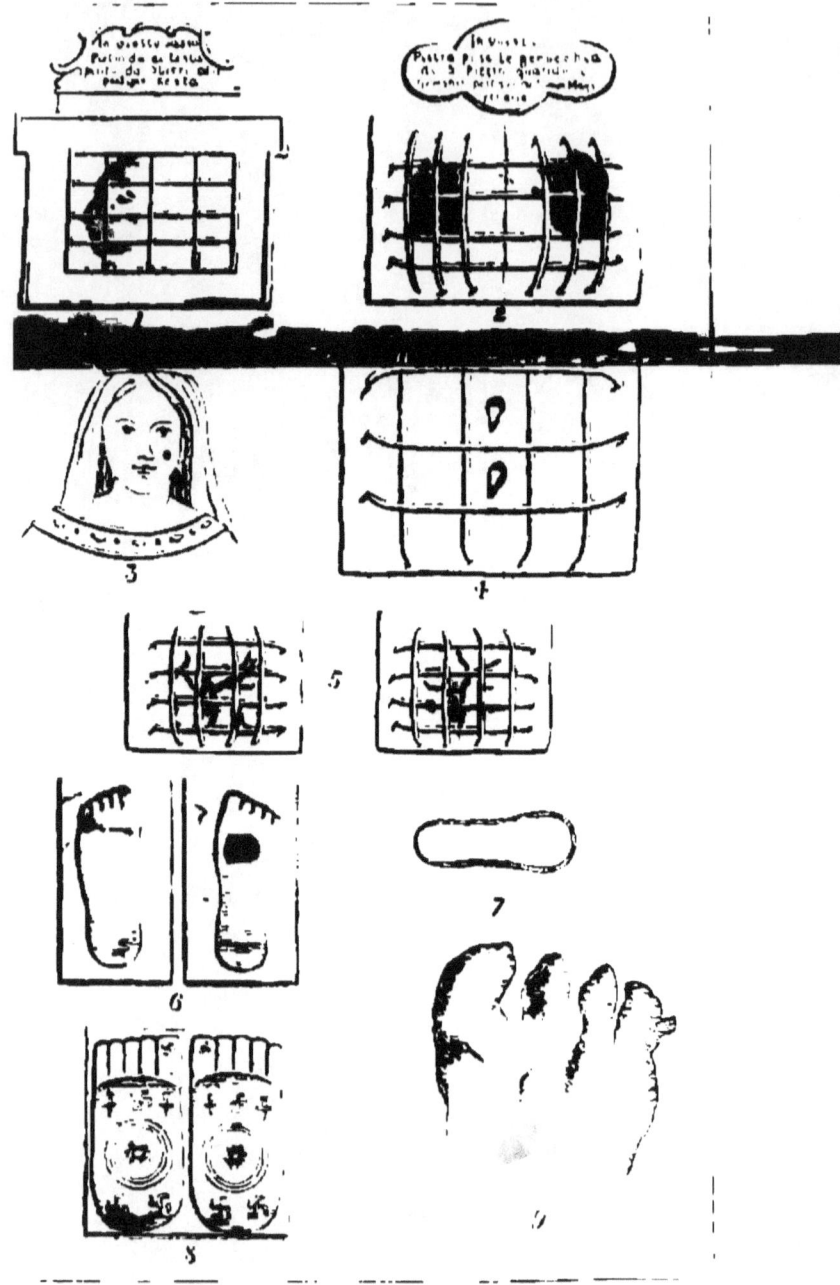

in religion, the so-called Christian in the West is in agreement with the Pagan of the East. Until a man is convinced of sin by the Spirit of God, and descries the Life which is the Light of men, he abides in darkness, whether he be Christian, Mohammedan, Brahman, or Buddhist.

On the opposite page we have given a few specimens of marks or impressions supposed to have been made by gods or supernatural powers. No. 1 represents the mark of Peter's face on the wall of the Mamertine Prison. No. 2, the marks of his knees in connection with the story of Simon Magus. The stone is preserved in the Church of Santa Francesca Romana, at Rome. Nos. 3 and 4, Mary and her tear, both from the Crypt of St. Peter's. The reference is to the story that she was once insulted by some youths who struck her upon the cheek with a ball. No. 5, Marks of St. Peter's knees. No. 6, the feet of Jesus from the Church " Domine quo vadis." The story is that Peter was in Rome during the Neronic persecution, and that the brethren, fearing for his life, besought him to fly. Moved by their entreaties, he was proceeding to leave the city by night, but as he came to the gate he saw the Lord just entering by it. Whereupon he exclaimed, " Domine quo vadis ? " that is, " Lord, whither art Thou going ? " And the answer was, " I am coming hither to be crucified again." Peter felt the rebuke, and turned back into the city; while the Lord left the impression of His feet on the place where He met the apostle. No. 7, the foot of Mary—very common in Spain and Italy. No. 8, the feet of Buddha—very common, nearly as much so as those of Christ. No. 9, the foot of Satan.

XXVII.

HOLY PLACES.

IN the previous chapter we had a remarkable example of the way in which superstition clings to places, in the case of the mark on the stone at Adam's Peak, which has been referred to their respective deities and saints by Brahmans, Buddhists, Gnostics, Mahometans, and Roman Catholics, successively.

The impressions on the rock at Hoosan Abdul, together with the spring and sacred tank, are another instance of the same thing. In early times, the locality was sacred to Buddhist and Brahman divinities; then, when the sword of Islam had passed over the conquered land, the honours of the place were transferred to two Mahometan saints. Finally, when the Sikh reaction introduced a renovated form of the old Hindoo creed, Buddhist, Brahman, and Mussulman, were all alike deposed, and the rock bore testimony to the miraculous power of Baba Nanak's hand.

These are remarkable illustrations, in a regular catena, of the tenacity with which natural religion adheres to localities and to wonders. Whether it be in the Mamertine Prison, at Rome, Jerusalem, Hoosan Abdul, Benares, Mecca, or elsewhere, the perceptible, the material, and the palpable, is that to which the idolatrous heart of man is ever prone.

The history of the world testifies to this fact on almost every page, and teaches us how men will risk their very lives to gain or defend that which they believe to be holy ground. Take the Crusades as an example—that marvellous psychological phenomenon. And the spirit which inspired them has scarcely died out. Even in the days of Louis Philippe we were on the brink of something like them; when, through priestly influence, the same "holy places" all but involved Europe in the flames of war.

And again, how much the question of the keys of the holy places had to do with the Crimean War. It is doubtless true, as Kinglake has it, that "a crowd of monks, with base foreheads, stood quarrelling for a key at the sunny gates of a church in Palestine, but beyond and above, towering high in the misty North, men saw the ambition of the Czars." Yes; but it was "the strife of the Churches" that inflamed the hearts of the Russian·people, and filled them with enthusiasm to obey the Czar. It was the reiterated assurance—confirmed by signboards purposely set up on the roads—that their march was in the direction of Jerusalem, which fired their zeal, and supplied them with a fanatical devotion.

Sanctuaries and miracles all men must have, until the Spirit of God has taught them to understand spiritual worship, and has removed from them the veil that is spread over all nations. If the Hindoos have their sacred tank, the Irish have their holy wells; if Baba Nanak has left the marks of his hands on the rock at Hoosan Abdul, Peter has also imprinted his knees on the stone which is built into the wall of the Church of Sa. Francesca Romana in the Forum. And such facts, multitudes of which could be easily collected, help to demonstrate the substantial unity of all natural religions, no matter what the differences of period, race, or mode of worship, may be.

The *religio loci*, or local superstition, finds its most abundant illustration in Rome itself, where in many cases the Christian performs his devotions at the sanctuary formerly used by the Pagan Romans. The Temple of Vesta, the goddess of fire, is now the Church of the "Madonna of the Sun;" that of the twin brothers Romulus and Remus is now dedicated to the twin brothers S.S. Cosmo and Damiano; that of Anna Perenna, the sister of Queen Dido, has become, with a slight alteration of name, the Church of Sa. Anna Petronilla, the mother of the Virgin.

"In converting the profane worship of the Heathen to the sacred worship of the Church," says the author of the Guide Book, *Roma Moderna*, "the faithful used to follow rule. Hence the temple of Rhea, 'the mother of the gods,' 'the good goddess,' they have dedicated to the Holy Virgin. In the place once sacred to Apollo now stands the Church of S. APOLL-inaris. The altar of Bacchus becomes that of S. BACC-o. On the site of a temple of Mars is erected the Church of Sa. MAR-tina, the inscription on it being:—

"'Martyrii gestans virgo Martina coronam,
Ejecto hinc Martis numine, templa tenet.'"

(Mars hence expelled, Martina, martyred maid,
Claims now the worship which to him was paid.)

The conversion of Apollo's temple upon Mount Soracte into the church and monastery of S. Oreste we have already noticed. But the great type of all these changes is the Pantheon. There it stands, almost perfect, a noble monument of the splendour of Heathen piety, dedicated by Agrippa "to Jupiter and all the gods."

But the ancient deities have been driven from their abode, and their place has been occupied by a new tribe.

Δῖνος βασιλεύει, τὸν Δί᾿ ἐξεληλακώς.

The king has been deposed, and a queen has succeeded; for Pope Boniface III. expelled Jupiter and all the gods, and conveyed the building to St. Mary the Virgin and all the saints.

XXVIII.

MODERN PILGRIMS.

IN talking of holy places, one's mind instinctively turns to the pilgrims who frequent them; and I am now going to say a word or two concerning these people—nothing, however, connected with famous stories and times long past, which my readers might get from other books, but merely a few trifling incidents of my own experience among modern pilgrims.

The year 1877 was the Jubilee at Rome, and, on the 5th of May, I found myself there in the midst of many pilgrims, French, German, Flemish, and some English—quite two hundred of them were in the hotel.

And what sort of people are pilgrims? Divest your mind, reader, of all association with Chaucer's *Canterbury Tales;* do not think of poor Ophelia's ditty—

> " How should I your true love know
> From another one?
> By his cockle hat and staff,
> And his sandal shoon."

For modern pilgrims are very prosaic persons, just like everybody else. Nor do they think of toiling along the hard road with peas in their shoes: they travel in first and second class carriages; nay, I have even seen them luxuriating in *coupés-fauteuils*.

After journeying from Pisa with about a hundred of them, I have lived among them ever since, and find that, as in Chaucer's time, they know how to enjoy themselves, and are by no means dolorous company. Yesterday was Friday, and a *jour maigre;* consequently we were not allowed flesh, but there was no reason to regret its absence. We sat down, a hundred and twenty in number, to a better dinner than that of the day before: there was plenty, variety, and delicacy, with abundance of good wine, and the meal was enlivened by much fun and talk. It was a strange fast!

But, to enter upon particulars, here is a specimen of a fasting *déjeuner à la fourchette*, or second breakfast.

Opposite to me sat a lady and gentleman, and, being curious to see how modern pilgrims fasted, I watched them. This was their meal:—A poached egg apiece; a boiled egg apiece; macaroni with sauce and grated parmesan for one; two little red mullets and lemon for one; artichokes *à l'huile* for two— with plenty of bread and wine. The lady finished her repast with a glass of Chartreuse.

A little incident set the opinions of these good people upon pilgrim-fasting in a still stronger light. The lady, a charming young Frenchwoman, put a piece of fish into her mouth, and I observed her delicate cheek flushing indignantly. "*C'est froid,*" said she; and with some little anger pushed the plate from her, as she called to the *garçon* to remove it.

So evidently, from my experience both of the dinner and of the *déjeuner*, fasting pilgrims are particular in regard to their meals, and must have proper sauces and adjuncts, with everything in plenty and everything *en règle*.

On my first Friday here I made an amusing mistake. The hotel possesses two spacious dining-rooms adjoining each other, and, on entering the principal one at dinner-time, I was confronted by the chief waiter, a very fat man, who—according to the custom on meagre days—without any preface, addressed every guest as he came in with the to me mysterious words, "*Gras ou Maigre?*"

Not being prepared for the inquiry, "Fat or Lean?" I was taken quite aback, and for the moment could not make it out, the absurdity of the connection between the very fat man and *maigre* helping considerably to push my mind off the scent. So, following instinctively, I suppose, the grossness of nature, I replied "*Gras!*" and sat down upon the nearest vacant seat. However, I soon repented of my choice, rose, and went into the other room.

The pilgrims at the time in Rome were mostly French. On one of their grand field days I went, at eleven o'clock in the morning, to see them assembling at the foot of the great Vatican stairs, the *scala regia*, on their way to an interview with Pio Nono, which, a long time before, had been arranged for that noon. Being over fifteen hundred in number, they spent more than an hour in assembling, during a part of which time the great bell of St. Peter's just above them was pouring forth its mighty voice.

The Pope met them in the ducal hall of the Vatican—a noble room, but, to the French, of inauspicious memory; for its painted walls commemorate the massacre of St. Bartholomew, 1572, when some thirty or forty thousand of their countrymen were slaughtered. The Pope of that time, Gregory XIII., went in solemn procession to the basilicas to thank God for the bloody deed, and ordered Vasari to record it in three large pictures. I have often seen them, but not lately, since the public are now excluded.

Among the many pilgrims, I met with one who greatly interested me, a very ancient man, and a senator of the kingdom, Monsignore Di G——, Bishop of C., in South Italy. I won his heart by certain little courtesies at breakfast, where we used to meet, and mention him to show how diverse Italian habits are to our own. His breakfast did not include anything to eat, but consisted of one cup only of black coffee, with a wine-glassful of brandy poured into it.

After breakfast he used to go to a neighbouring church, the steps of which he could scarcely ascend for very age. And, strange to say, he had no servant. One morning I followed him, with the intention of offering my arm to help him up the steps. But lo! he was leaving for Naples, after his light breakfast; and I could do no more than assist him into the omnibus.

The French pilgrims in Rome were from six dioceses. Among those at our hotel was the Bishop of Brieux, with his Breton flock. It was interesting to see so many bishops passing up the Vatican stairs, from France and other countries. Some of them were splendid in their apparel, and green, gold, white, purple, and violet, delighted the eye. Even military pomp must yield the palm to ecclesiastical. Soldiers have indeed the advantage of number and solidity of movement; but in beauty and costliness of dress the priests far surpass them. They are the most gorgeously attired men in the Western world, just as the Greek priests are in the Eastern: yet both of these are sworn to renounce the pomps and vanities of this wicked world!

There were but very few laymen among the fifteen hundred pilgrims; the number was mainly made up of priests and women. The latter were all in black, with black veils, the Court dress of the old *régime*, which was and is very strict. Many of both sexes were carrying bags, bundles, boxes, packets, and parcels—a proceeding which seemed a little inconsistent with Court dresses. However, the mystery was soon unravelled; for I noticed some persons carrying exposed in their arms the things which the majority had enclosed in cases. It appeared that the packages contained rosaries, medals, crosses, and such wares, which were being conveyed to the Vatican to receive the Pope's blessing, in order that they might thenceforth act as charms. It was curious to see how great a weight of these things some of the ladies were cheerfully sustaining. Now I understood the meaning of those cigar boxes and various parcels which I had seen priests and others carrying about the streets for some days previously.

In regard to the ranks of society from which the pilgrims came, I was surprised to see none, or almost none, of the peasant class; there were, perhaps, half-a-dozen well-to-do women from North Holland. No, on every side there were dress coats, and black veils thrown over the head. I did see one lady in white stockings, and another in boots, and a priest with a hole in his stocking—poor man, he had no wife to mend it!— but otherwise the dressing seemed to be unexceptionable.

Nevertheless, the pilgrims were not, so far as I could learn, drawn from the upper class of society, but seemed to be, for the most part, middle-class people of comfortable means. For instance, out of the two hundred who were staying at the same hotel with myself, there were but one or two families who were at all *distingué*.

However, that is a matter of little importance; the great fact before us is the vital power of Popery, which is able to make large bodies of people, from different parts of the earth, assemble to what they call the capital of Christendom, we the capital of Antichrist, for the purpose of doing honour both to it and to the Pope.

This is a grave matter, which demands consideration, and something more.

XXIX.

BLEEDING KNEES.

IN the French Journal, *Le Signal*, of November 22nd, 1879, I observed a notice of certain penances performed by women in Brittany. The penitents crawl on their knees many times round the sacred places of pilgrimage; and this act is called "mortification."

The Irish often perform this kind of penance by proxy, giving a few pence to a poor woman, who thereupon will go thirty or forty times round the sanctuary on bare knees. Of course this is not done without considerable suffering; the stones are reddened with the blood of the devotees; and frequently the recklessness produced by pain and exhaustion makes them indifferent to the indecent exposure of their person. Incapacity for their domestic duties, owing to the laceration and swelling of the knees, necessarily follows. Thus bleeding knees are to be seen around the holy wells, and at other places in Ireland, just as they are in Brittany.

Something of the same kind is beginning to be common in England, and for a kindred reason. Ladies, as a sort of meritorious penance—so they are instructed—kneel, in church or oratory, on the bare stones. The result is "the housemaid's knee"; and a case of this kind has lately fallen under my observation.

Now let us go back some eighteen hundred years, to the times of Heathen Rome, and we shall find a similar penance in fashion. Juvenal, in one of his Satires (vi. 522-6), speaks of a superstitious woman who is conscious of sin, and thus describes her efforts to expiate it:—

"She will break the ice and go down into the river in the depth of winter; she will dip herself three times in the Tiber at early dawn, and bathe her timid head in its very eddies; then, naked and shivering, she will go and crawl on bleeding knees over the whole extent of the Campus Martius."

How common such penances were among the Pagan Romans we may see in the following words of Tibullus (I. ii. 83):—

"I would not hesitate, if I had done wrong, to prostrate myself in the temples, and to give kisses to the consecrated thresholds; I would not refuse to crawl over the floor on my knees, and to beat my wretched head against the holy doorposts."

Bretons, Irish, English, and ancient Romans, are alike possessed of the universal idea of the natural man, that by his sufferings he can atone for his sins.

Dion Cassius relates of Julius Cæsar, that on one occasion he ascended the steps of the Capitol on his knees in order to avert an evil omen; the same thing was done by Claudius. Indeed, as Blunt remarks, "the practice of creeping upon the knees seems to have been a superstition generally prevailing among all classes, and is one among several expiatory rites."

On the steps of Ara Cœli, answering, in the present day, to those which were pressed by the knees of Cæsar and Claudius, one may even now occasionally witness the same penance in course of performance by modern devotees. But at a little distance are some much more frequented steps; I mean the Scala Sancta, or Holy Stairs, where, from morn to eve, numbers of persons may be seen laboriously toiling up the ascent in the old Pagan fashion.

We began this chapter with an allusion to superstition in Brittany; it might be expected to linger there, since some parts of the province are said to have been Heathen within the last two centuries. Indeed, from the first introduction of Christianity into that country, it would appear that Christ was degraded to a level with the old gods, as in so many other cases. The early missionaries made ineffectual efforts to overthrow the Celtic worship, and at last, tired of failure, changed their plans, and began to engraft their own faith upon the old idolatry of stones and fountains. These measures were successful; but that which resulted was not Christianity. The dolmen, or table-stone, was converted into a chapel; the menhir, or upright stone, into a pedestal for the crucifix—it often serves this purpose even now; the sanctity of the fountains was preserved, and the gods were gradually changed into Christian saints. Hence a strange jumble! Those who call themselves Christians are seen making pilgrimages to sacred fountains, the holy water from which is poured over the affected part of the diseased. And, in the depth of night, the barren woman hastens to some solitary stone, as her Hindoo sister does to the *lingam*, hoping to become a mother by virtue of her contact with it. See the article on Brittany in the *Handbook for France*, which goes on to describe the too obvious results of such a religion:—"The pilgrimage being over, and indulgence for past sins obtained, the penitents are no sooner shriven than they begin to run up a fresh score at the riotous festivals which follow these assemblies."

Roman Standard.

XXX.

ST. GEORGE AND THE DRAGON.

A CURIOUS instance of the percolation of Heathenism into Christianity is to be found in tracing out the myth of St. George and the Dragon. The following is Gibbon's account of the original of the hero:—

"George, from his parents or his education, surnamed the Cappadocian, was born at Epiphania in Cilicia, in a fuller's shop. From this obscure and servile origin he raised himself by the talents of a parasite; and the patrons, whom he assiduously flattered, procured for their worthless dependent a lucrative commission, or contract, to supply the army with bacon. His employment was mean; he rendered it infamous. He accumulated wealth by the basest acts of fraud and corruption; but his malversations were so notorious that he was compelled to escape from the pursuit of justice. After this disgrace, in which he appears to have saved his fortune at the expense of his honour, he embraced, with real or affected zeal, the profession of Arianism. From the love, or the ostentation, of learning, he collected a valuable library of history, rhetoric, philosophy, and theology; and the choice of the prevailing faction promoted George of Cappadocia to the throne of Athanasius. The entrance of the new archbishop was that of a barbarian conqueror; and each moment of his reign was polluted by cruelty and avarice. The Catholics of Alexandria and Egypt were abandoned to a tyrant qualified by nature and education to exercise the office of persecutor; but he oppressed with an impartial hand the various inhabitants of his extensive diocese. . . . The messenger who proclaimed at Alexandria the accession of Julian, announced the downfall of the archbishop. George, with two of his obsequious ministers, Count Diodorus, and Dracontius, Master of the Mint, were ignominiously dragged in chains to the public prison. At the end of twenty-four days, the prison was forced open by the rage of a superstitious multitude, impatient of the tedious forms of judicial proceedings. The enemies of gods and men expired under their cruel insults; the lifeless bodies of the archbishop and his associates were carried in triumph through the streets on the back of a camel; and the inactivity of the Athanasian party was esteemed a shining example of evangelical patience. The remains of these guilty wretches were thrown into the sea; and the popular leaders of the tumult declared their resolution to disappoint the devotion of the Christians, and to intercept the future honours of these *martyrs*, who had been punished, like their predecessors, by the enemies of their religion. The fears of the Pagans were just, and their precautions ineffectual. The meritorious death of the archbishop obliterated the memory of his life. The rival of Athanasius was dear and sacred to the Arians, and the seeming conversion of those sectaries introduced his worship into the bosom of the Catholic church. The odious stranger, disguising every circumstance of time and place, assumed the mask of a martyr, a saint, and a Christian hero; and the infamous George of Cappadocia has been transformed into the renowned St. George of England, the patron of arms, of chivalry, and of the garter."

St. George was thus turned into a military saint, but he was unprovided with a suitable history. However, "the deficiency," says Mr. Baring-Gould, "was soon supplied, just as the story of Hippolytus, son of Theseus, torn to pieces by horses, was deliberately transferred to a Christian of the same name, St. Hippolytus." Here is the fable, which we may compare with the history given above.

George was born in Cappadocia, and entered the army in early youth. He was put to death in the Diocletian persecution, enduring no less than seven martyrdoms, extending, with unheard-of tortures, over seven years; through which he converted the Empress Alexandra and forty thousand men!

But Christians are not the only persons who venerate him, and pray at his shrine. The Mussulmans also do so; and about the year 900, one of their number, Ibn Wakspiyu, translated an ancient Nabathæan volume into Arabic from the Chaldee. In this book there is much about Thammuz or Adonis, the Sun-god, and it is related of him how he was tortured, often put to death, and as often rose again.

Now in the month which after him is called Thammuz, his festival was held, and down to A.D. 900, at least, in Bagdad and other places a great wailing was made for him, especially —as in the days of Ezekiel, B.C. 594—on the part of the women. Owing to the remoteness of the time, no one, says Ibn, knows exactly what his story was, nor why they lament him. But he goes on to state, that what is said of Thammuz is the same as that which is told by the Christians of the blessed George.

"We have, then," remarks Mr. Baring-Gould, "the myth of St. George identified with that of Thammuz." The worship of St. George and its popularity in the East is mainly due to his being a Christianized Thammuz, the Sun-god, who, with the year, dies and lives again.

Thammuz, Adonis, Osiris, Baal, and St. George, were all names under which the sun was worshipped.

In the legend of St. George, two ladies are prominent—a widow with whom the youthful knight lodged, and an empress in whose house he died, and who was herself martyred. So, too, in the story of his prototype, Thammuz or Adonis, there are two ladies, Venus and Proserpine. Both of them are enamoured of him, and he divides the year between them, spending half of it with Venus on the earth, and the other half with Proserpine in the realms below. Mr. Baring-Gould thus cleverly draws the parallel:—

"It is, I think, impossible not to see that St. George is a Semitic god Christianized. A few little arrangements were necessary to divest the story of its sensuous character, and to purify it. Venus had to be got out of the way. She was made into a pious widow. Then Proserpine had to be accounted for. She was turned into a martyr. Alexandra the Empress accompanies George into the unseen world. Consequently, in the land of light he was with the widow, in that of gloom with the Empress; just as Adonis divided his year between Venus and Proserpine.

"As to the fable of the dragon, combat with these imaginary monsters belongs to all mythologies, whether Pagan, Paynim, or Church; everywhere there are dragons and their slayers, from Hercules and the Hydra, Apollo and the Python, down to the many specimens which may be found to-day in the fanes of China and Burmah."

St. George's encounter is said to have taken place on the coast of Syria, near Beyrout, not far from the scene of Perseus' famous exploit, the rescue of Andromeda, to which we shall presently have to call attention. It is commemorated in the following verses:—

> "O Georgi. Martyr inclite,
> Te decet laus et gloria,
> Per quem puella regia,
> Existens in tristitia,
> Salvata est."

That is,

> "O famous martyr George,
> Glory and praise to thee,
> Who saved the royal maid
> From dire calamity."

"Thus," says Mr. Baring-Gould, "sang the clerks from the 'Sarum Hours of the Blessed Virgin,' on St. George's day, till the time of Pope Clement VII. (d. 1534), when the story of the dragon was cut out." And well it might be; for the light of the Reformation had begun to shine, and was revealing its Heathen features.

The story of the encounter is as follows:—A lake near a town was infested by a monster, who had many times driven back an armed host, and who was wont to approach the walls of the city, poisoning by his exhalations all who came near him. At first sheep were thrown out to him as food, and, when they failed, men. And so at length the lot fell upon the king's daughter to be devoured; but as she was sadly awaiting her doom, St. George happily appeared, and, making the sign of the cross, brandished his lance, and forthwith assailed the dragon. There was a terrific struggle; but at last the monster was so thoroughly subdued that the saint bade the maiden pass her girdle round him, and lead him along. He followed her in the gentlest manner, and in this way was brought into the city, where his appearance produced the greatest excitement, and the Pagans fled in all directions. St. George, however, recalled them, and then appeased their fears by cutting off the dragon's head.

Of course the end of the story ought to have been that the maiden and her deliverer fell in love with each other, were married, and lived happily ever afterwards. But such a moral would not have suited the interests of the priesthood, and, consequently, the result is of a very different kind. The king and his people, twenty thousand men, besides women and children, are baptized; baptism being the great missionary aim of a Paganized Christianity.

Among Heathen myths similar to this Church fable, that of Andromeda is, perhaps, most exact in its parallelism. The lady, of course a great beauty, was the daughter of Cepheus, King of Æthiopia. Her mother, Cassiope, by vaunting her own beauty against that of Juno, had grievously offended that goddess. To punish her, an aquatic monster was sent to ravage the territories of Cepheus; and the oracle declared that nothing could stay the calamity unless the daughter of Cassiope were exposed to his fury. Accordingly Andromeda was chained to a rock at Jaffa, and left to her fate. But happily she had her St. George in the person of Perseus, who, on his return from the slaughter of Medusa, happened to pass that way just in time to rescue the doomed maiden from the jaws of death. But from this point the Heathen myth, following the course of nature, is far more picturesque and pleasing than its ecclesiastical imitation. The damsel and her deliverer are smitten with a mutual love, marry, and have a numerous and lovely offspring.

Thus the Pagan story, at any rate, leaves a pleasing impression; while the termination of the Church legend disappoints. The simple reason of the difference is that the latter is tortured into a form consistent with the ideas of a celibate priesthood, whereas the former closes in obedience to the sweet and hallowed law of natural affection. Enforced celibacy is a far worse enemy to our common humanity than either of the monsters slain by the two famous knights could possibly have been.

We have already alluded to the fact that the localities of both adventures are in Syria. At the beginning of the Christian era, the chains which bound Andromeda to the rock of Jaffa were exhibited to the credulous. And now, as the traveller crosses a stream a little to the north of Beyrout, his attention is directed to the scene of the conflict between St. George and the Dragon.

XXXI.

POPE JOAN.

THE story of the Dark Ages to which the title of this chapter refers, whether it be a true history or a fable, is so famous, and at the same time so characteristic of the period to which it is assigned, that it seems worth a few words.

A vivid reminiscence of my childhood, in the early years of this century, is a certain circular toy of Tunbridge ware which formed the centre of the round game of Pope Joan. After losing that association, I cannot remember to have heard the name of the Papessa for more than fifty years, and always regarded her as a fabulous personage. But at the end of that time, in 1878, happening to be in Siena, where the interior of the cathedral displays portraits of the Popes down to Alexander III., and having been told that the effigy of Pope Joan was once among them, I questioned the sacristan.

"Come here, sir," said he, politely, "and I will show you where she used to be."

So he took me with him to the great western door, and, after opening it to give light, pointed to a portrait on the north wall, near the west corner, and said, "There, sir, that was her place."

But if she were a fabulous person, how could she have found her way into that grand cathedral, and taken her place in the company of the Popes? By what means was the necessary sanction of the Bishop of the diocese, the Canons, and the other authorities of the church, obtained? I carried my difficulty to two friends who were learned in such matters. The first told me that for five-and-twenty years he had felt convinced that her story was a fact; the other observed, "There is every reason to believe it."

These answers disposed me to study the subject, which I did, though I can by no means claim to have waded through the whole vast mass of literature connected with it.

The story is as follows:—Joan was of English origin; she was beautiful, talented, and learned; but incontinent, an intriguer, and false.

While yet a girl she disguised herself as a male, and entered a monastery in order to join a monk for whom she had conceived a passion. Subsequently the lovers fled, and, after wandering hither and thither for some time, repaired to Athens with the view of perfecting themselves in Greek studies. There the monk died; and Joan, broken-hearted, but still disguised, went to Rome and opened a school. It was not long before she had the satisfaction of seeing her lecture-room crowded with literary and distinguished men, and of knowing that the city was filled with the fame of her extraordinary learning and ability, and with her reputation for piety. She rose higher and higher in public estimation, until at last, upon the death of Leo IV. (A.D. 855), she was elected Pope, and "reigned prudently during two years, five months, and four days." At the end of that time, when passing in a public procession near the Colosseum,—between it and the famous Church of St. Clemente,—she was seized with the pains of labour, fell to the ground, and died.

So runs the tale. Baring-Gould, in his amusing *Myths of the Middle Ages*, thus disposes of it:—"It need hardly be stated that the whole story of Pope Joan is fabulous, and rests on not the slightest historical foundation. . . . A paper war was waged upon the subject, and finally the whole story was proved conclusively to be utterly destitute of historical truth."

Such strong language from a clerical author, to whom the

present Premier, Mr. Gladstone, has granted a literary pension, ought to carry weight. But, though I would not contradict it absolutely, I am, at the same time, prepared to maintain that no one who has carefully and impartially sifted the evidence could be justified in making so unqualified an assertion as that which has just been quoted.

But our author makes another, which may be positively denied. It is, that "the great champions of the myth were the Protestants of the sixteenth century;" of whom we are then told that "they were thoroughly unscrupulous in distorting history and in suppressing facts."

The "myth" was, however, as we shall presently show, established and recognized by Roman Catholics centuries before the Reformation. And Mr. Baring-Gould's characterization of the Protestants is a shameful calumny, at which, however, we cannot profess surprise when we read his laudation of their persecutors, and find him describing the Papal system as "a Church where every sanctuary is adorned with all that can draw the heart to the Crucified, and raise the thoughts to the imposing ritual of heaven."

Why has not this writer, and why have not many others of the same class, honestly joined themselves to the Church which they delight to honour? Why have they remained in a communion which owes its constitution and its articles of faith to that Reformation which they are ever eager to vilify, and which Mr. Baring-Gould is said to have described as "a miserable apostacy"?

"The whole story was proved conclusively to be utterly destitute of historical truth."

Let us see how this statement bears the test of investigation. But before we adduce direct evidence, it would be well to inquire whether Rome was at the time so holy and so pure that such an episode would have been impossible, or, at least, in a high degree improbable.

The date assigned to Pope Joan is A.D. 855, and Marriott, in writing of that and the two following centuries, calls them "a period of darkness, both intellectual and moral (especially so at Rome itself), such as the Christian world has never known either before or since" (*Vestiarium Christianum*, LXXXIII). In support of this statement he quotes the testimony of the great Roman annalist, Cardinal Baronius, who, in commenting upon A.D. 912, writes as follows:—

"What at that time was the condition of the Holy Roman Church! How superlatively foul, when harlots, most powerful as they were most disgraceful, were ruling at Rome, at whose will sees were changed and bishops appointed, while—horrible and shocking to tell!—false Pontiffs, their lovers, were from time to time thrust into the Chair of Peter! Such men are entered in the lists of Popes only to record the lapse of time; for who could affirm that those were legitimate Roman Pontiffs who were lawlessly thrust into their office by whores?"

These are strong words, but they were not written by Protestants of the sixteenth century. Is it impossible that among the false Pontiffs Joan might have been thrust into the chair of Peter by some of her lovers, Cardinals who were quite aware of her sex?

"For a contemporary picture," says Marriott, "of what Rome then was,—a picture which more than justifies such language as the above—see the Sixth Book of the *Historia Luitprandi Episcopi*. He also adds that "Genebrardus, Archbishop of Aix (*Chronographiæ*, lib. iv., p. 553), speaks of this period of awful corruption, in the Papal See itself, as lasting for one hundred and fifty years, and through a succession of fifty Pontiffs."

With such testimony before us, we may surely dismiss the question of impossibility, and boldly affirm that no antecedent improbability can be alleged against the story of Joan.

For direct evidence to its credibility we shall rely upon these three facts :—

I. A medallion of Joan, set in its proper order among the portraits of the Popes, existed for some two and a half centuries in the Cathedral of Siena.

II. A statue was erected to her at Rome, on the spot where she is said to have died, and it remained in its place until the times of the Reformation.

III. Her reign is recorded, and her portrait given, with those of the other Popes, in the *Nuremberg Chronicle* (A.D. 1493).

(1) In regard to the medallion at Siena, I have already mentioned my own experience. Murray's *Guide* contains the following notice :—" Pope Zacharias was originally the bust of Pope Joan. It had the inscription, 'Johannes VIII, Femina de Anglia' (that is, 'John VIII., an English woman'). In 1600, it was metamorphosed by the Grand Duke, at the suggestion of Clement VIII. and Cardinal Tarugi."

There can be little doubt as to the truth of this statement, in proof of which we will adduce the testimony of the Jesuit Bower (b. 1686, d. 1766), who was Public Professor of Rhetoric, History, and Philosophy, in the Universities of Rome, Fermo, and Macerata, and also Counsellor of the Inquisition in the latter place. From his *Lives of the Popes*, London, 1759, we gather the following information respecting the medallion :—

That it was in its place at Siena in the time of Baronius (b. 1538, d. 1607).

That it was fixed between Leo IV. and Benedict III., and bore the inscription, " John VIII., an English woman."

That, at the request of the Cardinal Archbishop of the city, Tarugi, the features were altered in 1600.

And that some time previous to 1677, since every one knew that it had once represented the female Pope, it was broken or removed, in order that her very memory might be abolished.

The destruction of the figure took place in the Pontificate of Alexander VII. (1655-67), who, being himself a Sienese, was, perhaps, jealous for the reputation of his native town, and, therefore, finally removed the scandal from it.

After its disappearance in 1677, the learned Franciscan and Provincial of his order, Antonius Pagi, passed through Siena, and some curious particulars of his visit are given by Bower:—

"How great care was taken at Siena to abolish all remembrance of Pope Joan, as well as of the statue with which she was honoured in the stately cathedral of that city, will appear from what happened to the very learned Father, Antonius Pagi, as related by himself.

"Since Pagi, when passing through Siena in 1677, was very desirous of being informed upon the spot of every particular relating to the famous statue of the she-Pope in that cathedral, he applied for information to the religious of his own order. But, to his great surprise, they all pretended never to have heard of such a statue. Thereupon Pagi, finding that they declined —he knew not why—to enter upon the subject, repaired to the cathedral, and, addressing most of the prebendaries as they came out of the choir, told them that he wished to see the statue of Pope Joan, and begged that they would show it to him, since it might afford him some new light to confute the fable, and confound the heretics. But they all walked off, without so much as deigning to give him an answer.

"When they had gone, a man advanced in years accosted him, introduced himself as one who had long been attached to the cathedral, and said that since his inquiries were not prompted by idle curiosity, but by a desire for the good of the Church, he would furnish him with such information as might be thought necessary for so worthy a purpose, on condition that he undertook never to disclose the source from whence he obtained it. With this condition Pagi readily complied; and thereupon the old man answered all his questions, showed him the place where the statue had stood, and told him how it had first been changed into that of Zachary, and at what time it had been altogether removed, namely, in the Pontificate of Alexander VII., a native of Siena.

"Here I cannot help observing," continues Bower, "that the promise of secrecy insisted on by the old man, the clownish behaviour of the dignitaries of the Church in one of the most polite cities of Italy, and the shyness of the friars, averse to enter upon the topic of the female Pope even with a very learned man of their own order, who, they knew, would make a good use of their information, plainly show that an order had been issued by the Inquisition commanding all the inhabitants of Siena to observe a strict silence with respect to Pope Joan and her statue."

In 1699, Montfaucon, the learned French Benedictine monk, after an antiquarian tour in Italy, in the course of which he was received by the Pope with great distinction, returned home through Siena, and subsequently wrote as follows in his *Antiquities of Italy*.

"On a cornice in a row (in the cathedral) are the images of a hundred and seventy Popes, from the shoulders upwards, all in clay. The first is St. Peter (the first now is Christ), the last, Adrian IV. Order is not observed; for some are double, the Anti-Popes being inserted, and the true omitted.

"Pope Joan was formerly there; but, at the request of Clement VIII., the then Duke of Tuscany changed the name of Joan into Zachary.

"These heads of Popes were made and placed there A.D. 1400."

The reader will observe that this learned antiquary and very decided Papist does not speak, as is now the custom, of the story or fable of Joan, but mentions her as he would any other Pope—"Pope Joan was formerly there." This is not, of course, conclusive as to his opinion, and I have not studied his numerous folios sufficiently to know whether he has elsewhere expressed himself upon the subject. But his mode of speaking in the passage just quoted favours the idea that he believed in the existence of the female Pope, as he certainly did in that of her statue.

So much, then, for the medallion, which was unquestionably permitted to remain in the cathedral at Siena for some two centuries in its original condition as Pope Joan, and in its altered form as Pope Zachary for half a century longer. The fact that it was placed in such a position in A.D. 1400 certainly indicates a general belief, on the part of the ecclesiastics of the time, in the historical reality of the person represented, and an utter indifference to the scandal of her story. We now pass on to our second point, the statue in the street of Rome.

(2) In the King's Library at Paris there is a manuscript of John Burcardt, Bishop of Horta, who was "Master of Ceremonies of the Pope's Chapel" during the reign of five Pontiffs, from 1483 to 1506. Entirely and deservedly trusted by his employers, of whom he was a close observer, and with whose private life he had abundant opportunity of becoming acquainted, he was accustomed to amuse himself by writing a daily Journal of the proceedings of the Papal Court. Soon after the year 1785 an account of his manuscript, with extracts, was prepared by a Committee of French Academicians, and published by order of the King. In 1789 it was translated and published in England (London, R. Faulder), and from that edition I take the subjoined passage, dated Dec. 27th, 1487:—

"The Pope, returning in state on horseback, passed through the street in which the figure of Pope Joan is placed in memory of her lying-in. Now it is pretended that the Popes, in their cavalcades, ought never to pass through that street. The

Pope was, therefore, blamed by the Archbishop of Florence and some other prelates for having gone that way."

But this feeling was not universal among the dignitaries; for Burcardt relates that he talked about the matter to one bishop who said "that it was nonsense, and that the very mention of it savoured of heresy."

M. Brequigny, the academician who translates and comments on the extracts from Burcardt, remarks on the passage just quoted:—"The year [1487] produces a fact which appears to me worthy to be selected," that is, from the general matter of the Journal. And presently he gives his reason for the preference:—"It seems by this that at Rome there was at the time a general belief in the story of Pope Joan."

So late, then, as the end of A.D. 1487 the statue of the Papessa was to be seen in a street of Rome. And it appears to have remained there for many subsequent years; for when, about A.D. 1511, Luther visited the Imperial City, this scandalous exhibition was one of the many things which horrified him.

"Another day, passing down a wide street leading to St. Peter's, he halted in astonishment before a stone statue, representing a pope, under the figure of a woman, holding a sceptre, clothed in the papal mantle, and carrying a child in her arms. It was a young woman of Mentz, he was told, whom the cardinals elected Pope, and who was delivered of a child opposite this place. No Pope, therefore, passes along that street. 'I am surprised,' says Luther, 'that the Popes allow such a statue to remain'" (D'Aubigné's *History of the Reformation*, vol. i., p. 195).

Even Bower—whom we have already quoted, and who, like other post-Reformation Papists, endeavours to cast contempt on the story of Joan—makes this admission:—"We cannot doubt that a statue was to be seen in the place where Joan is supposed to have been delivered of a son."

He also mentions Theodore of Neim, who was secretary to two Popes, and who tells us that the statue was standing when he wrote, in A.D. 1413. "In his time," says Bower, "the fable of the female Pope obtained universally. Not that we can hence believe the story to be true, but only that it was believed when the statue was erected, as it was believed when the medallion was placed in the cathedral of Siena" (Vol. iv., p. 257).

So general a credence may well have produced the old monkish line—

"Papa Pater Patrum : peperit Papessa Papellum.'
"Popes father Fathers : but the Papess Joan
Mothers a Pope—brings forth a little one."

(3). We have now to notice the evidence of the *Nuremberg Chronicle*, a curious history of the world, brought down to A.D. 1493, the date of its publication. It is written in much abbreviated Latin, printed in black letter, and adorned with woodcuts. Besides numerous pictures of kings, legislators, poets, philosophers, and other celebrated persons, sacred and profane, it also contains portraits of the Popes and Emperors, the former beginning with Linus and ending with Alexander VI., who assumed the tiara about a year before its publication. A great curiosity it is, but very troublesome to read on account of its many abbreviations.

In this *Chronicle* Joan is found in her proper place among the Popes; her portrait is reproduced on the opposite page. In it she wears a triple crown, just the same as that of her brother Pontiffs; but she does not carry a staff with a double cross, as they do, since her hands are occupied with her child. No objection is made to her, nor is there any particular notice. About ten lines are devoted to her history, and she is described in the index to the volume as "Johannes Papa Septimus Anglicus mulier fuit in habitu virili." That is, "Pope John VII., of English extraction, was a woman in male disguise."

The *Chronicle* states that her Pontificate lasted two years, five months, and four days. And it further records, that, after her death, two things were observed with regard to the Popes. The first, that they never proceeded to the Lateran by the way of the street in which she died; the second, that from that date means were taken, at his election, to substantiate the sex of a new Pope.

The last clause alludes to the *sedes stercoraria* on which formerly the Popes were made to sit at their installation. From Burcardt's Journal we learn that this custom was practised as late at least as the coronation of Julius II., A.D. 1503.

Bower admits it as strong historic evidence of the general early belief in a Papess. It would seem that it must have originated in something of the kind, although a silly attempt has been made to explain it from Psalm cxiii. 7, a verse which was probably used to hide its real significance.

As to the conjectures mentioned by Bower to explain away the episode of Joan, they are as disgraceful to the Holy See as the story itself. "Aventinus," says he, "will have it that the fable originated in Pope John I., who was raised to the See by Theodora, an imperious courtesan. And Pauvinius is of opinion that Joan Rainiere, another famous courtesan, who with uncontrolled power governed both John XII. and the State, was in raillery called the she-Pope."

A comparatively recent Roman Catholic historian of the Popes, the Spaniard Lorenté, who wrote in 1822, is, I observe, quoted as accepting Joan, and placing her in the Papal succession of the year 855.

It will be noticed that we have supported all our arguments by Roman Catholic authorities. The Protestants of the sixteenth century did undoubtedly press their opponents with this as well as with other scandals of the Papacy, but they were by no means "the great champions of the myth"; and a more decided refutation of Mr. Baring-Gould's baseless charge could not be found than the words of the Jesuit Bower, who thus expresses himself in regard to Joan:—

"She owes her existence and promotion to the Roman Catholics themselves. By them the fable was invented; it was published by their priests and monks before the Reformation, and was credited upon their authority even by those who were most attached to the Holy See, St. Antoninus, Archbishop of Florence, being among them. *Nor did they begin to confute it till the Protestants reproached them with it.* Æneas Silvius (Pius II., died A.D. 1464) was the first to question the fact by saying that 'the story was not certain'" (p. 259). It will be noticed that the character of this negation is sufficiently qualified.

Thus even Bower, anxious as he was to get rid of the story, establishes several points in favour of its authenticity, and finds himself compelled to admit its possibility. And he speaks in just the same strain as other authors respecting the morals of the time, affirming that Rome "was profaned by the bullies, lovers, and bastards, of public prostitutes, who governed the city with absolute sway, and raised their favourites to the See of St. Peter" (p. 251).

The main points, then, which we have been enabled to extract from the testimony we have adduced are as follows:—

That Protestants neither invented nor popularized the story of Joan.

That if it were an invention, "it was invented and published by priests and monks before the Reformation, and credited upon their authority even by those most attached to the Holy See."

That the immorality of the Papal court at that time, and subsequently, made any iniquity possible at Rome.

That for some centuries the episode of a Papess seems to have been generally accepted as a historical fact in the Roman Catholic world.

That the Papists did not begin to confute the story until the Protestants reproached them with it.

That the name and portrait of Joan appear with those of other Popes in the *Nuremberg Chronicle*, a Roman Catholic work published before the Reformation, in A.D. 1493.

That a statue in commemoration of herself and her sad end was erected by her co-religionists on the spot where she died, and remained there for centuries.

That her medallion, duly inscribed with the words "Joannes VIII., Femina de Anglia," was placed in the Cathedral of Siena, and up to the year A.D. 1600 was to be seen there among the effigies of preceding and subsequent Popes.

In regard to the last two points I would ask, When in the capital of a country, and with the sanction of the authorities of that capital, a statue is known to have been erected in a public place, in commemoration of an event said to have happened on that spot to the ruler of the country; and when, in one of the most notable and splendid buildings of that country, the bust of the same ruler has also been seen, associated, in a complete collection, with portraits of the other rulers of the land—with such evidence before us, are we justified in affirming that both the event and the ruler so commemorated are fables "utterly destitute of historic truth"?

I think not; and must confess my own conviction that Joan is a historical person, and her story in the main a fact. This was the general belief for centuries, during those times of corruption when immorality was a very venial sin, and such a history brought no blush to the cheek. But the Reformation dawned, and the Word of God began to teach men to discern between light and darkness, between right and wrong: the Spirit convinced even the world of sin. A certain sense of shame and concealment, which in the case of the wicked is ever the companion of shame, ensued, and men strove to deny a fact of which they were no longer disposed to speak either with bravado or indifference. Hence the change in Roman Catholic writers in regard to this subject: they were no longer acquiescent or apathetic, but were stimulated by an intense anxiety to discredit so shameful a story—an anxiety sometimes leading to extravagance like that of the Bollandist Du Sollier, who talks of "fabella sexcenties jam exsufflata, convulsa, et obtrita." At the same time the whole tone of society was raised by the dissemination of the Holy Scriptures, a more healthful public opinion began to spread through Europe, and those who wished to obliterate the memory of Joan were helped by the fact that men now found it difficult to conceive of such a state of things as would render the intrusion of a female Pope possible. And so the story was speedily conveyed from the realm of fact into the dreamland of fable.

Roman Augur with Crozier.

XXXII.

THE ELECTION OF A POPE.

THE subject of the previous chapter brought before us the terrible corruption of the Papacy; we will now inquire into the process by which a new Pontiff becomes possessed of the chair of St. Peter.

In 1878 the whole Roman world was thrown into a state of excitement by the death of Pio Nono, and the consequent necessity of electing a new Pope.

But Rome was, from time to time, subject to similar excitements two thousand years ago; for in Heathen ages there was a Pontiff at the head of the world's religion just as there is now. Nay, in those ancient times he was even called by the same name as his modern successor. Julius Cæsar, as well as Leo XIII., had the title of Pontifex Maximus, or Sovereign Pontiff. When Pagan Rome assumed her Papal disguise, it was usual—as we have already seen—to change Heathen into Christian terms, though the usages continued to be the same; but in this case the name remained as well as the office.

"The ancient Romans," says Du Choul, "had many orders and colleges of priests, such as the greater and lesser Pontiffs,

Flamens and Arch-flamens, Augurs, Salii, and their colleges and presbyteries, like our Canons." They had also "their method of consecrating their Pontiff and other ecclesiastical dignitaries, just in the same manner that we consecrate our Pope, cardinals, bishops, archbishops, and others." "When the Pontifex Maximus died, the other priests—*petits Pontifices*—chose his successor, just as our Pontiff is at this day elected by the Cardinals. To the Pontiff were submitted all things sacred. His duty was to take charge of religion and of ceremonies, and, above all, to take heed that no strange customs prejudicial to the ceremonies of religion and of their gods were introduced."

Thus, then, according to the testimony of Roman Catholics themselves, the Heathen Pontiff was, like his successor the Pope, elected by a college and a sort of conclave of Cardinals; and with the selfsame object, that he might take care of ceremonies and of the gods, and keep out strange customs, or, in other words, extirpate heresy.

How energetically the Papal Pontiffs have taken care of the gods, and kept out "heresy" by treachery, faggot, fire, and sword, is too well known. If the Heathen Pontiffs persecuted the Christians fiercely, their successors have persecuted them fiercely and perseveringly, even up to our own times.

The proper number of the Cardinals who elect the Pope is seventy. In 1878 there were sixty-two, of whom thirty-six were Italians; four years earlier there were but forty-five. The necessary majority for the election of a Pope is two-thirds of the whole body; and the manner of procedure is to vote by ballot twice in the day, until the majority has been secured. The names of the candidates are written on slips of paper, which are then placed in a vessel in the Sistine Chapel. If an inspection proves the result to be indecisive, the papers are burnt, and the smoke issuing from them signifies to the expectant crowd that the election is not yet made.

"After each failure," says the *Daily Telegraph*, "the Conclave is the scene of the usual by-play of a contested election. Cardinals visit one another in their cells, and parties are dissolved and reformed for the next scrutiny. In this manner the fortunes of the various parties change twice a day. . . . Like an English jury, the Cardinals who elect are supposed to be entirely secluded from the world, though it is certain that in mediæval and later times they received communications which were intended to affect their choice. Unlike an English jury, however, they were not starved."

Before proceeding to the election the Cardinals have to take the following oath:—"I call Christ the Lord, Who is to judge me, to witness that I elect him whom I believe God would wish to be elected." Terrible words, when we call to mind the elections which such jurors have sometimes made!

"Ordinarily," continues the *Telegraph*, "only old men used to be elected to the Papal chair. In 1846, the favourite candidates in opposition to the late Pope were all more than sixty-seven, while he himself—Pio Nono—the youngest of the Cardinals, was only fifty-four. It followed that the Cardinals would be great in proportion as their future master lacked energy to make his will felt. Hence the brief reigns of Popes as compared with those of other sovereigns. For example, since the Conquest there have been only thirty-five sovereigns of England, whilst during the same period there have been over a hundred Popes. A darker reason is sometimes given. Italy was a land of secret poisoning, and a troublesome 'Holy Father' was seldom known to live long."

"In an election, that which every member of 'the Sacred College' pursued was his *own interest*. It little mattered whether they chose the best man or the worst. All they cared for was to ensure the election, either of him who could *lead them most ably the way they wished to go*, or of him who would most *passively follow the lead of the born rulers among* them. Next to a *stern* Hildebrand or a *domineering* Sixtus V., what best answered their purpose was a *profligate* Julius III. or a *tipsy* Gregory XVI. Often in the perplexity of counsels the election was virtually adjourned—namely, they chose what they called a dead Pope, '*Papa de tomba*,' some decrepit valetudinarian—a mere *stop-gap*. . . . Everything is keenly contested, and in order to keep out one whom some or many have cause to dread, mediocrity and insignificance become the pathway of success " (*Times*, Feb. 9th, 1878).

The same writer observes that " the Cardinals, in choosing a Pope, had to please first themselves, then the Roman people, then the Italian Princes, finally the European Monarchs. It was now the genius of a man, now the tact of a diplomatist, now the gold of a prince, now the will of a monarch, which preponderated; not unfrequently the craft of a mere subordinate agent.

" For hardly of less consequence than the Cardinal Nephews, Cardinal Protectors, Cardinal Princes, were often the 'Conclavists'—private secretaries, *valets, sick-nurses;* many of the Conscript Fathers are old, and need nursing—and others acting as *scouts, spies*, and *messengers* of the locked-up Cardinals, and in many instances, by a timely warning, or a lucky stratagem, forwarding or frustrating the combination of their employers, and determining the chances of a contested election."

After alluding to the intrigues and corruptions which have so often signalized transactions said to proceed by Divine inspiration, the writer quotes the following from Cartwright's *Constitution of Papal Conclaves* :—" Conclaves are filled with manœuvres practised by plotting Cardinals who have the visible impress of that cautious and cunning temperament which never operates but under a mask, and never contemplates to work otherwise than by stratagem."

But language so strong is not confined to Englishmen. We may gather testimony of the same kind from M. Petrucelli, in his *Histoire Diplomatique des Conclaves*, 4 vols., 1866. The author states that he has read more than a hundred thousand official despatches, most of them unedited, with the result that, for the general character of Conclaves, he endorses the report given to the King of Spain, in the sixteenth century, by Cardinal Mendoza, who had been present at three consecutive Papal elections, and had twice "a narrow escape" of becoming a Pope. The following is an extract from this Report:—

"I must declare that a Papal election is a school of deceit and malice rather than of religion. Princes at a distance do not know the thousandth part of what a Conclave is. Were a prince with his own eyes to behold the proceedings of a Conclave, he could not fail to be convinced, were he a God-fearing man, that it is to the Papacy—shamefully bought and sold as it now-a-days is—that all the evils of Christendom should be ascribed!"

In proof that this sad condition of things still continues in our own times, we may cite the testimony of the Ultramontane Marquis de Costa, Ambassador of Sardinia in 1829, at the election of Pius VIII. Writing to the Prime Minister of his master, King Charles Felix, he says—

"Flatteries, deceptions, treacheries, pledges and promises given and broken without a shadow of shame, all the ordinary incidents occurring at every Conclave, did not certainly fail to reproduce themselves in the present instance; so that I heard more than one pious, upright, and noble-hearted person declare that it would be impossible for any man of character to take an active part in a Conclave for more than once in his' lifetime, unless he were compelled to do so by the strongest sense of duty."

Chateaubriand, who was in Rome at the same time (1829), speaks to the same effect; and what we read in the works of M. Petrucelli and of Mr. Cartwright with respect to the election of Pius IX., in 1846, is sufficient to satisfy us that the usual intrigues were as much at work on that as on any previous occasion.

In the face of such iniquities, what can we say of the men who would dare to utter the terrible oath quoted above? And after their outspoken denunciations of the Conclave, could either Cardinal Mendoza or the Sardinian Ambassador have denied that it was "a synagogue of Satan"?

GODS IN THE AIR.

The upper cut, from a French original, represents the gods Apollo and Diana spreading the pestilence in defence of their votaries; the lower, from Raphael's great picture in the Vatican, depicts the gods Peter and Paul also helping their people from the air.

XXXIII.

ECCLESIASTICAL PAINTING—ITS SENSUOUSNESS AND PAGAN CHARACTER.

IN his charming work, *The Renaissance in Italy*, Mr. Symonds gives utterance to some weighty observations on the sensuousness of the Roman ecclesiastical system, some of which we will now submit to our readers.

"Intent," says he, "upon absorbing all existent elements of life and power, the Church conformed her system to the Roman type, established her services in basilicas and in Pagan temples, adopted portions of the antique ritual, and converted local genii into saints. . . . The Christianity she formed and propagated was different from that of the New Testament, inasmuch as it had taken up into itself a mass of mythological anthropomorphic elements. Thus transmuted and materialized, Christianity offered a proper medium for artistic activity" (p. 27).

"The spirit of Christianity and the spirit of figurative art are opposed, not because such art is immoral, but because it cannot free itself from sensuous associations. It is always bringing us back to the dear life of earth, from which the faith would sever us. It is always reminding us of the body, which piety bids us to forget. Painters glorify that which saints and ascetics have mortified "(p. 25).

"The old gods lent a portion of their charm even to Christian mythology, and showered their bloom of beauty on saints who died renouncing them. Il Sodoma's *St. Sebastian* is but Hyacinthus, or Hylas, transpierced with arrows; so that pain and martyrdom add pathos to his poetry of youthfulness. Leonardo's *St. John the Baptist* is a faun of the forest, ivy-crowned and laughing. Roman martyrs and Olympian deities, heroes of the Acta Sanctorum and heroes of Greek romance, were alike citizens of one city—the city of the beautiful and the human. . . . How the high-wrought sensibilities of the Christian were added to the clear and radiant fancies of the Greek, and how the frank sensuousness of the Pagan gave body and fulness to the floating wraiths of an ascetic faith, remains a miracle. . . . There are not a few for whom the mystery is repellent, who shrink from it as from Hermaphroditus" (p. 38).

Repellent, indeed! For, as our author presently remarks, "the thoughts which art employs must needs immerse themselves in sensuousness." Certainly they must do so, since art deals with the things that are seen; but true Christianity is concerned with the things which are not seen. And so the religion of Rome, being sensuous, depends much upon art; whereas the religion of Christ, from its spiritual nature, is altogether independent of it. Nay, art—I mean ecclesiastical art—is the deadly foe of faith, since it leads men away from the unseen, and from the Word of God, to the material and the sensual.

"Because," says Mr. Symonds, "painting sufficed for Mariolatry, and confirmed the cult of local saints; because its sensuousness was not at variance with a creed that had been deeply sensualized, the painters were allowed to run their course unchecked. . . In the pictures of Raphael, a new Catholicity, a cosmopolitan orthodoxy of the beautiful, was manifested" (pp. 32-36).

"The masterpieces of Titian and Correggio lead the soul away from penitence, *away from worship even*, to dwell on the delight of youthful faces, blooming colour, graceful movement, delicate emotion. . . How can the worshipper endure the contact of those splendid forms, in which 'the lust of the eye and the pride of life,' professing to subserve devotion, remind him rudely of the goodliness of sensual existence? The sublimity and elevation which art gives to carnal loveliness are in themselves hostile to the spirit that holds no truce with the flesh" (p. 26).

"A single illustration may be selected to prove how difficult even the holiest-minded and most earnest painter found it to effect the proper junction between plastic beauty and pious feeling:—Fra Bartolomeo, the disciple of Savonarola the Florentine Reformer, painted a *St. Sebastian* in the cloisters of St. Marco, where it remained until the Dominican confessors became aware, through the avowals of female penitents, that this picture was a stumblingblock and a snare to souls. . . . No other ideas but those of heroism, constancy, or faith, were meant; but the painter's art demanded that their expression should be eminently *beautiful*, and the beautiful body of the young man distracted attention from his spiritual virtues to his physical perfections. The picture was withdrawn" (p. 29).

Unfortunates, who under the pretence of religion are thus tempted by Pagan Apollos; or, if they be of the other sex, have set before them Venus the beautiful! For what is a St. Sebastian but an Apollo or a Perseus cast in the mould of manly perfection, and leading its beholder far from the quiet paths of spirituality? What is a recumbent Magdalene of Correggio, or of Guido, but an Aphrodite with dishevelled charms, dangerous to contemplate, and filling our excited imagination with the splendour and sensuality of Hellenic fable? Such, even before the rise of Greek art, must have been the effect of the giant imaged heroes of Egypt—those awful forms! Nor can we forget the solemn charge which Ezekiel brings against the wicked and corrupt Aholibah: "For when she saw men pourtrayed upon the wall, the images of the Chaldeans pourtrayed with vermilion, girded with girdles upon their loins, exceeding in dyed attire upon their heads, all of them princes to look to, after the manner of the Babylonians of

Chaldea, the land of their nativity: and as soon as she saw them with her eyes, she doted upon them, and sent messengers unto them into Chaldea" (Ezek. xxiii. 14-16).

All men naturally delight in the religion of the eye, and therefore it is that Rome, who for her own ends would sway the world—therefore it is that she abounds in imagery of every kind to satisfy the cravings of the corrupt human heart. By forms, whether of beauty or of hideousness, according to the taste of the worshipper, she seduces multitudes, and by means of their imagination holds them in thraldom. Nay, of such importance does she consider this among her other arts, that, to defend it, she sometimes mutilates the Word of God by striking out from her catechisms the commandment which says, " Thou shalt not make to thyself any graven images."

I have noticed a curious instance of this omission on the noble bronze gates of the Madelaine in Paris. The subject depicted upon them is the Ten Commandments, displayed in acts of human obedience and disobedience to the laws of God. For example, there are pictures in bronze of Cain's act of murder, of the stoning of the Sabbath breaker, and of the covetousness of Achan; but there is no illustration of the Second Commandment—that is suppressed. I could scarcely believe the testimony of my own eyes when I detected this.

XXXIV.

ECCLESIASTICAL SCULPTURE: ITS SENSUOUSNESS AND PAGAN CHARACTER.

IN the previous chapter we saw that art, though not evil in itself, has been made so in its ecclesiastical application, and that painters, with the sanction of the clergy, have done much to Paganize Christianity. We will now turn from painting to sculpture.

The pulpit of the baptistery of Pisa, a full-sized cast of which may be seen in the South Kensington Museum, is well known. It is the work of the great mediæval sculptor, Niccola Pisano, and is thus criticised by Mr. Symonds:—
"Carved upon this pulpit, Madonna assumes the haughty pose of Theseus's wife; while the High Priest displays the majesty of Bacchus leaning on the neck of Ampelus. Nor, again, is the naked vigour of Hippolytus without its echo in the figure of the young man—Hercules, or Fortitude—upon a bracket of the same pulpit."

While I agree with the criticisms of our author in regard to the wife of Theseus, she seems to me to be most fully represented in the panel of the pulpit next to the door, on the right. For there, yet more grandiose than elsewhere, the gentle Mary is represented as the haughty Heathen Queen, and made to assume the air and character of a proud Grecian beauty.

"These sculptures of Pisano (c. A.D. 1265)," continues Mr. Symonds, "are a symbol of what happened in the age of the revival of art. The old world and the new shook hands. Christianity and Hellenism kissed each other. . . . And yet they still remained antagonistic. . . . Monks leaning from Pisano's pulpit preached the sinfulness of natural pleasure to women whose eyes were fixed on the adolescent beauty of an athlete. Not far off was the time when Filarete should cast in bronze the legends of Ganymedes and of Leda for the portals of St. Peter's; when Raphael should mingle a carnival of more than Pagan sensuality with Bible subjects in Leo's Loggia; and when Della Porta should place the naked figure of Giulia Bella—the mistress of the infamous Alexander VI.—as an allegory of *Truth* upon her brother's tomb in the choir of St. Peter's.

"Filarete's gates, besides a multitude of living creatures, represent the best known among Greek myths, such as the Rape of Proserpine, Diana and Actaeon, Europa and the Bull, and the Labours of Hercules. Such fables as 'the Fox and the Stork,' 'the Fox and the Crow,' and old stories like that of the Death of Æschylus, are also included in this medley" (p. 108).

A medley indeed! Such incongruous minglings are, however, by no means confined to the gates of St. Peter's. I have seen them in many other places; as, for instance, at the cathedral of Como, the façade of which is adorned with equestrian statues of the Plinies. Another example may be found in the Certosa—that is, the Carthusian monastery —of Pavia, between that town and Milan, a rich and beautiful, but not very tasteful, building. On its façade I observed medallions of Alexander the Great, of the Roman Emperors, and of I know not how many other Heathen celebrities. But there are two delightful things at the Certosa—the nightingales in May, which seem to be ever singing, and the charming frescoes of Luini.

In 1874 I took a journey from Mentone to Perugia to

see the famous frescoes with which Perugino, the master of Raphael, adorned his native town about A.D. 1500. The most celebrated are in the little Sala del Cambio, or Exchange, and very delightful they are. But the strange grouping of sacred with profane much surprised me. Moses and David, Solomon and Isaiah, were matched with Numa and Leonidas, with Socrates and Trajan. Also Neptune and Venus and Apollo and the Sibyls were in the not very suitable neighbourhood of the Nativity and the Transfiguration.

But who were the Sibyls? They were mythical Heathen prophetesses, very popular at Rome, and in later years adopted into the Christian mythology; for the priest must appropriate everything that represents power. According to mediæval legends, they stand next in dignity to the prophets of the Old Testament, with whom they are made to alternate in Michael Angelo's celebrated work in the Sistine Chapel. Five are there portrayed—the Sibyls, Persica, Erythræa, Delphica, Camæa, and Libya; while the prophets chosen to be their companions are Jeremiah, Ezekiel, Joel, and Isaiah, with Jonah and Zechariah, one at either end. In the Church of Sa. Maria della Pace are four Sibyls, painted by Raphael, also in the vicinity of prophets; and in Sa. Maria sopra Minerva there are four more. "As in the Greek Church," writes Mrs. Jameson, "the sages of antiquity were admitted into the ranks of the prophets, the Latin Church acted in a similar way by the adoption of the Sibyls." She adds: "They are twelve in number; and the Church of St. Jaques at Dieppe has twelve niches reserved for the twelve figures of these Pagan witnesses to Christianity." In calling them witnesses to Christianity, she appears to refer to the supposed Messianic prophecies found in the Sibylline writings, but ought to have known that these are manifest interpolations, "pious frauds" of the second century, perpetrated in all probability by men who, like Jacob, did not deem the

Lord capable of carrying out His own purposes without the help of their miserable craft.

It would be easy to adduce many other instances of the union of Scriptural and Heathen figures in Romish churches; we will, however, mention but one more, in the Church of St. Augustine at Deauville near Havre. There, over the altar, and in heroic size, appears the patron saint; Vice and Error are chained before him, and he is supported on the right by Moses, Isaiah, Demosthenes, and Cicero, and on the left by Paul, John, Socrates, and Cato.

But if such comminglings of clean and unclean were allowed in churches, they must also have become common in private dwellings; and of this I noticed a strange illustration—though not in sculpture—at the South Kensington Museum in the summer of 1877. It was an elegant object of art—seventeenth century—styled "A domestic altar," and came from northern Italy. It was small, apparently of metal, gilt, exquisite in shape, and highly ornamented. The centre was a painting on agate, the most prominent of two domestic scenes for this domestic altar. It represented Mary suckling her child, with Joseph looking on—a very favourite subject, especially with Italian artists. The second scene—subservient, like all the other ornamentation of the piece, to the central group, and placed just above it—was made up of Vulcan, Venus, and Cupid, who, by the way, was not the son of Vulcan. Such were the three unholy Heathen deities evoked to be the companions of the Holy Family. I shrink from pointing out the exact parallelism.

On either side of the central group stood a man-at-arms.

Below it was Christ bound and bleeding, and supported by angels; but the latter were curious figments of the artist's fancy—female angels; in other words, Heathen genii.

Heathen Caryatides, also female, supported on either side the frame of the central picture. And the terminal ornament to this "domestic altar" was the shepherd Paris, with three naked Heathen goddesses, Juno, Minerva, and Venus, standing before him!

Had such a composition been merely intended to illustrate a Pagan myth, there would have been little fault to find with it. But when we know that it was used to beautify a Christian "domestic altar," what can we say but that the Christianity

which the altar represented must have sunk to the level of its Heathen embellishment.

It is worth notice that the female figures on the altar-piece were to the males in the proportion of eight to five. In regard to the peculiar angels, we quote the following from Mr. Symonds:—

"Correggio's angels are genii disimprisoned from the chalices of flowers, houris of an erotic paradise, elemental sprites of nature wantoning in Eden in her prime. They belong to the generation of fauns. Like fauns, they combine a certain wildness, a dithyrambic ecstasy, a delight in rapid motion, as they revel amid clouds of flowers."

But if the Church derived her idea of saints, angels, and devils from the Heathen, it was natural that she should seek their forms from the same source. What does the reader think of those in the cut on the preceding page? A sturdy tailless devil, and a sweet sentimental-looking angel! he may perhaps exclaim. No, they are neither devil nor angel; they are not even ecclesiastical, much less Scriptural, icons. They are purely Heathen fancies, and were found in one of the disinterred houses of Pompeii. The first is a satyr of the forest; the second is taken from a pleasing composition representing Thetis holding Achilles by the heel and dipping him in the Styx. An attendant is looking on, while the genius of the place—the figure which we have copied—winged, and with a circular nimbus, leans over a rock to contemplate the scene.

Such is the origin of conventional angels and devils. To the satyr the "Church" attached a tail, and he forthwith became the Prince of Darkness in the chambers of her imagery; while the Pagan genius, the nymph of the river or the grove, was transmuted into an angel of God.

Medal of Eugenius IV.   Medal of John Palaeologus II.

XXXV.

THE BRONZE GATES OF ST. PETER'S.

WE have recently alluded to the Bronze Gates of St. Peter's, of which, remarkable as they are, very few descriptions have been written. We propose, therefore, to give some particulars respecting them.

From the *narthex*—that is, the corridor forming the great vestibule which extends along the whole front of the church—there are several grand gates of entrance into the building itself. Of these, one is walled up, since it is never opened except in the year of Jubilee. Another, the central gate, is the ordinary entrance. A third, to the left of the last-named, is the bronze two-leaved gate, of which we are about to speak, and which is only opened on state occasions. It was wrought about the year 1447, by the Tuscan artist Antonio Filarete, for Pope Eugenius IV.

Its elaborate *relievi* are discoloured with age, save where exploring fingers, following out the various myths and floral traceries, have polished the brazen records, and made them plain. Higher up, and beyond the reach of touch, there is much that cannot be deciphered, even with the aid of a glass.

As works of art, these gates are inferior to those which Ghiberti executed, about A.D. 1440, for the Baptistery at Florence; they are, however, full of interest, and have somewhat of a Byzantine look. Of course they were originally made for the old cathedral, which stood on the site of the modern St. Peter's.

They exhibit a strange jumble of subjects—Scriptural, Traditional, Ecclesiastical, and Pagan; and, set as they are at the entrance to the chief of Rome's temples, form a fitting illustration of the more than semi-Paganism which one may expect to find within.

For subjects from Holy Scripture, there are our Lord and His mother; for traditional subjects, the martyrdom of Peter and Paul; for ecclesiastical, the Council of Florence, and other events in the life of Eugenius IV. There are also quantities of charming fruits and flowers, mingled with beasts, birds, forms of creeping things, and a multitude of other objects, often arranged as a setting to the more important and central tableaux, some of which we will enumerate.

First, there are several illustrations of our old friend Æsop—the Fox and the Stork; the Lion, the Fox, and the Ass; the Wolf and the Ass; the Wolf and the Lamb; and the Fox and the Crow, so pleasantly turned into verse by La Fontaine. In this scene, by the way, the cheese is curiously rendered. What the shape thereof was in Æsop's day and country I do not know; but here it resembles a big sausage, and is not very unlike those cheeses encased in reeds which are sold in the streets of Syracuse. Probably this was the prevailing shape in the times of the cunning artist.

Then we have fabled beings of another kind—loathsome satyrs, with whom are mingled Roman Emperors; nymphs not quite Christian, or even decent, in their propensities; a sacrifice to Proserpine and Bacchus; Circe extending her cup of enchantments; and Ulysses and the Syrens. Romulus and Remus are draining the dugs of the she-wolf; Phryxus and Helle ride to Colchis on the ram of the golden fleece; the hunter Actaeon surprises Diana and her nymphs as they are bathing in the translucent wave; unwilling Daphne is chased by Apollo; and well-pleased and brazen-faced Europa mounts the bull. Here, again, Nessus strives to abduct the fair Dejanira, and is slain by the poisoned shaft of Hercules; the Roman ruffians violently carry off the Sabine maids; and many other acts of woman-lifting, of violation, and of spoiling, are represented.

But over much of this sort, and especially over the adulteries of Jupiter, there figured in perpetual brass, I cast a veil. Homer does indeed make the shameless god recount his exploits, and that to Juno his Queen! Homer, however, was a Pagan, and had little opportunity of knowing better. But what shall we say of Christians, nay, of professed ministers of Christ, who deliberately record in brass and glorify such deeds of darkness, exposing them to the gaze of all men, on the gates of their most renowned and central church! It is scarcely possible to believe that they are there, and that for nearly five centuries, first in the old and then in the present cathedral, they have been advertising the sympathy of Papal with Pagan Rome to the nations who come up to worship, have remained as the brand upon the forehead of the woman, proclaiming her to be "the mother of the harlots and the abominations of the earth"!

For centuries the Popes, the Bishops, and the Clergy of the "Holy Catholic Church," as they are pleased to style themselves, have habitually passed and repassed those brazen offences, from generation to generation, and yet have given no sign of disgust or indignation. Surely ecclesiastical celibacy must be a thing very far removed from true purity and holiness.

But if purity and holiness be lacking, it is vain to expect honesty of purpose and truth, and of this we shall find a sad example as we turn from the subordinate subjects portrayed upon the gates to consider some of the principal *relievi*, four in number, which set forth the praise and glory of Eugenius IV, by recording certain events of his pontificate. The subject of one of these is the coronation of the Emperor Sigismund; those of the other three, some leading incidents in connection with the Council of Florence. "And," says the late Rev. W. B. Marriott, "the general idea which, evidently, it was intended herein to set forth, is that of the union in the person of the Pope, as God's vicegerent upon earth, of supreme power, *both temporal and spiritual*."

By the kind permission of Mr. Marriott's family I am enabled to present the reader with plates of three of these *relievi*. They are taken from drawings prepared by an Italian artist for his learned and interesting works, *Vestiarium Christianum*, and *The Testimony of the Catacombs*.

The first represents, in one of its compartments, the coronation of the German Emperor Sigismund by Eugenius IV. The Emperor is at the feet of the Pope, who is placing the crown upon his head, while his German attendants stand behind him. The whole is admirably executed, with careful attention to the costume of the time, the two groups being united by wreaths of flowers.

In the other compartment we have the procession of the Pope and Emperor through the city to the Castle of St. Angelo, the inferiority of the Emperor being signified by the placing of his name beneath his charger, while that of the Pope is seen above. To receive them the Governor of the Castle, bareheaded and banner in hand, comes forth mounted upon a noble charger. In my humble opinion he is the finest figure of this masterly casting, and the *chef-d'œuvre* of Filarete.

The second *relievo* is intended to illustrate the journey of

John Palæologus II. from Constantinople to Ferrara, and its castings are arranged in three groups.

On the left, the Emperor, having set out from his capital, is seen seated in his galley on the voyage. Beside him is Joseph, the Patriarch of Constantinople; trumpets are braying, and the rowers stand to their oars. Fore and aft may be seen the two-headed eagle, the standard of imperial Rome after her division into the Eastern and Western Empires—previously to that time she bore the single-headed eagle. In this case it may be the ensign of Sigismund, Emperor of the West, from whom Eugenius possibly borrowed the vessel; but more probably it is that of Palæologus himself, hoisted in his honour in the Pope's galley, by which he was conveyed to Italy; not the eagle which is now borne by Germany and Austria, but that which appears upon the standard of Russia, and signifies the claim of her Czar to be the Cæsar of the Eastern Empire.

The central group exhibits the landing of the Emperor and his suite in the Venetian territory, the Emperor wearing the great shaded helmet of the Byzantine Empire, called the καμηλαύκιον. Behind, and close to him, is the patriarch, clad in mandyas and cowl.

The third and last subject of this first set of scenes is the reception of the Emperor and Patriarch at Ferrara by the Pope. The Emperor is bare-headed, and on bent knee at the feet of Eugenius; the Patriarch stands humbly at the door, until it shall please the vicegerent of Christ to take notice of him; while the Pope wears his tiara and sits enthroned. Thus did it suit the pride of the papacy to represent the event, and in such a manner was Filarete commanded to perpetuate it. But, in the words of Marriott, "*this last scene is wholly imaginary, nothing of the kind having really occurred.* What actually happened was *the exact opposite* of what is here represented, and that in every particular, from first to last, almost without a

Ferrara.

THE COUNCIL OF FLORENCE

single exception." And in commenting generally upon the *relievi*, the same learned writer also observes, "In some important particulars they represent events, not as they really did occur, but as, according to Roman theory, they ought to have occurred."

The third set of scenes also contains three actions.

On the left is the Council of Florence, July 6th, 1440. In this scene, the Emperor is seated as well as the Pope; but the Papal supremacy and pride are still asserted and maintained. For while the Emperor's seat is placed on the ground, that of Eugenius is set on a raised dais, or platform. On the left of the Emperor stands the Patriarch, who died before the separation of the Council; the two orators, Roman cardinals, and others, fill up the picture.

The next group exhibits the Emperor and his suite leaving Florence after the termination of the Council, in order to embark at Venice. All are on horseback, and the dresses are very curious and suggestive. On the Emperor's left is the learned Bessarion, Archbishop of Nicæa, who, in spite of his learning and rank, stooped to be bribed by Papal gold.

The third group gives the last scene—the embarcation for Constantinople. Again the trumpeters appear, but the rowers are not yet in their places; nor is the sail—the great lateen sail, which is still in use—unfurled; for the ship is riding at anchor. As before, an ensign with the double eagle is at the prow; but above it floats the Lion of St. Mark, an indication, probably, that this galley, at least, was Venetian.

In heraldic details Filarete seems to be most minute and careful. But he has greatly failed in his figure of the Emperor ascending the ship. It is difficult to conceive such an absurd bundle of a man to be the same as the stately horseman in the central group. Both artist and Emperor seem to have been more familiar with equestrian than with marine affairs.

The last of the four *relievi* is divided into two compart-

ments—the first depicting the reception of the envoys from
Eastern Churches by the Pope; the second, the solemn entry
of the envoys into Rome.

Taken together, then, these tableaux are intended to exhibit
the supremacy of the Pope over Sigismund, Emperor of the
West, and Palæologus, Emperor of the East, together with
the Patriarch of Constantinople and all his clergy. And if
facts would not lend themselves to this purpose, they were
wrested until they became subservient.

Such are the bronze gates of St. Peter's, cast in commemoration of that Council of ill repute which was moved
from Ferrara to Florence A.D. 1440, the only Council which
ever met for the exclusive purpose of re-uniting Christendom.

It was arranged that there should be a joint declaration
of the Eastern and Western Churches on the disputed point,
the Procession of the Holy Ghost. A definition was drawn
up by the Latins, to which the Greeks agreed, and the latter
left the Council with the understanding that they were to
retain their own rites. However, it would not have suited
the purpose of Pope Eugenius to admit this: he delayed
the assistance he had promised them against the Turks, and
diplomatized until he thought he could tell Europe that they
had conformed to the Roman rite. Mr. Foulkes, in his powerful pamphlet, *The Church's Creed and the Crown's Creed*, thus
speaks of the whole transaction:—"Of all Councils that
ever were held, I suppose there never was one in which
hypocrisy, duplicity, and worldly motives played a more
disgraceful part. How the Council of Basle was outwitted,
and Florence named as the place to which the Greeks should
come; how the galleys of the Pope outstripped the galleys
of the Council, and bore the Greeks in triumph to a town
in the centre of Italy, where the Pope was all-powerful; how
they were treated there; and why they were subsequently
removed to Florence, would reveal a series of intrigues of

the lowest order, if I had space to transcribe them: unfortunately they were too patent at every stage of the Council for the real object of its promoters to admit of the slightest doubt. Between John Palæologus and Eugenius it was a barter of temporal and spiritual gains from first to last. One had his capital to guarantee from attack; the other his position in Italy to establish. Each hoped to be victorious through the other—Eugenius over the Basle fathers, Palæologus over the Turks. The more sailors and soldiers the Pope promised, the greater submission the Emperor engaged to extort from his bishops to the teaching of the Latin Church."

Such is the testimony of a learned Roman Catholic and upright man to the character of the council of Florence. And they are acts of this ill-conditioned assembly—not worse, however, so far as I know, than several others—which Pope Eugenius boldly commanded Filarete to execute in bronze for the gates of St. Peter's! Brazen deeds in brazen castings, and set, as we have already seen, in shameless framework of immoral actions—the latter illustrating the lusts of the flesh, the former the desires of the mind.

As for the Emperor and his followers, it fared ill with them on their return to Constantinople. So badly were they received that they were induced to disown their acts to their countrymen. "The very bishops who were parties to the transaction found it necessary to express their reprobation of it" (Grier's *Epitome*).

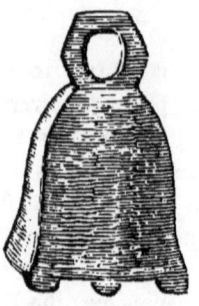

Bell from Padua.

XXXVI.

THE SHRINE OF ST. ANTHONY OF PADUA.

AFTER arriving at Padua and settling yourself in your hotel, the Stella d'Oro, your first business will be to step into a cab, and, as the driver is shutting the door, to say, "Il Santo."

In less than ten minutes he will set you down at the church of St. Anthony, who is "the saint" *par excellence* at Padua. He was born at Lisbon in A.D. 1231, and, though he lived but thirty-six years, is the same greatly-tried and wonder-working saint whose temptations Teniers and other Dutch painters have so comically portrayed. The Dutch evidently had a fancy for the grotesque side of Il Santo.

The vast church which contains his shrine, built from the designs of the famous Niccolo Pisano, is filled with remarkable works of art. It has seven domes, and is thus somewhat oriental in its appearance. The saint's sanctuary is, I suppose, the most splendid and the most popular in Italy. It is separated from the church by an arcade of round arches, on fine marble columns, supporting a magnificent screen, glittering with varied marbles, and adorned with exquisite sculptures.

This sanctuary, which is a side chapel, contains the tomb of the saint, and in front of it the general worship is carried on in the church by hundreds of devotees. But within the sanctuary, at the back of the tomb, a very strange ceremony is performed. The tomb is raised some five feet above the floor of the church, and is placed about eight or nine feet from the back wall, so that there is space to walk behind as well as on the other sides of it. During my visits to Padua—the last was in 1879—I have often rested upon a ledge which runs along the north wall, and watched the proceedings.

The suppliants approach, cross themselves, and then with the right hand touch the large perpendicular marble slab which forms the back of the tomb, the front and surface of it being used as the altar for Mass. They place either the tips of their fingers or the whole hand upon it, and, while carefully preserving their contact, recite their prayers for some minutes, apparently under the impression that virtue is flowing into them from the saint through their fingers. I have seen as many as ten right hands placed at one time upon the slab. Other suppliants stand near praying, and waiting until the departure of earlier comers shall have made room for them. On one occasion a very little lady was standing by me, and, seeing her need, I moved out of her way. She acknowledged the civility with a bow, and at once performed the accustomed rite, with hand uplifted to the shrine, which she could with difficulty reach. On another occasion a very odd worshipper presented herself, the oddness consisting in a mixture of grandeur and poverty: she wore a fine dress with a long sweeping train, but had no shoes on her feet. Often devotees may be seen rubbing their head against the stone, sometimes passing their hand over it, still more frequently kissing it.

It would be difficult to connect such worship with the Christianity of the New Testament; while in the splendid decorations of the shrine there is pure, or perhaps it would be more correct to say impure, Heathenism.

I allude to the marble arabesques, of which there are many executed in low relief, with exquisite skill, by an artist who seems to me a dangerous rival of Donatello. Nothing in marble can be conceived more beautiful than some of his female forms: in design as well as execution he exceeds Niccolo Pisano. On one of his works we may discern his name—"Matteus Allio faciebat."

There is of course the usual amount of beautiful women, bare to the hips, which terminate in foliage, large-breasted sphynxes, griffins, hippocampi, and other monsters—strange decorations, if the Lord Jesus is supposed to have anything to do with the place; but still not quite so mischievous, perhaps, to holy purity and undistracted worship as the following.

On the left pilaster of the shrine, sacrifices are depicted in three marble panels. In one, some thin-robed half-clad women are leading an ox decorated as a victim; in another there are two girls clothed in the same transparent drapery, with a Cupid raised on a stool, sacrificing at an altar. The third exhibits two other girls similarly vested, carrying a wreath, and apparently forming a part of the sacrificial procession. Above these are the three Graces in a state of nature, and far too beautiful for the place in which they are. Another group in the same perfectly nude condition, and of equal beauty, consists of two nymphs and a child; another of two nymphs and a youth wounded or languishing, and so on. All the figures are a foot or more in height.

On the inside of the other pilaster are figures too gross to be described. Suffice it to say that they are men playing on instruments, while women dance—a group corresponding to one on the opposite pilaster, where women are playing and boys dancing.

These incentives to passion in a so-called Christian church, one of the most frequented in Europe, and at a shrine of more than ordinary renown! And the priest every day celebrating the mass in close vicinity to such obscenities, as he has done for centuries!

How near is superstition to licentiousness; how ill-defined the boundary between Papal and Pagan Rome!

But here is in this church of St. Anthony another painful manifestation of Heathenism—the famous bronze Paschal Candelabrum of Riccio. It is a splendid specimen of art, but of Pagan art; yet great prominence is given to it by the clergy of this church; for it stands on the right of the high altar, from which it is separated only by another fine casting, the effigy of a bishop.

It was set up in 1516, and was the work of Andrea Riccio, the son of a Milanese goldsmith, whose portrait—the curls, from which he was called Crispi, escaping from his round cap—may be seen, in the choir of the church, in his noble bas-relief of David dancing before the Ark.

It is very lofty, and is raised on a pedestal of white marble. "Four Sphynxes," says Perkins, in his *Italian Sculptors*, "sit at the angles of the base, as if guarding the secret meaning of its ornaments, some of which Oedipus himself would find it difficult to penetrate."

Above the Sphynxes come four castings of Heathen subjects, in which naked men and women, Jupiter with lewd surroundings, sea-monsters, licentious triumphs of Neptune and Venus, and other Paganisms, are placed in offensive juxtaposition to the same number of Scriptural subjects just above them, the only figures which redeem the work from entire Heathenism. Yet even these are not all Scriptural: for one of them is Christ delivering souls from Limbo—the fable being treated by the artist in the same way as by the Limoges enameller in a plaque which may be seen at the South Kensington Museum.

Above these come Centaurs mounted by children; women in classic attire, or in no attire at all; winged genii, cupids, griffins, *et hoc genus omne.*

One cannot look at them without the thought—If such are the morals which Rome honours in Church, how must it be out of Church!

However, bad as Riccio's candlestick is, there might have been something worse; for Perkins tells us that another artist, Da Grandi, having produced a design for a sculpture to be erected in the same church, "its extreme Paganism so shocked the Commissioners that they dismissed him." How it could have been more Pagan than the candlestick, or even the shrine of the saint, I am unable to say.

Everywhere in that age the Church was mingled, not merely with the world, but with the Heathen world.

And, alas! the tide, which receded somewhat at the Reformation, is now returning upon our land with rapid advance.

XXXVII.

THE BURLESQUE SIDE OF SUPERSTITION.

SUPERSTITION is not without its burlesque side, and since St. Anthony furnishes several instances of the fact, we will, while the saint is before us, relate one or two of them, and also some others with which he is not connected.

In the *Daily News* of August 4th, 1879, a curious story appeared in reference to him. It was taken from the Lisbon *Revista Militar*—the official military journal of Portugal—and described, from the State Archives of Rio de Janeiro, the form of "conferring on good St. Anthony the grade of Lieutenant-Colonel in the Portuguese army by King John VI." This distinction was a reward to the saint for services rendered to the said army. "Therefore," runs the document, "we have resolved to raise (!) him to the rank of Lieutenant-Colonel of Infantry. He will receive the usual pay through our Field Marshal, De Cuntra. Given at our capital, August 1st, 1814."

Agreeably with this it is officially added, "that, from the date of his commission as an infantry officer, Lieutenant-Colonel St. Anthony has been borne on the strength of the Portuguese regular army down to the present day, somebody, or rather, a succession of somebodies, having regularly for sixty-five consecutive years drawn the pay of this eminent member of the Church militant."

But we will go back to the time when St. Anthony was still in the flesh. Then his miracles were countless; the Church at Padua is filled with representations of them, and some are very characteristic of the morals of the time. But the most famous of his wonders is his sermon to the fishes, a picture of which may be found on the south side of the church, near a vestry door. There they are, both saint and fishes, and I have stood gazing at them for a long time, fascinated, not exactly by their beauty, but by their quaintness. In the Borghese Palace at Rome there is a picture of the same scene by Paul Veronese.

The story is this. When the saint was at Rimini, the people would not hear him. Whereupon he repaired to the shore, and stretching forth his hand, cried, "Hear me, ye fishes; for these unbelievers refuse to listen."

"And truly," says the chronicler, "it was a marvellous thing to see how an infinite number of fishes, great and little, lifted their heads above water, and listened attentively to the sermon of the saint."

He addressed them as "Cari et sancti pisces," "Dear and holy fishes." And, continues the legend, at the conclusion of the sermon, the fishes bowed to him with profound humility, and with an appearance of reverent religion. So the saint pronounced his benediction, and the congregation dispersed.

While we are on the subject of fishes, we may mention the strange tradition respecting the John Dory. How this inhabitant of the sea got his name of John, I do not know; perhaps it was an affectionate tribute to his good fellowship, because he is such a capital dinner companion. According to some, the whole name is a corruption of the French *Jaune dorée, i.e.*, gilded, or golden, yellow; this, if not altogether right, may be so at least as regards the origin of Dory. The French, however, turn Golden John into a sort of a saint, only they do not call him St. John, but connect him with St. Peter. Hence it has been supposed, with some probability, that Dory is derived from adoré, *i.e.*, "worshipped." The story is that this was the fish out of whose mouth Peter took the tribute-money, and that the conspicuous marks on its side are the impressions of the apostle's finger and thumb.

There may seem to be a difficulty or two in the way. Troublesome quibblers, for instance, may suggest that the Dory is a salt-water fish, while the Sea of Galilee, into which Peter cast his net, is fresh water. They may go on still further to urge that the Sea of Galilee has no outlet whatever into the Mediterranean, and, therefore, request to be informed in what manner the Dory took his journey overland. They may also affect to think it improbable that the marks should appear in the Dory's children or grandchildren, though he may have displayed them in his own body; or they may, perhaps, even deny that the apostle's fingers could have left such impressions behind them.

But the first two objections are trifling, and no good purpose is served by disputing about trifles. Let them pass; and as to the others, see what Mr. Darwin has to say on the subject of transmitting impressions to posterity; remember, as we have already shown, that Peter left the marks of his head and knees upon rocks, substances far less impressible than the soft body of a fish, and where is the improbability of the story? The French Catholics found no difficulty; and, consequently, the fish was popularly canonized, and holds a proud pre-eminence among his fellows, something like that of our stately Sir Loin among joints.

If St. Anthony preached to the fishes, the birds also had their apostle in the person of St. Francis, whose sermon, addressed to them as "Brother Birds," is still extant. In the fine church dedicated to this saint at Assisi, there is a picture by Giotto representing the scene, among the audience in which I was particularly struck with the demeanour of a little wren.

But, before taking a final leave of St. Anthony and his church at Padua, we must mention one more of his wonders, the memorial of which, in the shape of a bronze by Donatello, may be seen in the Chapel of the Sacrament.

It is concerned with a mule at Rimini, of which we are told that, "rejecting the fodder which her master gave her, after a rigorous fast of many days, she prostrated herself before the Host which the saint was carrying to confound the heretic Bonvillo, who denied the real presence of our Lord in the Sacrament."

The audacious impudence of such a story—you can buy a book containing it in the vestry of the church—would be, we should think, sufficient to keep many other Bonvillos in the same kind of unbelief.

But a Latin work entitled *Historia Societatis Jesu* informs us that there have been pious asses as well as pious mules. Its author, a Jesuit of high repute, narrates as follows:—"A priest who was carrying the host to a sick man had to pass through a drove of asses. To his utter astonishment the beasts not only made way for him, but fell devoutly on their knees as he passed. They then formed into line, followed him in procession, and waited at the door till he had performed his ministration. Nor did they return to their pasture till they had received his benediction."

We may not inaptly conclude this chapter with a notice of the Feast of the Ass, which—together with the Feast of Fools, the Boy Bishop, and other buffooneries—was once an institution of the Church. Till I knew of it, I never could understand what Francesca meant by introducing a braying ass into his picture of the Nativity, which is now in the National Gallery. In the company of certain very ugly singing angels—neither angels, as we know them, nor human beings, can be anything but ugly when they have their mouths open—the creature stands, and in his fashion also sings, lifting up his ugly head. One almost seems to hear his discordant bray drowning the angels' song. But in former times such a voice was sometimes heard in Roman Catholic congregations, as

THE BURLESQUE SIDE OF SUPERSTITION.

we may see by the following extract from Hone's *Ancient Mysteries* :—

"*The Feast of the Ass*, anciently celebrated at Beauvais every year on the 14th of January, commemorated the flight of the Virgin into Egypt with the Infant Jesus. To represent the Virgin, the most beautiful girl in the city, with a pretty child in her arms, was placed on an ass richly caparisoned. Thus mounted she preceded the Bishop and his clergy, and they all went in grand procession from the cathedral to the church of St. Stephen. On entering the chancel they ranged themselves on the right side of the altar; the mass immediately commenced, and the *Introit, Lord, have mercy upon us, Gloria Patri*, the Creed, and other parts of the service, were terminated by the burden of Hee-Haw, Hee-Haw, in imitation of the braying of an ass; the officiating priest, instead of saying *Ita Missa est* at the end of the Mass, concluded by singing three times Hee-Haw, Hee-Haw, Hee-Haw," and was answered by a general braying from the congregation.

From the Missal composed for the service of this Feast by an Archbishop of Sens, who died in 1222, these additional particulars have been gleaned :—

"The Anthem being concluded, two canons were deputed to fetch the ass to the table, where the great chanter sat to read the order of the ceremonies, and the names of those who were to assist in them. The animal, clad with precious priestly ornaments, was solemnly conducted to the middle of the choir, during which procession a hymn in praise of the ass was sung in a major key." Its first and last stanzas have been thus Anglicized :—

> "From the country of the East
> Came this strong and handsome beast,
> This able Ass—beyond compare
> Heavy loads and packs to bear.
>   Huzza, Seignor Ass, Huzza!

> "Amen! bray, most honoured Ass,
> Sated now with grain and grass:
> Amen repeat, Amen reply,
> And disregard antiquity.
>   Huzza, Seignor Ass, Huzza!"

Another *Feast of the Ass* was anciently celebrated in France, in honour of Balaam's ass. At one of them, Warton tells us, "the clergy walked in procession on Christmas Day, habited to represent the prophets and others. Moses appeared in an alb and cope, with a long beard and a rod. David had a green vestment. Balaam, with an immense pair of spurs, rode on a wooden ass, which enclosed a speaker. There were also six Jews and six Gentiles. Among other characters, the poet Virgil was introduced singing monkish rhymes, as a Gentile prophet and a translator of the Sibylline oracles. They thus moved in procession through the body of the church chanting versicles, and conversing in character on the nativity and kingdom of Christ, till they came into the choir."

Palm Sunday, the Festival of Christ's entry into Jerusalem, was another time at which the ass was prominent. In reference to the celebration of this day in England, Hone quotes from an old book the words:—"Upon Palme Sundaye they play the foles sadely, drawinge after them an asse in a rope, when they be not moch distant from the woden asse that they drawe."

Some kind of performance with an ass used to be almost universal at this festival. At Easter 1879 the Naples correspondent of *The Times* wrote thus:—

"All the incidents of Palm Sunday, when Christ entered Jerusalem riding upon an ass, are, as it is well known, dramatized. One marks the progress of civilization in the diminution of these ceremonials. Time was when the Neapolitans were accustomed to place an ass at the head of the procession with a figure on it. This is now omitted, and the procession of priests enters the church followed by the mob, who rush in after them."

XXXVIII.

ORVIETO AND TRANSUBSTANTIATION.

ONE of the least known and yet one of the most interesting cities of Italy is Orvieto. Its name is probably a corruption from Urbs Vetus, a city of ancient Etruria. Its situation, on a highway between Rome and Florence, is remarkable and picturesque. It is built on a lofty plateau of rock, precipitous on every side, which being strengthened by fortifications rendered the city impregnable during the middle ages.

Thither in troublous times—and such were frequent—the Popes were wont to flee—like Bishop Hatto to his castle on the Rhine—that the rocky fastness might afford them security against their foes. Indeed, at different periods, no less than thirty-two Popes are recorded to have sought refuge in this stronghold, from the lofty steeps of which they could defy all assailants.

Nor were they likely to suffer from the calamity most incident to such a site—want of water; for the place contains a magnificent well, constructed by Langallo, and called San Patrizio, after St. Patrick. This well is similar to the grand work of the Sultan Saladin at Cairo, and is probably unique in Europe. It is cut in the rock, and winding round it in an outer walled circle are two sets of steps for mules, one descending, the other ascending, with a door to each on the top. The stairs are paved with brick, and sufficiently lighted by seventy window-shaped openings looking into the vast shaft.

The shaft itself is open to the top, and is a hundred and seventy-nine feet deep and forty-six in diameter. It is a noble work, and its proportions and symmetry are most striking.

The well at the fortress of Königstein on the Elbe is fine, but is not to be compared with that of Orvieto. There is, however, a remarkable likeness between the German and the Italian fortresses in regard to their respective precipitous sites. In 1879 I passed with my daughter almost directly from the latter to the former, and we were much struck by the similarity of their appearance.

Even the visitor who does not care for antiquities can scarcely fail to be interested in the curious and picturesque city of Orvieto, in the well, and in the beauty of the surrounding country. The well, which would seem less uncommon in the East, but is a wonder in the West, should be visited in passing, as you approach or leave the hotel, since the distance is considerable. Nor must the Etruscan Cemetery, lately unearthed, and described and figured in Dennis' *Cities of Etruria*, be neglected. It is of curious construction, very ancient, and perfect. Fragments of pottery are lying here and there, and also large wrought stones, some of which appear to have been connected with Phallic worship. When I visited the place a young mother and her little daughter were waiting to show us the Cemetery, both of them very interesting, and, though southerners, fair as the moon.

In 1263, when Urban IV. was residing at Orvieto, the Roman world was excited by the report of a wonderful miracle said to have taken place in the neighbouring town of Bolsena, and hence called the miracle of Bolsena. To understand it we must remember that the doctrine of Transubstantiation had now been promulgated for nearly fifty years, but was not so universally received as its supporters wished. The story runs as follows:—

A young Bohemian priest, who was somewhat sceptical in the matter of the dogma just mentioned, was staying at Bolsena, and, while celebrating mass there, beheld blood in abundance flowing from the broken parts of the wafer, and also bubbling from the cup, just as it is now represented in the Church of Sa. Christina. Moreover, the blood flowed freely over the pavement of the chapel—a dark, damp, half-subterranean place—in which the miracle occurred, and its stains are still shown under a grating on the floor—at least they were as late as 1879, when I saw them.

Of course the priest was immediately converted, and betook himself to Orvieto to make the wonder known to the Pope, and to get absolution for his former unbelief. Then Urban sent the Bishop of Orvieto, in whose diocese the miracle had taken place, to fetch its signs, the wafer and the linen, which were carefully conveyed to Orvieto.

Thus was a bold and well-timed falsehood, of a kind suitable to the age, devised for the purpose of popularizing the useful doctrine of Transubstantiation. Nor was the Church slow to follow up its advantage, and to make the most of it. Urban went forth in state to meet the evidences of so great a wonder: the red-stained napkin—or corporal—was exhibited; the wafer bearing the marks of a copious enundation of blood was set before the eyes of the people. Who could doubt proofs so clear? A church, the splendid cathedral of Orvieto, was ordered to be built in commemoration of the prodigy. And Ugolino Vieri, the great artist of Siena, was commissioned to construct a reliquary—with a façade like that of the cathedral, worthy of treasures so inestimable; a task which he executed with marvellous skill and rapidity.

Chiefest of all, a bull was published (1264), directing that the event should be commemorated by the perpetual observance of a new festival, that of Corpus Christi—the body of Christ—which has given its name to one of the colleges at Oxford. It is known in France under the name of the Fête-Dieu, or God's Festival, when Le bon Dieu, as the French call it, or in other words, the wafer, is carried through the town, and people at the windows exclaim, "God is passing!"

In so suspicious a manner, by a report of what had happened in "a dark and dirty vault"—for so the chapel is described in Murray's Guide—situated in an obscure country town, and on the testimony of a foreign stranger, was the imposture of Transubstantiation confirmed. Devised to suit the gross darkness of the age, and followed up with the most determined and unblushing effrontery, the story was successful.

The reliquary, to which we alluded above, is a great curiosity and a marvel of art. It is large, no less than four hundred pounds of silver having been used to make it. Its chief beauty lies in the statuettes, and especially in the enamels, with which the front is covered. Though it is more than five hundred years old, the lustrous blue, as brilliant as can be conceived, which is the prevailing colour, is still fresh and perfect, except in the case of one enamel. This, from the handling to which it has been subjected by being carried every year with the wafer in the procession of Corpus Christi, and possibly sometimes to the sick, is nearly obliterated. A piece of red coral, or something like it, marks externally the precise spot where, within, in the upper part of the reliquary, the miraculous host is said to be preserved.

M. Darcel, in his interesting *Notice Des Emaux Du Louvre* (Paris, 1867), speaks of Ugolino's tabernacle as the most remarkable work of that age which has come down to us, and also gives his opinion that the peculiar lustrous enamel was probably discovered by the accidental falling of a few drops of water upon the heated metal. "But," says he, "no one interested in these things can ever see them, since, with the exception of two days, they are kept under the custody of four keys, which it is impossible to unite." The Guide Books also state that considerable difficulty is experienced in getting a sight of the relics.

However, a secret was disclosed to me, which enabled me to accomplish the task with the greatest possible facility. On arriving at Siena one day from Rome, after having just passed, as at other times, under the very walls of Orvieto, I met a French gentleman at dinner, who told me that he had seen the relics, and that the landlord of the *Belle Arti* had arranged the matter for him. I at once wrote to the landlord of the *Belle Arti*, begging him to perform the same kind office for me, and on the next day started for Orvieto..

But before describing the visit, let me put together the dates of the events which have been enumerated in connection with the historic cathedral of the place.

    A.D. 1215. The term and doctrine of Transubstantiation adopted and confirmed by the fourth Lateran Council.

    1263. The miracle of Bolsena.

    1264. Bull of Urban IV. for the establishment of the festival of Corpus Christi.

    1290. The Cathedral of Orvieto founded.

    1309. The Cathedral opened for service.

    1338. The silver Reliquary made.

    1357-63. The Chapel of the Reliquary adorned with mural paintings made expressly with reference to the sacrament of the Eucharist.

These historic dates connected with the Cathedral of Orvieto are by no means unimportant, closely united as that edifice is with the doctrine of Transubstantiation, which it will be noticed is, comparatively, a modern innovation. On that dangerous deceit, as the Thirty-first Article of the Church of England calls it, rests another fable, that of Priesthood, and on the fable of Priesthood is raised the mighty and overshadowing fabric of the Church of Rome.

XXXIX.

THE CATHEDRAL OF ORVIETO.

Part I.

UPON my arrival at Orvieto I went to the *Belle Arti*. Imagine an hotel named the Fine Arts in England! But what do we northern barbarians know of such matters!

The hotel proved to be an old palace, and I soon found myself installed in a noble painted chamber, one of its apartments. The head waiter did the honours of the house for his master— an artist; hence, no doubt, the name of the inn—and procured the permission to view the relics, for which I had asked.

He was a young Italian, a nice obliging fellow, who had recently been connected with a tragic event in French history. Serving as valet to Monseigneur Darbois, Archbishop of Paris, at the time of the Communist *émeute*, he was imprisoned with his master. At the final scene, when the Archbishop was shot, he was present, and had he been a Frenchman would have been executed with the prelate; but the Italian Embassy at Paris interfered, and he was saved.

"Did you not," said a lady to me; "Did you not observe an expression of melancholy about the young man, marking him as one chastened by suffering?" Women are of quicker perception than men. Yes, I did observe it, after the remark, and still see it with my mind's eyes.

The shade on the man's countenance put me in remembrance of the fine delicate and melancholy face of Platina, the man of letters and historian of the Popes. He appears in a great mural picture of Melozzo da Forli in one of the rooms of the Vatican picture gallery, the third on the left as you enter, in the midst of a wicked surrounding of Roveres and Riarios. Poor fellow! he had a painful retrospect; for having been suspected by his evil master Pius II., a previous Pope, he had been stretched on the rack.

But to return to Orvieto. At ten o'clock in the forenoon I repaired to the Cathedral by appointment, having previously visited it, both the day before and early the same morning, to acquaint myself with localities. Of the façade I will only say that there is, perhaps, nothing in Italy to equal it. Designed and executed, as it was, by artists of inimitable skill, its materials—marble, mosaic, and bronze—are worthy of their handling, for it is a miracle of art. Its site, too, is admirable, being free from any surroundings.

Of the interior, the transept is the most remarkable part, and is formed by two chapels, both of them shut in by gates. The one, the chapel of the Sacrament, or of the Santissimo Corporale, is so called because within it is deposited the corporal, or napkin, stained with the blood of Christ (!), as well as a piece of the wafer from which the blood flowed.

Both of these chapels are entirely covered with grand or curious frescoes. That of the Sacrament—with which we have at present to do—has two series of pictures, besides a noble one of the Crucifixion which is walled up and apparently in part destroyed, as also are other valuable works in the same church.

The pictures on the right of the chapel give the history of the miracle of Bolsena. The unbelieving priest is massing, and in blank astonishment at the appearance of blood flowing from the cup and wafer. Next to this, bishops are seen examining the blood on the altar. Then the Bishop of Orvieto conveys the signs of the miracle to the Pope, who goes forth and meets him on the bridge of Rio Chiaro—or the Brook Clear—which is just under the walls of Orvieto, and over which one still passes in journeying westward. In this last scene the white

gloves of the Pope are conspicuous. Two or three other pictures complete the series.

The pictures on the left wall represent the administration of the sacrament to the sick and others, depicting some curious miracles. For instance, the host flies out of the priest's hands into the air, while Christ appears just above it, and an angel is preparing to catch it in a napkin. Again, the priest elevates the host above his head, and it becomes a little Christ; the same wonder is repeated as he holds it before him; and a Christ is also seen coming out of the cup. Indeed, there is a prodigality of wonders—far too many.

Among them is the history of a young Jew, a convert. He is first seen at the sacrament with other lads: then his irritated father seizes him violently by the neck, and throws him, head foremost, into a fiery furnace. But lo! he is miraculously delivered from the furnace, and his mother, supposed apparently to be a Christian, exhibits him to the astonished people.

But there is one thing in this remarkable series which is most interesting, and is yet unnoticed in the guide books. In a picture of the communion, *the cup is being administered to the laity*. I had a careful water-colour drawing of this picture made upon the spot by Professor Ferrari.

A Roman Catholic friend, who had joined me in examining the pictures, looked at this one in astonishment, and exclaimed, "Why, they are giving the cup to the laity!" "Yes," said I, "I was waiting to see whether you would observe it."

These pictures exhibit red wine in the cup. In the Church of Rome the wine ordinarily used in the present time is as frequently white as red. Yet our own people, I think, are so superstitious that many of them would be shocked if they were offered white wine at the Lord's Table. Tent wine—that is, *vino tinto*, or tinted wine—is with us considered to be most correct, because, as I have heard it said, it most resembles blood!

In the Orvieto pictures of the administration of the cup to

laics, it is to be observed that an assistant, and not a priest, stands holding in his right hand the cup, and in his left a small glass vessel, or cruet, containing the wine. In one case the acolyte is in the act of administering to a youth who, in company with several others, is on his knees.

Now the date given as that of the completion of these pictures is A.D. 1363. Up to that time, therefore, it must have been usual to administer the cup to the laity in the cathedral of Orvieto, the city of the Popes.

By what authority, then, did the clergy of the Church of Rome withdraw the cup from the laity, after the latter had received it for so many centuries? Surely the Communion as at present administered in that Church is only a mutilated rite, and no sacrament at all.

Early one morning in this very same chapel, with the picture of the laity partaking of the cup in full view, I saw a woman receiving, not the sacrament, but the bread. Nothing could have been more irreverent than the whole proceeding. While looking intently at the pictures, I had not noticed that a white cloth had been spread upon a desk, indicating that a communion was about to be celebrated. A priest with an acolyte came up suddenly to the altar near which I was standing, and the latter commenced some form of words with his eyes fixed—naturally enough, poor child!—upon the stranger.

Meantime, the priest took a host—previously consecrated—out of the *cibório* or pix, gabbled some short office as fast as he could, and at the same time employed his hands in folding the *corporal*. He then took a wafer to the kneeling woman, who was the only communicant. The acolyte followed him, and while he administered, held a napkin under the woman's chin. Then the priest returned to the altar, locked up the cibório, made his obeisance, and, with the boy at his heels, was off as quickly as he had entered. It was the most rapid administration I had ever seen; the whole ceremony did not occupy more than three minutes.

There were two things like fruits upon the altar. They were, I suppose, the appendages called apples—hollow ornamental vessels, in the shape of fruits, which are filled with hot water to warm the priest's hands in cold weather.

XL.

THE CATHEDRAL OF ORVIETO.

Part II.

THE hour appointed for my inspection of the reliquary had passed, the service was over, the music had ceased, the clergy were waiting; but of the laity a few visitors only were present in the great church.

"For whom are you waiting?" said I to the sacristan.

"For a Milor Anglais, sir," he replied, "who appointed to come and view the holy relics."

"Le voila," said I, pointing to myself, and enjoying the joke, "Je suis le Milor Anglais."

Four priests, two of whom were, I believe, canons, together with four attendants bearing six candles, were awaiting us, and upon our arrival at once formed into procession, and moved towards the Chapel of the Sacrament. Upon entering it they arranged themselves before the reliquary, and commenced to intone an office. I was taken by surprise, and not a little shocked; first at the profanity of prayers to the Almighty in the presence of, and in honour of, this gigantic fraud, and then at the thought that I was in a way paying for these prayers—a thing I had not realized.

The office was short, and at its conclusion we mounted some temporary steps to a platform before the reliquary, about six feet from the ground. A priest had preceded us for the purpose of unlocking the great outer case in which the silver shrine is enclosed: for it is offered to the public gaze only, I believe, once in the year.

There are two things to be seen: a stained piece of linen—the corporal—stretched, framed, and glazed; and the front of the reliquary. The linen, perhaps fifteen inches square, is in no way remarkable. The slight stains upon it may have been of blood, or of anything else; nor has the cloth the appearance of age.

The priest was very courteous, and indeed, with one exception at Rome, I have never met with priests who were otherwise. He gave us plenty of time, and with a taper enabled us to see each of the many rich enamels. This occupied some fifteen minutes, and on descending I was vexed to find that we had been all this time detaining the other clergy, since a closing office was customary, of which I had not been aware. When this had been completed the ceremony was over, the doors were locked, and we departed from the chapel into the body of the church.

Having thus noticed the materialistic confirmation of the materialistic dogma of transubstantiation by the sensuous fable of Bolsena, and its connection with the famous cathedral of Orvieto, let us now pass to the opposite transept formed by the splendidly decorated Chapel of the Madonna, a chapel which has no equal in Italy or the world.

On the vaulting are some noble works of Fra Beato Angelico, among which I was especially struck with a majestic figure of Christ surrounded by a group of saints, which, although it was painted five centuries ago, seems as fresh as if the brush had been only just laid down.

All the side walls were executed by Signorelli, an artist scarcely known in England, but possessed of transcendent powers. They exhibit several great and splendid compositions, excellently wrought, and of about the same date as the work of Angelico.

It would be a great pleasure to dwell at length on these grand conceptions of a lofty imagination, and to expatiate on the brilliancy and rich variety of the illustrious artist's creative powers as exhibited by them; but this would be beside our purpose, which is to call attention to the strange mixture of Heathenism with such sublime Christian compositions as The Resurrection, The Judgment, The Fall of Antichrist, and The End of All Things. For while these imposing frescoes are painted immediately under the vaulting of the ceiling, there is just beneath them another series of pictures partly allegorical—from Dante—and partly Pagan!

Five Heathen poets have been introduced by the painter, and one Heathen philosopher, Empedocles of Agrigentum— that is, Girgenti in Sicily. The poets are Homer, above as you enter, and Lucan on the right; the latter is, however, I suppose, now destroyed, because a Cardinal's tomb has been placed against the portrait. On the other side of Homer is Empedocles, a very perfect and interesting picture, the left arm of the philosopher resting on the lower part of a circular window, out of which he is leaning sideways, and looking upwards at the picture above him, " The End of All Things."

On the left wall also are portraits of Dante and Virgil in square painted frames, surrounded by many smaller illustrations of Dante's adventures with his conductor Virgil in the nether regions, and of other subjects from the *Divina Comedia*. All kinds of strange and fabulous forms and conceits are to be seen there; it is a wonder-land of captivating romance. And such is the character of the ornamentation which, with gorgeous arabesques, sphinxes, and monsters, surrounds all the portraits. In some of the persons introduced into these decorations Signorelli seems to be illustrating the lines of the *Inferno*, when in speaking of Hector, Aeneas, Lucretia, Brutus, Empedocles,

Saladin, and other heroes and heroines who were shut up in Limbo, Dante says :—

> "Souls with sedate and placid eyes were there ;
> And looks of dignity around they cast ;
> Seldom they spake, but sweet their voices were."

And, perhaps, in selecting some of the illustrious persons whose imaginary portraits he has painted, he was thinking of the lines :—

> "Four mighty shades I saw come us toward,
> Their aspect neither grief nor joy betrayed.
> 'Observe him well who bears in hand the sword'—
> To me the master kind his words addressed—
> 'Before the three who cometh as their lord.
> 'Tis Homer, sov'reign poet unsurpassed.
> Th' other is Horace of satiric fame ;
> The third is Ovid ; Lucan is the last.'
>
> * * * * * * *
>
> The beauteous college thus I saw unite
> Of that lord paramount of loftiest style,
> Who soars above the rest with eagle flight."

Scenes from their own writings embellish the portraits of the Heathen poets. Thus Homer is decked with subjects from his shield of Achilles ; Lucan with cameos from his Pharsalia ; and so on.

Passing now to the right wall, we find ourselves face to face with those acquaintances of our boyhood, Ovid and Horace. Elsewhere we should have liked to see them : here we cannot help exclaiming with surprise, What in the world has brought you into a place of this kind?—you, Ovid, with your Art of Love, and not too decent stories of Metamorphoses ; and you, Horace, too often saying what you had better have left unsaid? And we fancied we heard them reply just as naturally, "Ask the Pope, the bishop, and the priests, who ordered us to be placed here. It was none of our doing. We do not feel at all comfortable, having been accustomed to society of a different kind. The place is not to our taste, as you seem to know; we told Signorelli as much, when he wanted to put us here. But he said the priests liked our writings so much that they would have us. So here we are doing penance."

Ovid occupies a part of the wall just opposite to Virgil; while Horace faces Dante. All the poets are represented as standing at inter-columnar and open windows.

Ovid's head is crowned with laurel; his clothing is a tunic with a short black cloak thrown over it; and his finger is pointing to a passage in an open book which he holds. Four small circular compositions—*tondi*—in chiaroscuro, taken from his works, surround him.

In one of them Pluto is seen in his gloomy chariot, beneath the shadow of Ætna, anxiously gazing around to see whether "earth-shaking" Typhon is working mischief in his fiery realms.

Then Venus appears, calling upon Cupid to inflame the infernal king with his ardent shafts.

Quickly the consequence of the mischief follows in the rape of Proserpina, fair daughter of Ceres, who is seized and hurried away by her captor as she is gathering flowers in the beautiful plain of Henna, a central spot of Sicily. Take this fable in one way, and the history of the world is ever repeating it, in the premature death of the young. The subject has peculiar charms for the poet and the painter. Not long ago, in the waiting-room of the station at Turin, I was looking at a vast picture illustrating it, which there adorns the wall, and which had this legend:—

"Dis, dark as Erebus, black as an Æthiop, with powerful arms seizes the damsel fair as the morning, bright as the snows of her native Ætna. She shrieks, she cries. To her mother, to her companions, but most of all to her mother, she calls for aid. In vain! The grisly king hurries her away; and flowery Sicily for ever vanishes from her eyes."

Then, as Ovid has it :—

> "The gathered flowers, from her rent vesture falling,
> Do strew the ground."

And lovely those Sicilian flowers are, as any one who has seen them can testify. I have by me a list of some which the fair maid would have been likely to cull in spring, and among them is the exquisite little blue iris which adorns the ruined theatre at Taormania and other heights of Sicily. It grows, too, in the flowery land of Palestine, especially on the vast porch of the ruined Church of the Templars, at Jerusalem, which has been ceded by the Turkish Government to Germany, and in clearing which at the time thirty thousand ass loads of rubbish were carried forth.

Next in the series of pictures comes Ceres in her chariot, the mother of the maiden, seeking with torches for her lost child. Possibly the origin of the fable may have been as follows :—

Ceres, a queen, or potent lady with landed possessions in the island, by growing corn for which Sicily was famous, and the cultivation of which she probably introduced, is afterwards revered as a goddess of corn. She has an only daughter who dies at an early age, or, in the language of the myth, is forcibly carried away by Pluto, the god of the dead. There is a grand funeral ceremony at night, with a torch-procession, the Queen being the prominent mourner.

It was, then, probably, by teaching the rude Sicilians the method of cultivating grain that this queen, or lady, became a benefactress to the island. The people sympathised with her in the loss of her child, and decreed that the funeral should be annually commemorated at Henna, where the daughter died. A torch-procession was the principal part of the ceremony, and by it for centuries the sorrows of the distracted mother were kept in remembrance.

Time rolled on, and a new religion was introduced; but festivals are more tenacious than faiths, and often survive them. Under the new *regime* the feast of torches becomes the feast of candles; the name only is changed, and the festival, still held in February, is called Candlemas. I have witnessed it in the Pontificate of Pio Nono, when the tapers were given out by the Pope himself.

While in Sicily I met with another instance of the persistence with which ancient customs linger on. At Messina I saw a person surrounded by a densely-packed crowd of men and boys, to whom he was reciting verses of their poets. It was marvellous to see the rough fisher-boys, with upturned eyes, hanging on the lips of the reciter. But it was no new sight; two thousand years ago their fathers were wont to delight themselves by listening to the verses of Euripides, just as they do now to those of Tasso or Ariosto. Indeed, it is recorded that some of the Athenian prisoners captured at Syracuse, and condemned to work in the neighbouring quarries, were for their powers of recitation freed from bondage, in spite of the bitter hatred with which the Syracusans regarded the invaders of their island.

But, to return to the chapel of the Virgin. Its painted walls are adorned with many other Heathen fables besides those which we have mentioned, and among them with the story of Orpheus, " the sacred interpreter of the gods."

There you may see the impassioned minstrel making his perilous descent into Hades, and lulling the ever-watchful triple-headed guardian of Pluto's realms to slumber with the enchanting notes of his lyre. Now his resistless spell soothes the pains of Tartarus, and anon it is stealing gently over the Infernal Powers, and subduing even their pitiless hearts.

"Stern Proserpine relented, and gave him back the fair."

Then, rejoicing in the attainment of his object, he begins his return to the regions of day, closely followed by her for whom he had dared so much. But, alas, impatient youth! he breaks the law of the grim deities; ere the permitted time he turns to look upon his Eurydice—and in a moment all is lost; she is snatched from his embrace for ever.

But how near is the sublime to the ridiculous! Signorelli's strict orthodoxy has caused him to make a ludicrous jumble, and instead of representing Eurydice as vanishing away, or, at least, surrounding her with evil genii—such for example as may be seen on Etruscan tombs—he has introduced ecclesiastical devils! There they are, three of them, making greedy havoc of the poet's love, whom they are seizing neck and limb.

In my time I have examined the devils of many a painter, and must certainly pronounce these of Signorelli to be the most malevolent I have ever noticed. Some of the most comic—and ecclesiastical devils are often intensely comic—are those in the narthex of the grand old Basilica of St. Lorenzo, the Church of the Cemetery, at Rome; they are occupied in plaguing the unfortunate St. Anthony, and appear to be drawing considerable amusement from their occupation. Another very ludicrous person of the same class is to be seen in the porch of the cathedral at Berne. He has a Swiss basket upon his back, in which he is carrying off to the abode of woe a doomed bishop. Still more strange—the bishop looks out from the basket, and gives his professional blessing to the people as he is being hurried away.

But among the various species of ecclesiastical devils, which are generally either of the human or the bestial type, there appears to be also a feathered tribe, living in trees like birds. Montfaucon, in his *Antiquities of Italy*, mentions them in connection with the Church of Sa. Maria at the Porta del Popolo in Rome. "In the inscription set up in the choir," he says, "we have this account, which for its singularity is here inserted." He then gives the original Latin of the in-

scription, together with a translation to the following effect:—
"This altar was solemnly erected by Pope Paschal II.—A.D. 1118—in this place by Divine inspiration, by which he soon drove away the tall devils who, sitting on a nut tree—*nucis arbori insidentes*—cruelly insulted from thence the people as they passed by—*transeuntem hinc populum dire insultantes.*"

The inscription then goes on to state that the Church of Sa. Maria was built on the site of the Pope's altar. Certainly Montfaucon does not seem to be far wrong in characterizing this account of "tall devils" perched upon a nut tree and insulting the passers-by as singular.

There are some strange devils among the decorations of Fairford Church in Gloucestershire. Among them is the grimmest I have ever seen—a grand monster in painted glass at the west end, who is called Beelzebub. Upstairs, again, there is a very comical little one—smart, a beau in his way, in a gay mauve mantle—walking daintily on tiptoe, and playing a violin. One of his companions has a blue tail, and is wheeling away a woman in a barrow to a place to which she is very unwilling to go. However, she cannot help herself. The barrow is two-wheeled, with eight spokes to each wheel, and is particularly well made; the woman is robed, and sits gracefully in it.

But the idea of the barrow is by no means exclusively "Christian." Mrs. Hamilton Grey, in her *Sepulchres of Etruria*, describes a tomb found at Tarquinii, and dating back to some seven hundred years before Christ. In it is a figure robed in white, wearing a conical white tiara, and with one hand upraised apparently in the act of benediction. "Had it been drawn in our days," remarks Mrs. Grey, "it might have passed for the Pope." And in this same ancient tomb there is also an evil genius, or Heathen devil, wheeling off a soul to the judge of the dead in a hand-barrow, just as at Fairford Church. Truly, men unenlightened by revelation have much the same ideas respecting religious matters, whether they dwell in Etruria or in Gloucestershire; whether they are now alive, or passed out of the world some two or three thousand years ago!

The same tomb exhibits another curious parallel to Mediævalism. The soul of a person deceased is seated in a handbarrow ready to be carried off, and an evil and a good genius are struggling over it, the one pushing the barrow in the way in which he wishes it to go, while the other strives to impel it in an opposite direction.

In the narthex of the Church of St. Lorenzo at Rome there is a similar scene on a larger scale; the devils think themselves triumphant, and are capering about in delight at the prospect of carrying off the sinner upon whom they have set their mind, and who is none other than the Emperor Henry II. But St. Laurence, the patron of the church, suddenly bethinks himself of a golden cup which Henry had recently offered at his shrine, and casting it into the balance turns the scale. The emperor's sins kick the beam, as his merits weigh down the opposite scale, and the rashly exulting devils are disappointed of their prey.

But we have digressed at too great length, and must close our chapter on the Chapel of the Virgin without attempting to describe the many other Heathen decorations of the walls.

Mask from the Cathedral of Orvieto.

XLI.

THE CATHEDRAL OF ORVIETO.

Part III.

PASSING from the Chapel of the Virgin into the body of the great church, we find this part disfigured by a number of gigantic marble statues of modern date, ranged by the columns along the middle aisle, and for the most part executed in as bad a style as those of Bernini in St. Peter's. The original decoration consisted of beautiful frescoes, arabesques, and reliefs, thoroughly Heathen in character, but excellent in design and execution.

One of the statues, that of St. Paul, is a bad imitation of the Farnese Hercules at Naples!

Within the rails of the apse are two others, of life size or larger, by Mochi, representing the salutation of Mary by the angel. These are described in the guide books as "celebrated"; but in neither figure is there anything to admire; indeed, I never saw anything more repulsive than the face of the Virgin. "She is represented as starting from her seat at the salutation of the angel, her eand grasps the chair with almost convulsive energy, and her countenance wears a disagreeable expression of indignation."—*Murray*.

The last-mentioned feature puzzled me. I looked, and looked, but could not understand that expression of anger, and, probably, never should have done so had I not, when staying at Bologna on my way north, gone to the public library to search for De la Valle's *History of the Cathedral of Orvieto*. The librarian politely set before me a small quarto, printed at Rome in 1791, and, as I turned over its leaves, my eye rested on some Latin verses which supplied the desired information. They were as follows:—

> "Pennatum properare ducem vocemque salutis
> Improvisa timet : nec sponsa innupta Tonantis
> Esse velit. Thalamos fugiat, tædasque recuset
> Ferre maritali dextrâ. nisi pronuba sanctos
> Virginitas et Divus Amor jungant Hymenaeos."

Which we may, perhaps, freely render :—

> "Down from the stars the winged leader hastes :
> His voice of salutation frights the ear
> Of her astonishment. Nor will she be
> The Thund'rer's unwed bride. Let her the bed
> Avoid. Let her the torch refuse to bear
> In matrimonial hand, nor yield except
> Married Virginity and Love Divine
> The holy wedlock join."

Here is a strange origin for Christian statuary, one of the scandalous amours of Jupiter! De la Valle, in commenting upon the lines, makes no observation on the angry expression with which Mary meets *pennatum ducem*, "the feathered Mercury," alias the angel, nor does he note their Heathen character. On the attitude of Mary, however, he remarks: "Her movement may best be compared to that of a Spartan virgin from the antique."

This group certainly affords a fitting illustration of the

principle which is maintained throughout the whole cathedral of Orvieto, nay, throughout the whole system of Rome. But Romanists do not always approve of it. While travelling from Munich to Dresden with my daughter, in 1879, we fell in with Monsignor B——, Prelate of the Pope's household, who knew Orvieto. Upon our speaking of the Heathen character of the Cathedral, he observed, "*Cette Cathédrale est un Christianisme paganisé.*" He had seen it with his own eyes, and was able to judge for himself.

And I had intended, reader, that you to some extent should be enabled to do the same, and with that view employed an Italian artist to copy a few of the decorations. But some of his drawings proved too indelicate to be retained, though I had cautioned him to be careful in his selection. However, on the opposite page I have given an example, from the font, of the generally Heathen character of the ornamentation.

Voluptuousness mingled with sportiveness pervades the whole building. Among the arabesques is a humorous but improved repetition, on a small scale, of the fountain of the manikin at Brussels; also a copy of Donatello's charming laughing boy, with bronze water works, which is now in the Museum at Arezzo, and which has been imitated in "a domestic fountain" to be seen in our own South Kensington Museum.

But one brilliant work of Mosechino is specially conspicuous. It is a beautiful group of figures in white marble—women and children—in highest relief and nearly of life size. It forms a reredos, or back, to a large and prominent altar in the transept looking west. I cannot enter into details: it must suffice to say that the women are as voluptuous and enticing as skill could make them, and are placed just before the eyes of the officiating priest.

Naked youths in pairs crown the pediments of the side chapels, where, not to mention sundry questionable arabesques, beautiful female forms in colour, and *décolletées*, help to make up the ornamentation.

Such a style of decoration might be more suitable in a theatre, though even there it would be highly objectionable. But for a house of prayer it would be difficult to imagine anything more incongruous and demoralizing.

Blood drops from St. Christina's feet, preserved in a glass case in her church at Bolsena.

XLII.

BOLSENA.

FROM Orvieto to Bolsena is a drive of two hours, over high ground commanding splendid landscapes at the beginning and at the end of the journey. First one looks back on the picturesque city of Orvieto, which from one point bears a striking resemblance to the south-east corner of Jerusalem. And then the close of the drive reveals the lake, with its blue waters and islands, on which one descends, by a winding road, to the poverty-stricken and rarely visited little town of Bolsena, the scene of the famous miracle which we have already described.

Both town and miracle are the better known for Raffaelle's great picture of the latter in the *stanze* of the Vatican. Yet the artist has not shown the slightest regard in his composition either to place or person; for as to person, he has introduced into the picture his contemporary and liberal patron the warlike Julius II., and as to place, he has depicted a spacious and well-lighted building, whereas it is a dark half-subterranean chapel belonging to an insignificant church, that of St. Christina, which has the credit of the transaction.

On arriving at this church one is a little surprised to find, just outside the door, a sculptured Roman sarcophagus ornamented with Bacchic figures in bold relief, and so indelicate that they seem extremely unsuitable neighbours for a Christian place of worship.

The chapel itself, in which the Bohemian priest was officiating when blood flowed from the wafer, is low, vaulted, and green with damp. It contains, however, one work of art well

worthy of attention, a composition of Robbia's relating to the history of Sa. Christina, and consisting of several small figures, which cannot, however, be examined without the aid of lights. The altar, occupying the place of one anciently dedicated to Apollo, and the exact locality of the miracle, are covered by a stone baldachino, or canopy, supported by four columns of red marble. In front of this altar, let into it, and protected by an iron grating shown in the cut, is a stone impressed with a hideous pair of feet, very similar to those of the " Quo vadis " at Rome. The legend is that the feet of a certain Christian lady of the neighbourhood, named Christina, were attached to this stone by her persecutors, and that she was then thrown into the lake. But the stone, contrary to its nature, willed not to sink but to swim; and the saint, standing upon it, was thus conveyed in safety to the opposite shore, where she landed, leaving the prints of her feet upon the stone as indubitable evidence of the truth of the miracle. I remember to have seen a duplicate of the footprints in the lower church at Assisi.

Besides the blood-memorials of the miraculous wafer and cup which we have already mentioned—the stains on the pavement covered with a grating—there are also others kept in a gallery of modern date up a flight of steps. Since, therefore, I had asked to be shown everything that was to be seen, a messenger was despatched to fetch the priest, who presently appeared—a good-tempered dark little man. He at once robed himself, and proceeded, according to custom on such occasions, to light candles while the by-standers devoutly crossed themselves. Next came a short office, the people kneeling, and then the evidences or remains of the miracle were disclosed. They were kept in a sort of press, and were revealed by the drawing up of blinds. On the top of the press was a representation of a large cup with blood welling abundantly from it. The relics appeared to consist mainly of pieces of stained linen, on which were spots said to be drops of the blood of Christ, and to exhibit—each of them—His lineaments! We strove to discover a likeness to any human figure, but without success; however, some of those who were present affirmed that they could discern it, and certainly had the general belief on their side.

In looking through the *Graphic* of January 7th, 1883, I observed a curious parallel to this fancy. It was an account, by the Hungarian traveller Count Szechényl, of a syringa tree growing in China which is believed to have worked many miracles, and on which a mandarin is said to have discovered a leaf bearing a perfect portrait of Buddha. M. Huc, the Jesuit missionary, also makes mention of this tree.

Another testimony to the close connection of all natural religions! To whatever race or clime they may belong, their principal characteristics are ever materialism and credulity. In Europe, the natural man sees a miraculous Christ in a spot on a dirty piece of linen; in Asia, he discerns an equally miraculous Buddha on the leaf of a tree.

It was in 1879 that our party drove from Orvieto to Bolsena. In former days I remember passing through the place on the journey from Rome to Siena by the *Malle Poste* when the road was patrolled by soldiers on account of the brigands—even now it is not particularly secure. The Austrian Envoy had just been robbed of his effects, and even of his decorations, and, which was still worse, his postilion had been shot through the leg. This was in 1852.

The town, if one may dignify it by such a name, is situated near the lake—"the great Volscian Mere" of Macaulay, and the largest lake in Italy—at the bottom of a hill of unusual length and steepness. A carriage and pair of horses may be obtained for a visit from Orvieto at a very moderate rate—from twenty to five-and-twenty francs for the day. There are some curious Etruscan tombs between the two places, but off the highroad, which is good though hilly. The singing of the nightingales is enchanting, and reminded me of the Certosa of Pavia.

Leo X., who was a sporting man, used to fish at Bolsena and hunt at Viterbo, greatly shocking his Master of Ceremonies by riding out of Rome in boots. On such occasions he resided, not in the Castle, the picturesque ruins of which still remain on and within the walls, but in one or other of the two lake-islands where the Farnese family had villas.

The whole neighbourhood of the lake is now desolated by

malaria, and, so far as population is concerned, almost a desert.

When we entered the town, we were surrounded by a squalid set of half-clad miserables, from whose bodies we were quickly covered with—insects of provoking activity. Among them, however, was one old man of a higher type, who, while I was buying some coins from him, showed me a letter from his daughter in London. She was the wife of a tradesman in the Haymarket, and I afterwards called upon her with a message from her father, and found her a well-to-do, handsome, and respectable woman, and a great contrast to her country cousins at Bolsena.

There is no hotel in the place; the want of a railroad has caused its glory to vanish, since it is no longer a considerable thoroughfare. We dined in a large upstair room, at a rough, strange kind of place to which our driver took us; but we were not badly entertained. I wished to taste those classic eels, for eating the greatest possible quantity of which a certain Pope was in the habit of preparing himself *secundum artem*, like an old Roman; but we were unable to procure any. There was, however, an abundant supply of another fish, which the Papal fisherman Leo X.—a poor successor to him of the Galilean lake—must often have captured and consumed. So, with good bread and excellent wine, we ate the delicate long-snouted *tenca*, fried as English cooks can fry neither fish nor anything else—for Italians are famous for their *frittura*—and as we ate talked of Leo X., and longed for the pleasure of Roscoe's good company. For our excellent wine we paid less than half a franc a bottle, and for the remainder of our repast in proportion.

A charming drive back to our hotel at Orvieto concluded a day of great enjoyment.

XLIII.

BRIGANDAGE.

IN the previous chapter, mention was made of the prevalence of brigandage in the neighbourhood of Bolsena in 1852. It was not, however, until a recent visit to that part of the country that I fully realized the insecurity of the south of Italy.

We were about to make an excursion from Orvieto, and one of our party was the lady of an Italian Colonel quartered in the town. When the carriage which she had kindly ordered for us drove up, I was surprised to see a soldier seated on the box. In reply to my inquiries she said, "The Colonel thinks it will be as well for him to accompany us." The region through which we drove was indeed wild, and very suggestive of brigands, after they had been mentioned to us; however, nothing unpleasant occurred.

Just as we were starting the lady said, "Look down the valley: you see that nice house not far from the city walls? Well, for five years its occupants have been wishing to visit their estate in the neighbourhood—some eight or ten miles away—but they dare not, for fear of being murdered." It was a case of *vendetta*, as I afterwards understood.

But what the lady then told us was a still darker story. Signor A—— B——, a gentleman well known in the place, was awakened from sleep one night by some men, who presented a letter, which he was requested to read at once. Calling for a light, he looked at it, and then, folding it up again, observed that he would peruse it in the morning. "That will not do," replied the messengers, "the letter is concerned with your father, who is in the hands of banditti." "Indeed," said the son; and, bestirring himself immediately, he read, or thought that he read, the letter. "Yes," said he, "and at such a place I am to meet them and pay the ransom. Let us go at once." The horses were saddled, and they soon arrived at the appointed place; but no one was waiting. Again the son referred to the letter, and found that he had misread it, and ridden in the wrong direction. He then betook himself to the place which had really been mentioned, but when he arrived on the spot the time fixed for the payment of the ransom had passed, and the corpse of his father lay on the ground pierced with many wounds. The son, a considerable landed proprietor, has since the murder been shunned by his acquaintances.

Not long after this excursion, I was journeying with my daughter to Perugia. When we were near the lake—the ancient Thrasymenus, the scene of the dire defeat of the Romans by Hannibal—we were joined by a pleasant and intelligent French woman, a Sister of Charity, who was returning from a visit to her friends in Paris and on her way to Todi, where she had been labouring for some sixteen years. In speaking of the state of the country, she told us that she had known of six recent assassinations by brigands in the neighbourhood.

There are two causes, at least, which contribute to this miserable state of insecurity. One is that the Italians do not choose to recognise it. "Brigandage, sir!" said an Italian senator to me sixteen years ago—he was a Prince Somebody, but I forget his name, whom I was in the habit of meeting daily at a *table d'hôte* in Florence, and who knew England well— "Brigandage, sir! There is no such thing either in Italy or Sicily." Could one have conceived such perversity!

Another cause is the rarity of capital punishment—the miserable pusillanimity, or softness, or whatever you like to call it, —which persists in giving the colouring of extenuating circumstances even to the most atrocious murders. Man will be wiser than God; therefore, man must suffer. The primeval law of the Almighty is, "Whoso sheddeth man's blood, by man shall his blood be shed." The nations, and Italy among them, say, "Nay, it shall not be so": and the result is that unrestrained murder stalks fearlessly abroad.

One is glad to see this suicidal opposition to God given up in some parts of the world. Three of the Swiss Cantons have lately repealed their rebellious law against capital punishment. Experience has taught them that to spare the murderer's life does not conduce to the welfare of society. But in our own country the development of a mawkish feeling, which amounts to rebellion against God, is deplorable. Scarcely a malefactor, no matter how atrocious his crime, is sentenced to death without a number of people, wiser than the laws, than the administrator of the laws, and than God Himself, the Author of laws, raising a mischievous clamour for a reversal of the sentence, and so doing their best to frustrate the great Legislator's method of removing the guilt of blood from the earth.

We add a few particulars of Italian brigandage to illustrate the relations which have subsisted between it and the Romish Church.

A clever French writer, M. De Santo-Domingo, travelled in Italy about the year 1820, and, during his stay in Rome, moved in high ecclesiastical society. He was a strong Gallican and good Roman Catholic, but not a Papist. Consequently, being a firm partisan of the Bourbons, he does not hesitate to cast severe blame upon Pius VII. for, in effect, dethroning that family by consenting to officiate at the coronation of Buonaparte. This he does in his work called *Roman Tablets*, which is a collection of facts and anecdotes of manners, society, and government at Rome; and is of so caustic a character in its treatment of the upper classes there, that on his return to Paris the author was prosecuted before the Cour Royal—apparently at the instigation of the Pope's nuncio—fined, and imprisoned.

The book was suppressed; but it had already run through several editions, making a great stir upon the Continent, and had been translated into English—London, 1826.

In arraigning the government of the Pope, he observes in regard to brigandage, one of the crying evils of the day: "Travellers will testify to the truth of my assertion that almost every brigand possesses a house, a piece of ground, some cattle, and a lawful wife. They obey a chief who exercises over them the power of a dictator; they also experience all the advantages which result from absolute power. They are dressed in a uniform manner, and wear suspended on their breasts a silver heart, containing some holy relic, and bearing on the outside, in relief, the image of the Virgin."

Our author then gives a short account of the robber-bands which ravaged the country during the time of Pius VII., whose Pontificate lasted from 1800 to 1823.

Their fame was, I suppose, fairly diffused; at any rate, a vivid remembrance of my boyish days is connected with sundry popular prints, exposed in the shop windows, and representing combats between the Pope's soldiers and the brigands—for even these usually too good friends were wont sometimes to quarrel, and in the conflicts which ensued—if one may trust the prints—the women took no small part, manfully aiding their husbands.

One of these bands was under the leadership of Diecinove, a wretch who signalized himself by his horrible cruelties, craving more for blood than for gold, and subjecting his victims to prolonged tortures before he killed them. There was not a place in the environs of Rome where he had not spread terror and carnage. This monster proposed an armistice with the Papal government, and his offer was eagerly accepted.

"As soon as he and his companions had received from the holy Father their pardon as assassins, and their absolution as Christians, they resolved, now that they were protected by the shield of impunity, on visiting the theatre of their exploits, to view again the villages still reeking with the blood which they had shed. This they did, and, since they abstained from murder and pillage, demanded money on their departure from each place as a reward for their lenity: nor had any one the rashness to refuse them. Thus they continued to rob without risk, and in a manner under the protection of the government, which was fully informed of their conduct, but was willing, nevertheless, to grant the same amnesty to other bands of assassins.

"The chiefs Masocco and Garbarone, again, displayed an infernal genius in the invention of new crimes, and on my arrival at the city of Fonnino, their ferocious exploits were the one theme of conversation. The Pontifical government, having failed to capture these monsters, did not blush to treat with them as between nation and nation, and the Cardinal Secretary of State was deputed to carry on the negotiations. He had an interview with Masocco and his lieutenants near Terracina, and these men would have been content to receive the pensions and lucrative employments which were offered to them.

"But Garbarone, the other chief, not finding the conditions sufficiently advantageous, redoubled his depredations, and abandoned himself to his ferocious disposition. Again deputations were sent from the court of Rome, with still more seducing offers, to entice the banditti to accept a pardon and the remission of all their sins. Garbarone received the proposals with disdain, and answered them by fresh outrages, so that all that part of the country was filled with cries of distress.

"At last the rector of Terracina, a man greatly esteemed for his piety and virtue, armed himself with a crucifix, and went in search of the brigands. He succeeded, partly by his eloquence, but more especially by his offers, in persuading them; and then, not content with his first success, wished also to reform them, and with this view conducted them to his college, where the children of the richest families in the neighbourhood were being educated. At first the banditti showed great zeal in all pious exercises; the soul of the good rector melted with tenderness at their penitent behaviour, and he confessed them and administered the sacrament to them repeatedly.

"Suddenly the scene changed. After having fully informed themselves of the resources of the families to which the children with whom they were living belonged, they, one night, carried them all off to the mountains. The rector was absent, and on his return discovered too late that he had introduced wolves into the fold.

"The evening before the occurrence of this catastrophe at Terracina, I stayed there for some hours, and, on my arrival at Valatri, took a seat in the public conveyance for Rome, and entered into conversation with Signor Fasani, a Roman, who spoke much of his happiness in his son.

"When we reached Rome, Signor Fasani and myself took lodgings in the same hotel. The next morning he entered my room, pale with anguish. 'Yesterday,' said he, 'when I was speaking to you of my son, he had been carried off by a horde of assassins.' Before I could reply, a letter was brought in, and he started as he recognized the handwriting of his son. The message was as follows :—' My dear father, do not be unhappy. I am in good health, and among very good people, who take the greatest care of me, and pay me the greatest attention : but if you do not send me two thousand crowns immediately, they will kill me.'

"Hastily collecting all the money he could, he sent it off, with a promise that the remainder of the stipulated sum should be forwarded as quickly as possible ; and the fathers of the other children, who had received similar letters, did the same. The brigands released the greater part of their prisoners, and retained but three, of whom one was twelve years old, another thirteen, and the third fourteen. Signor Fasani's son was one

of these three, and the following is his narrative:—' When the robbers, after having taken us from the seminary, found that we could not walk as rapidly as themselves, they lifted us upon their shoulders, and did not halt until they had reached the mountains. On the way they met with some shepherds, whom they ordered to bring two fat sheep. After the repast, of which we partook, they recited a short prayer, in which they returned thanks to St. Antonio for having assisted them to carry out their plans. Then one of them read a book, in which, among other histories, was that of an adventurer called Ricardo, whose extraordinary enterprises excited in them transports of admiration. Afterwards they kissed the image of the Virgin, which they always carry about their person, and lay down to sleep.
. . . I had now seen twelve of my companions released; myself and two others only remained, and were kept tied together by the arms with a cord. The second in command of the band, observing that I was uneasy in mind, said, "Fasani, keep up your spirits: we are thinking of putting an end to your captivity. Meanwhile, preach us a sermon on death." I obeyed as well as I was able, little thinking that I was pronouncing my own funeral oration. When I had finished, the brigand dragged us to a little distance among a group of rocks which overhung a precipice, drew his poniard, and buried it in the bosoms of my companions. In their fall the cord which tied us together pulled me also to the ground, and I fell covered with their blood. I threw myself at the feet of the assassin, implored his pity, and begged him in the name of St. Antonio to spare my life. All this took place with the rapidity of lightning. He suspended his poniard, and appeared to hesitate. "Do not stab him!" cried the chief, "it will bring us ill luck: he has invoked St. Antonio. And he is the last. Let us offer a votive picture to St. Antonio."

"'I was then unbound: the chief spoke kindly to me, and gave me a ring, and this pass.'

"The child showed me the pass, of which the following is an exact copy:—

"'Every detachment of the company is commanded not to stop the bearer, Fasani.

>The Trinity, Virtue,
>Fidelity.
>Ant: Mattai
>Ed: Aless: Massaroni.'

"If," the French narrator very justly observes, "the lad had simply invoked the name of God, he would have been murdered. By employing the name of St. Antonio he was saved!

"Another head of a company of brigands was Bardone. This man was trained from childhood by his mother to deeds of blood, and no single act of generosity can be recorded to his honour. On the contrary, he added refinement to his cruelty. After he had exhausted all possible crimes, he wished to abdicate the dictatorship of the mountains, and made an offer to the Pope to do so provided he received as compensation a furnished house, a pension, and a public employment, with a supply of absolutions and indulgences. The Holy Father assented to his conditions, and the robber-chief made his entry into the capital of the Christian world, surrounded by a curious multitude, who felt a keen interest even in his murders. For at Rome—and alas! of late in England also—men generally transfer to the murderer the pity which is due to the victim. Place one of them between an assassin and the assassinated, and he will at once sympathise with the former, and say, 'Poor fellow! he has killed a man!'

"Bardone found a house prepared to receive himself and his wife near the bridge of St. Angelo, and the office of prison-keeper was assigned to him. He is still living in the same place, and walks in the streets of Rome with as much unconcern as if he were an honest man. Why should he not? Has not the holy water cleansed him from all the blood with which he was polluted? Can he feel remorse after having received from the Sovereign Pontiff the absolution of all his crimes?

"A number of his brethren in crime enjoy the same advantage of citizenship. Four of them lately presented themselves at the door of the Cardinal Secretary of State's carriage to demand an augmentation of pay, threatening that, if their demands were not conceded, they would return to the mountains. The Cardinal promised them everything.

"And thus," observes our author, "Rome has again become what it was at its origin under Romulus, an open asylum for robbers. In this respect the Pope resembles Romulus: the latter, however, founded only a profane city. But by what fatality is this place, where the religion supremely. excellent above all others (?) has established its throne, become the rendezvous of ruffians, brigands, and the most atrocious assassins, the receptacle of all the vices most degrading to humanity, the common sewer of the most filthy depravity?"
—*Roman Tablets.*

This is indeed strong language for a confirmed Roman Catholic to use, and it needs no further comment from us.

XLIV.

THE PERSECUTING SPIRIT OF ROME.

"WHY, you are a thorough persecutor!" said an acquaintance of mine to a young clergyman who had been expressing himself strongly on the subject of intolerance. "Yes," was the reply, "I am ready to burn, or to be burned."

Such a feeling is, I suppose, common enough to the natural man. Whatever his convictions may be, he is disposed, if he has the power, to force them upon others, and, should he meet with resistance, is often irritated by it to such a pitch of fury that he is ready for deeds of fiendish cruelty. There is nothing more terrible than the *odium theologicum* ; nothing more unlike the love of Christ; nothing which more plainly illustrates that profound knowledge of the human heart which led Satan to say, "Ye shall be as God."

And in this point there is the closest resemblance between Pagan and Papal Rome. How cruelly the former dealt with Christianity as soon as she discovered its true nature we have learnt from our childhood: the Ten Persecutions are a household word. But were Trajan or Diocletian worse persecutors than some of the Popes and the monarchs and prelates who followed their example? Did the gardens of Nero present a more atrocious spectacle than the Quemadura di la Cross? was the Colosseum more cruel than the innumerable torture-chambers of the Inquisition? Nay, in this point, as in so many others, Pagan and Papal Rome are in perfect agreement.

As a specimen of the persecuting spirit of the latter, we may quote a passage from Pascal the younger. In his *Cases of Conscience* that writer is urging upon good Roman Catholics the duty of denouncing to the Inquisition any of their kinsmen or relatives who may be suspected of heresy, and by way of encouragement gives them the following example:—

"Year after year the people of Italy and Spain are summoned to kneel before the altar of St. Ferdinand of Castile, and to bless God for 'the model king' who, when a heretic was burned, came forward, and with his own royal hands heaped fagots upon the pile."

This fact is also mentioned in the *Roman Breviary*, and is thus commended:—

"In him—Ferdinand—the virtues of a king shone out brightly—magnanimity, clemency, love of justice, and, above all, zeal for the Catholic faith, and a burning desire to protect and propagate its religious worship. He showed this especially by the vigour with which he pursued heretics. He never allowed them to exist in any part whatever of his dominions. And when they were discovered, he himself with his own hands carried the fagots to burn them."—*Breviarium Romanum*, Roma, 1843. See Feast of St. Ferdinand III., on the 5th of June.

Such are the models which Rome lifts up for imitation, such the persons whom she delights to canonize.

However, another Spaniard, Cyprian di Valira, tells us of a nobleman of Valladolid who surpassed even this "blessed example." For he denounced *his two daughters* to the Inquisition; and, when they had been condemned, asked and obtained permission to furnish fagots for the pile from his own forests. At the execution, after he had seen the victims safely chained to the stake, he kindled with his own hand the fire which was to consume his children!

But since we have been quoting examples of Spanish bigotry, my readers may, perhaps, be interested in the following extract from the *Daily News* of May 15th, 1869. It was given to me by Mr. A. Guinness, who has recently authenticated it at the office of the paper, and relates to the famous, or rather infamous, Quemadura di la Cross, or Burning Place of the Cross, at Madrid :—

"While the Cortes were debating upon religion, the workmen of the corporation of Madrid were laying bare one of the most conclusive historical records of the awful deeds committed in its name by the fanatics of olden times, who sought to perpetuate Catholic unity by the destruction of all who opposed it. I allude to the time of the Inquisition, when the Church of Rome believed that the best way to put down error was to burn the heretics. In making some new streets it became necessary to cut through the spot where tradition recorded that the burnings of the Inquisition used to take place, and which has always gone by the name of the 'Quemadura de la Cross,' or 'Burning-place of the Cross.'

"These excavations have not only confirmed tradition as to the spot, but have revealed something of the sad and cruel deeds themselves. The remains of the fires have been exposed in regular layers of long black bands, some of them 150 feet in length, and of varying thicknesses, with the spaces between them, which are from one to two feet, filled in with earth. A new road had been cut right through the spot, at a level of some twenty or thirty feet, and the cutting thus effected having been neatly faced leaves the original sandstone and clay formation on each side like a wall. There the black bands I have alluded to are distinctly seen, and at first sight seem like geological strata. There is, however, nothing of the coal formation in the hills on which Madrid is built. It is 2,400 feet above the level of the sea, and the formation is exclusively sandy limestone. One must seek in other than geological causes the presence of these black bands or layers. They are the veritable remains of the Inquisition fires—pulverised and blackened earth and coal, greasy even yet with human grease. Pieces of burnt clothing, calcined bones, and partially burnt hair have been taken out. All Madrid has been to the spot, and thousands have carried away some of the black mass itself, or of the cruel records found in it.

"To-day's *Imparcial*, speaking of it, says:—'It is the place where Catholics, pious and bewitched monarchs, permitted rational human creatures of all ages and conditions, and of both sexes, to be burnt alive, the victims of implacable Inquisitors, slippery monks, and impious defenders of the faith, as those executioners of human thought called themselves. It is where that unjust and dark Tribunal did its work, where they caused men and women, boys and girls, accused of sacrilege, heresy, compacts with Satan, and such like, to breathe their last in the midst of horrible torments. There the coal whose remains we now see, after being blessed by the Dominican fathers, burnt all who did not think or believe as the king and the monks thought or believed, or who would not serve the interests of tyranny, royal or clerical. There, in the bands one over another, in the manner of geological strata, we see, mixed up with fatty black earth, pulverised remains of muscles consumed by the live coal, calcined bones, remains of garments singed by the flames, halters stiff with coagulated blood, locks of hair imperfectly burnt—irresistible witnesses to the fact that brothers of ours expired amidst the flames, their hearts beating with energetic protests against men worse than hyænas, judges of perfidious heart and granite soul, who condemned them to die amidst agonies without number, and in the name of Christ delivered them to those fires.'"

Thus, while in the land of Assyria, in response to the efforts of Rassam, Smith, and other successors of Layard, earth was giving up her long-buried witnesses to the truth of the Old Testament histories—at this same time the hands of labourers at Madrid were laying bare proofs of cruel outrage perpetrated in the name of Christ upon innocent persons by the most terrible secret tribunal which the world has yet seen.

XLV.

MODERN JESUITISM.

IN Pagan times the great opposition to Christianity was carried on by the secret societies of the initiated, who at first tried to stamp out the new religion by persecution, and then, more successfully, to corrupt it by foisting themselves among its teachers and counsellors.

A striking parallel is found in the secret society of the Jesuits—that indefatigable Order which undoubtedly saved the Romish Church from destruction at the period of the Reformation, and has ever since proved the chief stay and strength of the system of disguised Paganism which we have been endeavouring to expose. But energetic as its members showed themselves to be in times that are past, it is probable that they were never more so than in the last few years. To their exertions we may refer the fact that the tide of Popery is again setting in upon the Protestant countries of England, America, and Germany.

Some five-and-twenty years ago a priest, in the course of conversation with an English lady at Teneriffe, remarked,—" Your nation will soon lose its Protestantism, and return to the bosom of the true Church. In about twenty years the change will be in rapid progress, and I will tell you how you may know that it is going on. You will see crosses put up everywhere—in your churches, in your churchyards, and in your houses."

Alas! the sign is indisputably before our eyes, and there is too much reason to fear that the prediction is proving true.

With that patient persistence which would be likely to

characterize highly-educated men, trained to regard their individual efforts as a mere contribution to the action of a vast and skilfully-directed organization engaged in carrying out a plan which will avowedly require many years for its accomplishment, the Jesuits have worked on. They have gradually secured a great influence over the Press; they have become clergymen and ministers of various denominations, and whenever, in such positions, it did not seem advisable to infuse their own tenets into their teaching, they have been content to be orthodox for the sole purpose of spreading that doctrine of tolerance and Christian charity which is ever upon their lips, until they have accumulated sufficient power to enforce obedience to their own iron tyranny. For they ever recognize the fact that it is as important for their object to attenuate Protestant feeling, and to enfeeble Protestant organization, as it is to propagate their own views. Nor, it is to be feared, are they unmindful of that rule of their Order which directs them to spread revolutionary sentiments, and to encourage sedition and anarchy, in those countries in which the supremacy of the Pope is not recognized. Hitherto the British empire has been their great obstacle, but the result of their labours may now be seen in every part of it, both at home and in the colonies and dependencies.

We cannot, however, in this book enter into the details of their history; but before dismissing the subject would just point to the remarkable parallel between the Jesuit revival in Europe, about A.D. 1600, and the so-called Catholic revival which is now vigorously progressing in England.

The Jesuits, we know, were the chief agents in rolling back the tide of spiritual light which flowed from the Reformation; and principles identical with theirs, employed first by Dr. Pusey and the Oxford Tractarians, and since by the whole body of the sacerdotal clergy, have in our own country opposed, and to a considerable extent checked, the flow of evangelical truth which some forty years ago was bidding fair to cover the land.

In both cases the spiritual revival was counteracted by a Catholic revival.

But let facts speak for themselves. About forty years ago, Mr. Dodsworth, who, more honest than his fellows, openly left the Church of England for that of Rome, wrote as follows to his friend Dr. Pusey :—

"You have led us on to that Church system of which Sacramental grace is the life and the soul. By your constant practice of administering the doctrine of penance ; by encouraging auricular confession, and giving priestly absolution ; by teaching the propitiatory sacrifice of the Eucharist, and the adoration of Christ really present upon the altar ; by your introduction of Roman Catholic books, rosaries, crucifixes, and devotion to the five wounds ; by seeking to restore monastic life—I say by teaching and practice you have done much to revive among us the system eminently called Sacramental."—*Dodsworth's Letters to Pusey*. Pickering, 1850.

"Done much," indeed ! Every doctrine and practice mentioned by Mr. Dodsworth is in direct opposition to the Articles of the Church of England. Yet it was through the persistent use and propagation of them by a clergyman, under oath at the time to believe and teach those Articles, that the "Catholic revival" sprang into life and grew in the Church of England !

Whether Dr. Pusey, and other leaders of the movement, actually belonged to the Society of Loyola or not, will perhaps never be disclosed until He comes "Who will both bring to light the hidden things of darkness, and make manifest the counsels of the heart."

XLVI.

CONCLUSION.

WE must now, for the present at least, bring our subject to a close. Of prepared material we have, indeed, sufficient for several additional chapters, but this is an age of brevity, and enough has been said to show that the transition from Paganism to Popery effected but little change in the principles and practice of Rome, and left her religion much the same as it was before, save that Christian names and terms were now given to the Heathen deities and rites.

Would that the eyes of Englishmen could be opened to the fact; sturdy efforts might then, perhaps, be put forth to counteract the sleepless propagandism by which our land is being filled with Popish churches, monasteries, convents, and schools. And alas! the evil is not confined to our land: in the United States of America, Rome is making even more rapid progress, so that some statesmen are beginning to feel alarm at the possibility of her power becoming paramount. If, again, we turn to Germany, the prospect is still gloomy: for we find that, after a desperate and ineffectual struggle of ten years' duration, Prince Bismarck is virtually surrendering to the Pope. Everywhere in the so-called Protestant countries Rome seems to be triumphing; while in other parts of Christendom, where she is better known, her influence is gradually yielding to the pressure of Secularism.

What shall the end of these things be? Earth has need of her rightful King, and Christians should pray more earnestly, " Come, Lord Jesus!"

But in preparing to meet Him, let us take heed that we fall not into the errors of human religion, and remember that it is no mere Church-holiness which we need: it is not that which is made to consist in obedience to certain rules of man's invention, or in submission to some human system; not that which is derived from membership with one church or another; not that which deals with meats, drinks, saints' days, Lent, seasons, hours, priests, altars, and buildings made with hands.

Such things pertain to man's method of holiness, to the holiness of the Scribes and Pharisees, of which Christ teaches that, unless ours exceeds it, we shall in no wise enter the Kingdom of Heaven. But God's method sweeps them all away, and directs us for the attainment of holiness to two things only, to the Holy Word, and to the Holy Spirit, Who can apply that Word so as to make us thereby believers in Christ Jesus, and members of His holy and invisible Church, nay, members of His own body, of His flesh and of His bones. And if we be thus created anew, sin is washed away, and we have the unspeakable privilege of living for our Lord now, the joy of knowing that nothing can separate us from the love of Christ, and the certainty that we shall shortly enter the gates of glory, and dwell in the golden city for ever. For did not our Saviour pray—

"Father, I will that they also, whom Thou hast given Me, be with Me where I am; that they may behold My glory which Thou hast given Me: for Thou lovedst Me before the foundation of the world"?

Crown 8vo, cloth, 7s. 6d.

A HISTORY OF THE JEWS IN ROME.

B.C. 160—A.D. 604.

By E. H. HUDSON,

Author of "The Life and Times of Louisa, Queen of Prussia," "Queen Bertha and Her Times," etc.

"The book is well-written, and should prove a great accession to many who cannot afford to read long histories, and yet wish to extend their knowledge on such subjects."—*British Quarterly Review.*

"A very remarkable book. . . . Certainly one of the ablest historical works ever written by a woman."—*Morning Post.*

"Miss Hudson gives a full and interesting account of the Sacred People in New Testament times, and the story continues with unflagging interest during the life and death struggle between the Church and Paganism. The book is very readable and interesting."—*Church Bells.*

"It embodies the result of wide reading and study, and contains much interesting matter."—*Scotsman.*

"As a comprehensive and popular survey of the period considered, we know no better book."—*Literary World.*

"A *résumé* of general Jewish history from the time of the Maccabees to the rise of the Papal power, a sketch of Roman history for the same period, a description of famous Roman edifices, and a history of the Jews in Rome. Miss Hudson studied her subject in Rome, and she describes many things from her own observations in the eternal city."—*Glasgow Herald.*

"The whole matter is full of interest."—*Christian World.*

"The chapter on the Barbarian invasion is well written, while the way in which the purer theology and loftier morals of the Jewish people, and subsequently of Christian teachers, told upon the usages and life of the Romans; and how the chequered fortunes of the Empire affected the condition of the Hebrews and the Christian sects, are suggestively and thoughtfully worked out."—*Daily Telegraph.*

"There is much interesting matter to be found in the book."—*Guardian*

LONDON: HODDER & STOUGHTON, 27, PATERNOSTER ROW.

WORKS BY DR. DE PRESSENSÉ.

Seventh Edition. Unabridged. Crown 8vo, 7s. 6d.

JESUS CHRIST:
His Times, Life, and Work.

More than one-third of the volume is occupied with a full discussion of "Preliminary Questions," including—1. Objections to the Supernatural; 2. Jesus Christ and the Religions of the Past; 3. The Judaism of His Time; 4. The Sources of the Gospel History. Having thus described His relation to ancient and contemporary history, the author proceeds to unfold the life of Jesus, depicting its scenes with a vividness derived from a visit to the Holy Land. The result is a work which has been referred to by Canon Liddon "as a most noble contribution to the cause of truth," and by the *Contemporary Review* as "one of the most valuable additions to Christian literature which the present generation has seen."

Cheap Edition. In Four Vols., price 7s. 6d. each.

THE EARLY YEARS OF CHRISTIANITY:
A Comprehensive History of the First Three Centuries of the Christian Church.

COMPRISING—

I. The Apostolic Age.
II. The Martyrs and Apologists.
III. Heresy and Christian Doctrine.
IV. Life and Practice in the Early Church.

"The author's keen spiritual insight, his rich eloquence. and his epigrammatic characterisations have given him, among his compeers, perhaps the very foremost place as a Church Historian and Apologist. His work, both in France and England, holds a place of its own, and with a power, completeness, and eloquence not likely soon to be surpassed."—*British Quarterly Review.*

"The student who cares for a subject, which is becoming one of ever deepening interest, will find his pains amply rewarded, if he gives a close and attentive perusal to M. de Pressensé's pages."—*Spectator.*

"The four volumes of this work are a splendid addition to our stores of church history. . . . We so highly appreciate the book that we place it among those which every student should possess. It fires the soul to read the great deeds set forth in such stirring words. A fitting and worthy sequel to Pressensé's Life of Christ."—Rev. C. H. SPURGEON in *Sword and Trowel.*

LONDON: HODDER AND STOUGHTON, 27, PATERNOSTER ROW.

www.ingramcontent.com/pod-product-compliance
Lightning Source LLC
Chambersburg PA
CBHW031327230426
43670CB00006B/262